P9-CJK-222

THE
TREE
OF
CULTURE

RALPH
LINTON

THE
TREE
OF
CULTURE

ABRIDGED BY
ADELIN LINTON

VINTAGE BOOKS

A DIVISION OF RANDOM HOUSE

New York

VINTAGE BOOKS

are published by ALFRED A. KNOPF, INC.

and RANDOM HOUSE, INC.

© ADELIN LINTON, 1955, 1958

PREFACE

DR. RALPH LINTON devoted four years of the spare time salvaged from a busy life to writing the original edition of this book. However, the concepts were evolved and the data accumulated during forty years of work in anthropology, archaeology, and ethnology, and studies in anthropological theory and personality and culture. This book was an attempt to synthesize the experience, the reading and thinking of a lifetime into one volume tracing the evolution of culture from its multiple beginnings at the subhuman level through its divergent lines of development. This project required not only broad knowledge, but also considerable temerity. Anthropological data have been accumulating with such amazing speed in recent years that few scientists venture to deal with the material except as specialists in particular areas or periods.

The title of the book refers, not to the familiar evolutionary tree with a single trunk and spreading branches, but to the banyan tree of the tropics. The branches of the banyan tree cross and fuse and send down adventitious, aerial roots that grow into supporting trunks. Although the banyan tree spreads and grows until it becomes a miniature jungle, it remains a single plant, its various branches traceable to the parent trunk. So cultural evolution, in spite of diffusion and borrowing and divergent development, can be traced to its prehistoric origins.

Because of space limitation in this Vintage edition, the labyrinthine growth of the tree of culture has had to undergo considerable pruning. The root material (the prehistoric stages on the way to Homo sapiens and the slow changes that marked man's progress from food-gathering and hunting to farming and husbandry) has been considerably curtailed. Some of the foliage (the descriptions of technologies and social organization) has been cut back. We have had to concentrate on the main branches.

It was found necessary to omit the chapters on the

New World. Because North and South America were the last great land masses to be populated, their cultures lagged behind those of the rest of the world. At the time of the discovery, the northern tribes were still uncivilized in the sense that they had no cities or empires. South of the Rio Grande, where the migrants had domesticated a crop (maize) on which a stable economy could be based, civilized living had developed. The arts of the Mayas, their knowledge of astronomy and mathematics, were as advanced as anything in Europe at the time. The Incas, with their amazing ability to organize and direct masses of people, had established the first totalitarian empire. However, the superior technology of the Europeans completely overwhelmed these cultures, which were therefore prevented from sending down their own roots and forming independent trunks in the banyan tree.

The original edition of *The Tree of Culture* was nearing completion when Dr. Linton died on December 24, 1953. In 1948 a grant from the Wenner-Gren Foundation for Anthropological Research had made possible the transcriptions of the lectures on which the book is based. Although Dr. Linton himself made use of these transcripts only as a guide and outline, they proved invaluable for the completion of the book, a task that I undertook after his death. That it is not the book it might have been had Dr. Linton been given time to complete it and edit it himself is undeniable. I did my best to make it as nearly as possible what he had hoped and planned. In my work on the present edition I have tried, in so far as possible, to maintain the spirit and scope of the original.

ADELIN LINTON

048310

CONTENTS

Contents

THE
TREE
OF
CULTURE

1 IN
THE
BEGINNING

THE primary purpose of this book is to set down what we know about the origins and growth of what the anthropologist calls culture: the mass of behavior that human beings in any society learn from their elders and pass on to the younger generation. However, before going into this, it is worth while to say a little about the origins and qualities of the animal responsible for this curious behavior. This is the more necessary because there is, as always, a lag between what the scientist knows and what the nonscientist believes. The battle between the anthropologists and the antievolutionists, which in any case was mainly shadow-boxing on the part of the antievolutionists, has long since been fought and won. Outside of a few geographical or intellectual back districts, no one questions today that we are descended from some sort of animal. The main problems are what sort of animal, and what line human evolution has followed. We can dispose of one popular misunderstanding immediately. It is certain that man is not descended from any anthropoid ape now extant. These apes are not our ancestors but are cousins whose line of descent branched off from our own at least a million years ago.

In the attempt to reconstruct human ancestry we have to rely on the evidence of a few fossils, eked out by what we know of the processes of evolution, and by the fairly clear picture which we have of the pattern of primate development in general. It would be nice if we had

more early human and semihuman fossils, but it is unlikely
that the supply will ever be very large. Until very recent
times, in fact, until man learned to raise his own food, he
was a comparatively rare species. Our semihuman ancestors were even rarer since they were not as well
equipped for exploiting their environment as the first true
men. Fifty square miles to support each individual would
be a conservative estimate even in favorable territory.
Moreover, fossilization requires special conditions. A body
which lies out in the open becomes one more item in the
economy of nature by way of buzzards, jackals, and all
sorts of other carrion-eaters.

In spite of these difficulties, a moderate number of
human and subhuman fossils have been found. These are
merely points along an evolutionary trajectory. By sight-
ing from one to another of these fossils we can extend this
evolutionary trajectory from ourselves back to the remote
past. From everything that we now know, it seems that
our remote ancestors were monkeys. Those who are an-
noyed by this may take comfort from the fact that, at
least, the founders of our family line were educated in the
higher branches.

The first step in the direction of man came when
these little beasts took to a new method of travel. Instead
of jumping from branch to branch, they began to swing
from one branch to another in much the fashion of an
athlete on flying rings. This brought about important
changes in structure which really laid the groundwork for
most of the later and more specific features of man's bodily
development. In branch-swinging, the body hangs from
the arms and is thus brought into a quite different position
from that which it has in animals that travel on all fours.

This resulted in a series of structural adaptations. The
body became shorter and more compact so that it could
be swung for long distances from the arms like a weight on
the end of a string. The pelvis took over the task of supporting the viscera, which had formerly been held up by
the sling-like abdominal muscles, and became deeper and
more bowl-shaped. The shoulder joints, which had previously had only a moderately free rotation, as in modern

monkeys, were loosened until they developed the sort of articulation which makes it possible for man today to throw a baseball. This was a tremendously important development since, among other things, it extended the range of man's aggression through the thrown rock and spear and the swung club. Lastly, the frequent elimination of individuals who could not judge distances when jumping or grab branches successfully led to a steady development of patterns of stereoscopic vision and of neuromuscular coordination. In other words, most of the things which made the modern man physically the sort of animal that he is today got their start in this branch-swinging adaptation.

At some time during this branch-swinging period the human and anthropoid lines separated. While the ancestors of the anthropoids were following the tree road, our ancestors took to the ground. We have no way of telling why they did this, but we do know that during the Miocene geological period, the time when the human and anthropoid lines separated, there were very extensive climatic changes in many parts of the world. It is possible that rather than our ancestors leaving the trees, the trees left them. However, the one thing that we can be sure of is that our ancestors came to the ground after their arms and eyes had become fairly well adjusted to tree-swinging but before their bodies had become so well adjusted to it that they could not start out handily on another tack. Even the earliest semihuman fossils which we have show the modern human style of leg and foot fully developed, while such ancient forms as the Neanderthal man had arms which were relatively shorter than those of modern man.

From the physical point of view man is merely another large terrestrial primate. He is actually not as far evolved in terms of structural specialization as his cousins the anthropoids. He is set off from the other members of his order, and indeed from other mammals in general, by his tremendous ability to learn, to think, and to communicate to others what he has learned and thought. In such matters, just as in his physical structure, it is possible to see him as the end product of certain generalized evolutionary

trends, but here the record is even more incomplete. The
break which separates man from the nearest animals in
all these respects is so enormous that the differences become not simply quantitative but qualitative.

In rating these special human abilities most people today would probably put intelligence first. This is a direct
reflection of our current cultural values with their stress
on reasoning ability, as shown in I.Q. tests. Actually, the
two most important human qualities are probably super-
lative learning ability and language. It is wonderful to be
able to solve problems by reason rather than trial and error, but we tend to forget that the results of thinking can
be no more valid than the premises with which the process
starts. These premises have to be learned, usually from
other people. The ability to learn is by no means limited
to human beings. Its high development in our species is
the culmination of a recognizable evolutionary trend. All
living forms respond to their environment with either
instinctual or learned behavior.

At the lower levels of evolution, most behavior is
controlled by instinct, although even such lowly forms as
earth worms and cockroaches can learn a little. As animals
increase in the complexity of their nervous systems, there
is a progressive shift from instinct to learning as the dominant factor in their behavior. Instincts practically disappear by the time one reaches primates in the evolutionary
scale. When we get to humans, who are the ultimate products of the evolutionary trends toward more and more
complex neurological organization, automatic unlearned
responses seem to be limited to reactions controlled by the
autonomic nervous system. These would include such
things as the digestive processes, adaptation of the eye to
light intensity, and similar involuntary responses. The
fewer instincts a species possesses, the greater the range of
behaviors it can develop, and this fact, coupled with the
enormous capacity for learning which characterizes humans, has resulted in a richness and variety of learned behavior which is completely without parallel in other species.

Thanks to the works of modern psychologists, we

understand the processes involved in learning fairly well. Unfortunately, we know considerably less about thinking. This process seems to represent a reorganization of previously learned responses to meet an unfamiliar situation. The same end can be accomplished by trial and error but much more slowly and clumsily. The rudiments of thinking ability are found in many mammalian species other than man. Primates, and especially anthropoids, are better at it than most other animals, but here again the gap which separates even a stupid human from the most intelligent anthropoid is tremendous. Anthropoid reasoning reaches at best the level of that of a three to four year old human child.

The use of language is very closely associated with the superior thinking ability of humans. In his ability to communicate, man differs even more from other animals than he does in his learning or thinking. Most mammals make sounds or have movements expressive of such emotional states as hunger, anger, fear, pleasure, or pain. These are recognized by other individuals of the same species and serve for communication, as anyone who has kept pets can testify. However, man is the only species which has developed communication to the point where he can transmit abstract ideas. The symbols which we use are normally verbal, and we usually think of speech and language as synonymous, but the same sort of communication can be achieved in other ways. It is only necessary that the symbols used should have the same value for both communicating parties. Thus, the sign language of the Plains Indians can be used for such complicated purposes as giving geographic information, preaching a sermon, or making a proposal of marriage with suitable financial guarantees. However, such developments in communication are atypical. Most human language is based on speech. Although research has shown that speech begins with the shaping up and fixing of articular phonetic patterns which fall within the range of chance variation in the sounds made by the child, most of speech has to be learned by imitation. It is a curious fact that there is no mammalian species other than man which imitates sounds. The almost

insurmountable difficulties which have attended all efforts
to teach apes to talk seem to be due to the impossibility of
getting them to imitate sounds.

We know absolutely nothing about the early stages of
development of language. It is safe to conclude that the
use of language is exceedingly old, but unwritten languages
disappear without leaving a trace. By the time that writing
appeared, in Egypt and the Near East, about 4000 B.C.,
the evolution of language was complete. The earliest
languages which have left a record were as complex in
their grammar and as adequate for the conveyance of
ideas as any modern ones. Moreover, everything indicates
that during the early part of human history there were far
more languages spoken than there are at present. Each of
the small local groups in which early man lived probably
had its own language.

The so-called primitive languages present a truly be-
wildering array of concepts expressed in grammatical
form: such things as gender based on shape or consistency;
singular, dual, and plural pronouns and verbs which ex-
press multiple ideas by slight modification of a few roots.
In almost grammarless languages, such as Chinese or English, a larger vocabulary becomes necessary. The enormous vocabulary of English is a necessity if the language
is to be used to convey precise ideas. Equally grammarless
Chinese, with a much more limited vocabulary, has the
brevity and uncertainty of meaning of a cablegram.

In spite of such differences, we have abundant evidence that any idea can be conveyed in any language.
The differences lie in whether the society has been familiar
enough with the idea, or sufficiently interested, to coin a
single term for it. Thus, to convey the idea of an airplane
in an aboriginal Australian dialect would require several
hundred words, while in English a single word would do
it. However, it would take quite as long to convey in English the idea of Alchuringa ancestor which could be conveyed by a single Australian word.

The symbolic system created by language is a tremendous aid to the individual in thinking, although the concepts embodied in the structure of the language in which

he thinks are likely to have their effects on the outcome. This is a field which is just beginning to be explored by the emergent science of semantics. Thus, the fact that there is no inanimate gender in Indo-European languages makes all their speakers animistic in their approach to abstractions. If our grammar divided the contents of the universe into animate and inanimate, as do the Algonquin languages, our philosophers would have been saved from wandering into many logical bypaths.

Most of our thinking is done in words, although other symbols can also be used. Thus the artist or musician operates with a different, nonverbal, set of symbols and has corresponding difficulty in describing his creative processes. With the aid of symbols it is possible for the individual to solve problems and arrive at results without going through the slow and clumsy process of overt trial and error. The use of words in thinking is very much like the use of mathematical symbols in calculation. Mathematical symbols make it possible to solve all sorts of problems without weighing or counting actual objects. Word symbols make it possible to determine the results of particular actions without actually performing them.

The human combination of extreme learning ability and language has made it possible for our species to accumulate and transmit from generation to generation a wealth of knowledge and tested behavior patterns which no other species can even approach. In other mammalian species, offspring can and do learn a few simple forms of behavior by imitating their parents, but the possibilities are limited both by the parents' inability to transmit abstract ideas and by the relatively short time that parents and young are together. In humans, the child's dependence on and consequent association with parents must continue for ten to twelve years as a minimum. Before the first third of this period has passed, the child has acquired language and the parent can thus transmit to him the proper responses not only for situations which arise while they are together but for those which may arise in the future. Parents can tell children about all sorts of things which can happen and what to do when they do.

Since humans are the most intelligent and also the most easily taught of animals, one would expect them to be the most highly individuated. No two persons are exactly alike in their physical and mental potentialities, and certainly no two individuals, even identical twins reared in the same family, have the same experiences. Human beings are thus potentially less alike than the individuals of any other species. It is most surprising, therefore, that they have chosen to live in closely organized groups whose members carry on a variety of specialized activities but are mutually interdependent for the satisfaction of practically all their fundamental needs. Many other mammalian species live in herds or packs, but the organization in these is minimal. The only division of activities is that devolving upon the two sexes by their different roles in connection with reproduction, while social control is a simple matter of the poorer fighters giving precedence to the better ones. To find anything which even remotely resembles the complexity of human societies, one must go to the social insects, such as the ants and the bees. Here the cooperation which is necessary for the survival of the community is assured by the physical specialization of the various groups of workers, fighters, and so forth, and by a high development of instincts. Since humans lack such instincts, it becomes necessary to subject them to an extraordinarily long and elaborate training if they are to function successfully as members of a society. We are, in fact, anthropoid apes trying to live like termites, and, as any philosophical observer can attest, not doing too well at it.

ON THE WAY TO HOMO SAPIENS

W E D O not know where the first recognizable representatives of our species appeared, but we can be fairly sure that it was not in some small, clearly delimited area. There was no Garden of Eden. Subhuman fossils which might be in our line of ancestry have been found as far apart as China, western Europe, and South Africa, and we can be fairly sure that various subhuman species occupied all the temperate and tropical parts of Eurasia and Africa. We do not know which of these is our ancestor or whether two or more subhuman species may not have contributed to the making of modern man. It seems that when any two primates of opposite sex and of the same or similar species meet, their normal reaction is to make a pass at each other, and if the various species of semihumans did not mix their genes, it was probably not for lack of trying.

As has been said before, the fossil record is exceedingly fragmentary, but the earliest remains of our own species which have been discovered show them to have been like modern men in every respect. Apparently, these first representatives of Homo sapiens were like ourselves even to the extent of having the same psychological potentialities. The great difference between their way of life and ours was due to the difference in the amount of knowledge which was available for them to learn and transmit.

Since our species emerged, it seems to have made most of its environmental adjustment by way of changes in its learned, transmitted behavior. It has, to be sure, produced physical varieties partly in response to environmental factors which it could not handle in any other way, partly, it seems, by chance, but none of these changes have been very far reaching. Their results are to be seen in what we call the races of mankind.

According to the most recent estimates the beginnings of culture, as shown by tools and traces of fire, go back at least 600,000 years. Men of our own species have been in existence for at least 100,000 years and the earliest culture which can be positively ascribed to them already shows a greater variety of tools and weapons than are in use by some tribes still extant. For all but the last seventy-five hundred years of this enormous time span, all human beings have lived by hunting and food-gathering. The importance of this phase of man's economic development in setting the patterns for later lines of cultural evolution can hardly be overestimated, and it is regrettable that we still know so little about it.

One who has the temerity to plunge into the huge and highly technical literature dealing with the earlier stages of human history cannot fail to be struck by the contrast between some nine-tenths of the Old World, for which information is either entirely lacking or woefully inadequate, and a few small areas, France and England in particular, which have been studied in extreme detail. The material on these areas bristles with the names of local cultures, each beloved by its discoverer, whose interrelations are matters of vigorous dispute. The nonspecialist cannot be blamed for feeling that he has wandered into a maze which has no exit.

That Europe should have been the part of the world whose early history was most intensively studied was a historic accident, a by-product of the invention there of the scientific method. However, it was in many respects a regrettable accident. One may question whether any other part of the world which was occupied by early man offers a poorer guide to the reconstruction of cultural evolution. It is fairly certain that man did not originate in Europe, and there is abundant evidence that throughout most of history the continent has functioned as a receiver rather than a donor of new cultural developments. The four glacial advances and three glacial retreats which alternately forced man out of and lured him back into Europe made the development of culture appear there as a series of discrete episodes rather than as a continuing process. To attempt to apply the typologies and chronological sequences derived from study of European materials to central or eastern Asia or Africa south of the Sahara can only lead, as it has led, to confusion. This is even more the case when one tries to apply European typologies to American materials.

The settlement of America occurred in such recent times and the cultural developments in the New World were so independent and in certain respects distinctive that it is best to postpone any discussion of American prehistory. Culture began and underwent most of its early development in the Old World. The most striking fact about this early Old World record is that even in the most ancient times of which we have knowledge there were already a number of cultures. These cultures existed not only in different areas but also, in some cases, within the same geographic area. In the same area varying cultures may have belonged to groups who exploited different environments, such as forest dwellers and prairie dwellers, or may represent occupations by different peoples at time intervals too brief to be revealed by the geological record.

Neanderthal man is the best known of all early human varieties. His slightly bent knees, forward thrust head, and massive chinless jaw decorate innumerable museum walls, and his presumed habits are favorite material for writers of science fiction. His evolutionary position is uncertain, but the last Neanderthalers are much less like ourselves than the earlier ones. Except for a brief flyer into North Africa, Neanderthal seems to have kept fairly well to northern latitudes and he was able to stay in Europe through the first half of the Fourth and last Glacial. He was human enough to interbreed with our own direct ancestors in Palestine, where the two varieties of man shared the Mousterian culture, and the best explanation for his differences seems to be that he was a sub-Arctic human variety in process of developing into a distinct species. Most of the things that distinguish him from our own ancestors can be paralleled in northeastern as contrasted with southwestern varieties of other Eurasian mammalian species of wide distribution.

In any case, the behavior of Neanderthal seems to have been thoroughly human. During the bitter weather of the Fourth Glacial he took to caves wherever these were available, and since his ideas on sanitation were rudimentary, to say the least, he has left considerable evidence of his living habits. Bones from his meals, ashes from his fires, and lost and broken implements were simply trodden into the floor of the cave, forming in time deposits several feet thick. The implements from these deposits include triangular flakes, smooth on one side, which could have been used as spear points or knives, and other flakes with a curved edge showing signs of use as scrapers. Several caves have yielded artificially shaped spherical stones, two or three of these of nearly the same size often found close together. There can be little doubt that these are the remains of *bolas*. Simple as this weapon was, its invention must have involved considerable observation and ingenuity. Such an appliance is a far cry from a simple implement like the hand axe.

It is safe to conclude that the Neanderthalers made many wooden objects and probably had containers made from bent bark or even crude basketry. Moreover, in view of the glacial climate of Europe during much of their stay, they probably wrapped themselves in animal skins. It may be noted in this connection that arthritis was common among the middle aged.

Only a few facts about their way of life can be deduced with any certainty. They must have had some sort of band organization like that of the most backward hunting peoples today. Several hearths are often found on the same level in a cave, indicating that several families lived together, and hunting the big game which was their favorite food must have required the cooperation of a number of men. It is idle to speculate on how the Neanderthal bands were organized or what their family groups were like, but frequent evidences of cannibalism suggest that anyone outside the band was considered, quite literally, as fair game.

At the close of the last glacial, a new people entered Europe, bringing with them a new culture and ushering in a new archaeological period, the Upper Paleolithic. The retreat of the ice had left the continent cold and comparatively dry. Most of it was park country, open plains with woods in the river bottoms and clumps of trees where depressions held the melting snow. Such territory is particularly favorable for grazing animals, and there were tremendous game herds comparable to those which covered the African highlands at the time the first modern European settlers arrived. It must have been a region of cold winters and hot summers, and much of the game probably moved north and south every year with the changing seasons. The newcomers were primarily hunters and had equipment which was a great improvement over that of their Mousterian predecessors.

Although the Neanderthal people had camped in the mouths of caves, the Cro-Magnon people of the Upper Paleolithic were the first to penetrate their depths. They carried on ceremonies in the deep galleries for the increase of game and for success in hunting. Their artists often worked in places that were so inaccessible that it seems unlikely that they ever expected their work to be seen after they finished it. Probably, the drawing, as an act of creation, was supposed in some way to reinforce the creative powers of the species. In addition to these remote and hidden figures, which must have been the work of individual medicine men, there were veritable cave temples, chambers which were elaborately decorated with series of paintings, and even with animals modeled in clay.

It is improbable that these earliest Europeans carried on systematic warfare. There were certainly amicable contacts between the various local groups, perhaps somewhat like the get-togethers of the modern Australian aborigines, in which past offenses and jealousies are worked off by relatively harmless formalized fights. That they met and traded is proved by the finding of objects far from their source. Sea shells from the Mediterranean were treasured as ornaments and were traded as far as Central Europe. There was also a trade in seal skins between some point on the French coast, perhaps Brittany, and Spain, since we find in the Spanish caves, far south of the range of this particular species, seal skulls with no other bones. Presumably the skins were traded with the heads attached.

As in the case of Neanderthal man, we have no concrete knowledge on the social or political organization of these people. We may assume that, as in the modern hunting peoples of the Circumpolar zone who are certainly their cultural descendants, all adults were married. Since in a culture of this sort where the main food supply was big game there would certainly be more widows than widowers, it is probable that the best hunters provided for the surplus by taking care of several wives. As regards government, the obvious importance of magic in the culture suggests that, again as with the modern hunters of the north, the most important individual in the community and the nearest approach to a chief was a shaman. Such men were specialists in magic who knew how to make charms and cast spells, and could even, on occasion, send their souls out of their bodies to see what was happening far away.

The equipment of ancient hunters and food-gatherers, though crude by modern standards, enabled our species to occupy a much greater range of environment than any other mammal. People who were still at this technological level reached all parts of the world which did not require long ocean voyages and settled nearly all the regions which are inhabited today. In the process they encountered a wide range of climates and natural resources and adjusted to both. It is highly probable that by the end of the Mesolithic there were more distinct languages and cultures in existence than the world has seen since. However, all these cultures were subject to certain limitations inseparable from the hunting and food-gathering economy.

2 BASIC INVENTIONS

FIRE AND TOOLS

THE use of fire and the making and using of tools are common to the whole of mankind and differentiate humans sharply from all other animals. Fire is, of course, infinitely older than man. It may be started by volcanic action, by lightning, by spontaneous combustion, or even by the friction of two dry branches rubbing in the wind. Most animals are afraid of it. Man tamed it and used it for many millennia before he learned how to create it. Fire, once acquired, was kept going for as long as possible, a practice still characteristic of many peasant groups. It is simple to preserve fire by means of rotten wood, lichen, or stems with pithy centers, such as the dry fennel stalk with which Prometheus stole fire for man. The Australian aborigines and the Oceanic Negritos regularly carry fire when they move camp; while among settled villagers the fire on the hearth, unless temporarily extinguished for ceremonial reasons, is kept going for as long as the house stands.

Once fire had been tamed it became man's most useful servant and his collaborator in the earliest chemical processes and a whole series of manufactures. We are prone to think of the main utility of fire to earliest man in terms of heat and light. However, since the earliest fire-users were denizens of tropical or warm temperate regions where heat was not important, and since they rose and retired with the sun, heat and light were not of much importance. Fire may have assisted in giving protection against the large carnivores, but its main value was certainly in connection with technology.

The earliest technological use of fire was in connection with woodworking. Poles could be pointed by careful burning and scraping away of the char. Green sticks could be straightened and hardened by use of fire. The discovery that fire which had once taken hold on a block of wood could be controlled and directed made possible a new method of shaping wooden utensils, canoes, and furniture. Except for the time involved, it was fully as effective as the work that could be done with nonmetal, cutting tools.

Fire is also highly useful in the clearing of land and the felling of timber for use. Needless to say, it is also the basis for most of the more elaborate later developments in technology. It has made possible first pottery, then metallurgy, and eventually a tremendous number of technological processes which depend on chemical reactions which take place in the presence of heat.

Several European writers have expatiated on the value of cooking as an aid in the tenderizing of meat, an idea which reflects the troubles of modern man and his bridgework. Even today such people as the Eskimo live largely on raw meat and have no difficulty in masticating it. Actually, any form of animal food which is eaten cooked can also be eaten raw, with the possible exception of a few sea foods. The difference is simply a matter of jaw muscles and taste preference. The real importance of fire to the food supply lay in its use in the preparation of vegetable foods, especially those which permitted of preservation.

Roots, which lend themselves better to storage, with very few exceptions require cooking to make them edible. Even such mild roots as sugar beets or potatoes can cause uncomfortable intestinal upsets if consumed raw. Taro, the great staple of the Polynesians, is filled with salicylic acid crystals which make it exceedingly irritating unless cooked, while manioc, the staple crop of the South American jungles, contains hydrocyanic acid, an exceedingly deadly poison which has to be destroyed by heat. The various seed crops such as grains and legumes are, with few exceptions, quite inedible without cooking. These are the crops which lend themselves most readily to long term preservation and storage and which, therefore, are a society's best insurance against famine. They are also forms which, first as wild plants and later as domesticated ones, range far north of the tropics. It was the use of fire which made it possible for our ancestors to change from the predominantly frugivorous diet of our anthropoid ancestors to the predominantly seed and root diet of our own species. By making many new food plants available, it increased the food supply and also extended the human range into more northern latitudes and into arid regions where the heavy starch supply characteristic of the seeds of many desert plants could become a human staple.

The use of tools or, more correctly, the making and saving of tools, reflects the peculiar qualities of the human mind much more directly than does the use of fire. The use of tools is not an exclusively human characteristic; the great apes employ sticks and stones which may come to hand for poking and pounding and some very curious examples of tool using have been recorded even among insects. However, as far as we know, there is no animal which ever shapes a natural object to adapt it for use as a tool or which saves an object which has been used once to use again. The human tool is one more manifestation of the curious quality of the human mind which makes us conscious of past and future and able to plan our behavior with an eye to both.

Even the simplest tools require some little skill for their manufacture, as will be discovered by anyone who tries to duplicate even such a simple object as a properly balanced club or stone chopper. The wide range of tools and appliances which are made by the members of even the simplest human societies is made possible by the universal pattern of specialization.

One who reads any of the numerous descriptions of the life of very ancient man must be struck by the importance attached to stone tools. In fact, the first of the great periods into which human history is usually divided is known as the Stone Age. This is not because early man used stone so much more than he did other materials. A glance at the cave man's actual equipment would probably have shown wooden clubs and spears, bark baskets, skin bags, and fur clothing, with only an occasional stone knife, scraper, or chopper. However, everything except the knife, scraper, or chopper was made of perishable materials. Only stone, and later bone, has survived for the record. Early man's stone implements were mainly used for making other things. They were primary tools, like the modern axe, hammer, plane, and knife. Also, it is interesting to note that all our modern hand tools were developed long before the dawn of history, and that most of them have changed their original forms very little.

The use of tools and fire gave man an incomparably greater control over his envioronment than any other mammal. This made possible an unparalleled extension of his range. There is no other warm-blooded animal which is so widely distributed, unless we count man's friend, the dog, whom he took with him in his wanderings. In particular, the development of hunting equipment made it possible for him to penetrate into northern territory never reached by any of his vegetarian primate ancestors. Man is able to subsist on a meat diet, and such groups as the Eskimo are able to thrive in a region where the only possible vegetable foods are berries, rock lichen, and reindeer moss. The last can only be eaten after it has been processed by partial digestion in the reindeer's stomach. This tremendously wide spatial spread has also enabled Homo sapiens to convert himself from a decidedly rare species to an exceedingly numerous one. There is no other large mammal now extant which can approach him in numbers. In fact, with modern science operating to prevent the operation of the factors which once held human populations in balance with their food supply, the most serious problem which confronts man at this writing is how to keep his numbers down to the point where the earth's resources can provide the average individual with a good life.

DOMESTICATION OF PLANTS AND ANIMALS

THE invention of food-raising ushered in the second great period in human history. It transformed Homo sapiens from one of the rarest to the most numerous of mammalian species. It also resulted in a tremendous accelearation in the rate of cultural development. This was no doubt due in part to the surplus of time and economic resources which food-raising made available, but it may also have been linked with population increase.

Early students of the evolution of culture believed that the domestication of animals preceded agriculture. After man the hunter had tamed his prey, according to their somewhat romantic formulation, woman, the plant-gatherer and homemaker, gently diverted him from hunting and herding and persuaded him to settle down to planting and plowing. However, it seems fairly certain that, with very few exceptions, agriculture preceded animal domestication. It is almost impossible to tame animals and attach them to a human group as long as this group is continually on the move in search of food. It was not until humans had begun to raise crops and settle down that they tamed most of the domestic species which we have today.

The most notable exception to this rule is the dog. The association of man and the dog began in Mesolithic times and may well have been a symbiotic relationship. The dog, with his keen senses of hearing and smell, could track game and give warning of enemies and was rewarded for this by being thrown the scraps of the hunters' feast. At the same time, as any dog owner will recognize, the personality patterns of the two species were so similar that it was easy for them to come to understandings and form mutual attachments.

The other exception to the rule that agriculture precedes animal domestication is the reindeer. These animals provide a reliable food supply throughout most of far northern Eurasia in a region where agriculture is impossible. Because of the reindeer pattern of migration in dense herds, it was possible for human groups to attach themselves to these wild herds, protecting them from their natural enemies, the wolves, and killing from the herd with as little disturbance as possible when food was needed. Reindeer are not difficult to tame, although they never become completely reliable and have to be rebroken for use after a single season free on the range. Their utilization other than as a source of meat seems to have been developed in imitation of cattle- and horse-using nomad peoples to the south with whom the reindeer herders were in contact.

The domestication of other animal species did not occur until humans had established settled village life. There can be little question that domestication began with the keeping of pets, and that the original motives were not economic. Even today, there are many uncivilized peoples who keep a great variety of pet birds and animals simply for the amusement and emotional outlets which they provide. Young animals are cute and appealing. The hunter who has killed a mother animal for food often brings the cubs home for his children to play with. Young humans and young animals always have an affinity for each other. However, as animals of most species grow older they either run away or become troublesome and go into the pot at the first sign of food shortage.

Various species differ in their adaptability. In order to become domesticated the species has to be tough enough to survive abuse and neglect, and capable of forming sufficiently strong attachments to either people or places so that they will stay around the village even when unconfined. Not all species are capable of this sort of adjustment.

It is important to note that the real test of domestication is whether a species will breed in captivity. Many animals which can be tamed and even put to economic use cannot withstand this test. Thus, elephants have been tamed and used for at least five thousand years. In the

Gilgamesh epic, a Mesopotamian religious poem which goes back to at least 3500 B.C., there is mention of what must have been a tame elephant "that shakes off its blanket." Although the taming and training of elephants are so ancient, until very recently it has been impossible to breed them in captivity. Even now in Nepal, Burma, and other regions where elephants are used as work animals, great areas are maintained as elephant preserves in which the animals live and breed wild. The young adult elephants can be trained easily when caught, and this holds even for African elephants, who were never tamed by the natives.

It is an interesting fact that no economically significant animal species was domesticated within historic times. As a matter of fact, a number of species which were domesticated at one time have been allowed to revert. For example, the Egyptians herded various species of gazelle and antelope with their cattle. However, these animals proved to be less productive of milk and meat than cattle and their domestication was dropped. The Egyptians also domesticated the hyena, which is quite dog-like in its behavior, and makes a good hunter and tracker. It is hard to say why the hyena was allowed to revert to a wild state unless its odor was too strong for even the olfactorally callous early Egyptians.

The fact that we always refer to early man as a hunter and food-gatherer reflects the importance which humans attach to meat, much as does the listing of meats as the principal dishes on any menu. Actually, early man was not primarily a hunter except in those fortunate localities where game was plentiful, or in the far north where vegetable food was scanty or lacking. In most parts of the world human beings have depended much more on seeds, roots, or fruits than on meat. The regions where food-raising began were those in which the population was already heavily dependent upon wild vegetable foods and where they had become accustomed to the laborious processes involved in gathering roots and seeds. In places where game was plentiful even the taking over of agricultural techniques already developed elsewhere met with strong resistance, since hoeing is a much less entertaining occupation than hunting.

The full complex of plant domestication involves a whole series of techniques: planting, cultivation, the use of fertilizer or fallowing, and, in arid regions, irrigation. However, instead of a progressively logical evolution of agriculture in which people always began by planting, then learned to cultivate and fertilize, the distribution of these techniques among living primitives is irregular. Each technique is found alone in one group or another as an initial step in their emergence from simple food-gathering.

For instance, in Australia the natives made the discovery that if they threw peelings and shoots scraped off in preparing wild yams in a place where the soil was black, they would find a yam patch growing there when they returned to the camp site the following year. They replanted tops deliberately, but they never cultivated or fertilized yam patches. This haphazard planting was their only agricultural achievement.

In British Columbia, on the other hand, the Indians did no planting except for the occasional scattering of tobacco seeds on burned-over ground by some of the southern tribes. However, they prized sweet clover and skunk cabbage as greens. The skunk cabbage is one of the first plants to appear in the spring and its shoots were in demand for cooking with dry salmon which had been kept since the previous spring run. It probably improved the flavor. A woman who discovered a good patch of clover or cabbage would fence it, weed it, and put up various ingenious scarecrows to keep the deer away. Other women would respect the patch as her property. However, it never occurred to anyone to try to plant or fertilize such patches.

The use of fertilizer is one of the rarest agricultural techniques, yet it was used by the Indians of our own Atlantic coast. The New England tribes put a herring in each hill of corn when they planted, then went off to hunt, leaving the corn to its own devices until they returned to harvest any which had survived weeds and insect pests.

In the Rocky Mountain plateau the Paiutes neither planted nor cultivated, but they irrigated. They were fond of pig-weed, which they used as greens in the spring and as seeds in the autumn. The Paiutes built small dams at the heads of shallow valleys to impound the winter snow water. The pig-weed grew in the valleys below the dams and each band had an official irrigator who made the rounds of the pig-weed patches from time to time, and if they seemed to be getting too dry, would poke a hole in the dam, let some water run down over them, and then fill up the hole again.

It can be seen from the foregoing that there was no one neat pattern in the development of agriculture. Each crop and each climate presented its own problems which had to be solved.

In the development of food-raising the region extending from northwestern India across Asia Minor and south to the Red Sea and the Sinai desert was of outstanding importance. Seven or eight thousand years ago this whole region seems to have been park country. However, game was not plentiful and the population apparently relied heavily on seeds for its food supply. The region contained a great variety of wild grasses among which were the ancestors of our modern wheat, oats, rye, and barley.

The presence of polished sickle flints in Mesolithic sites shows that the people were reaping grain even before they began to cultivate it, although these grains are among the easiest domesticated plants to grow. At first the sowings were mixed, but as agricultural technique improved, and particularly as the grain growing population shifted out of Southwest Asia into other regions, the different kinds of grain were gradually sorted out. Barley seems to have been the favorite Southwest Asian crop in early times, but as farmers moved northward they found that barley did not do as well as wheat and changed their staple crop accordingly. North of the zone where wheat did best, rye and oats, which had originally been weeds sown unintentionally with the wheat, could still produce good crops. Oats flourished the furthest north of all. There were, of course, further adaptations through the development of particular varieties suited to particular soils or local variations in climate.

All the later cultures which traced their origins to this Southwest Asian area were primarily grain-raisers. However, a few other plants were domesticated in the same general region. A number of plants of the beet-cabbage family were brought under domestication, as well as the onion and cucumber. Apples, pears, almonds, and a bit later, grapes, figs, and dates were cultivated here, and also flax. There were two species of flax: one raised for its fiber, the other for its seed. Although the oil pressed from this seed (linseed oil) has now been relegated to industrial uses, it seems to have formed part of the diet of Neolithic man, whose food supply was notably short in fats.

A second and quite independent center of plant and animal domestication occurred in Southeast Asia. The staple lowland crops were taro, yam, banana, and breadfruit. The coconut also belongs to this region; but since it grows only close to the sea, it was not of economic importance on the mainland. In the Pacific Islands, however, it became a veritable staff of life.

Two animals domesticated in Southeast Asia have become exceedingly important in world economy. These are the pig, also domesticated independently in the West, and the chicken. Both seem to have been domesticated for religious rather than economic reasons. Even today they contribute little to the local food supply. The people in Southeast Asia practiced what is called haruspication: divining from the entrails of animals. The Romans also used this method. Before the Senate opened, the priests would sacrifice an animal and examine its internal organs. The Roman substitute for a filibuster was for the diehard minority to have the augur announce that the auspices were bad and the Senate should not meet that day.

The chicken also seems to have been domesticated first for magical reasons. Its ancestor, the wild jungle fowl, also had the trick of crowing from time to time during the night and always just before dawn, at the time when all ghosts must hurry back to the earth.

In the mountain regions of Southeast Asia a different type of agricultural economy was developed. The first crops raised by the hill people seem to have been yams and certain varieties of rice. The cultivation of dry rice is generally believed to have begun in Assam. Where the domestication of irrigated rice began is still unknown, but the fully irrigated rice complex involved the use of a domestic animal, the water buffalo. This animal can be used as a source of milk, meat, and traction in tropical regions where cattle cannot survive. From Southeast Asia, rice culture was carried northward into China and eventually to Korea and Japan. In all these regions it became the basis of a dense and stabilized population.

Most of our familiar domestic animals seem to have been brought under control in this same Southwest Asian region. Various breeds of cattle, sheep, goats, and donkeys were also developed here from the local wild species. The pig also may have been domesticated here although, if so, there was a second independent center of pig domestication in Southeast Asia. In any case, the pig did not figure in Southwest Asian economy to anything like the extent which it did in Southeast Asia or in the forested regions of western Europe. In the same region but at a much later time the dromedary camel was added to the local equipment.

Horses had been introduced into this region by 3000 B.C., but were still rare animals used for display or in war. Their first domestication was certainly not in this region. The backward trail seems to lead to the Central Asian Steppes, but horse-taming may have been an exceedingly ancient and widespread practice. Horses run in bands made up of mares and young animals, dominated by a single stallion. Since stallions are always anxious to add new mares to their harems, tame mares would be valuable to horse hunters as decoys, and domestication may have begun in this way.

The utilization of horses for anything but food or decoys seems to have been later than that of cattle, for the first pictures of horses in use show a type of harness obviously based on the ox yoke. This arrangement was by

no means satisfactory, since the yoke or breast strap inter-
feres with the horse's breathing, but it was not until the
Middle Ages that the invention of the horse collar in
northern Europe made possible a really effective use of
horse traction. Until fairly late in history horses were not
ridden at all, and it was still later that an effective saddle
suitable for military use was developed.

The ancient people of Southwest Asia were also responsible for the invention of milking, one of the most
revolutionary economic developments in human history.
This invention seems to have been made only once. The
American Indians failed to develop it in the regions
where they had a potential milk animal, the llama, and
even in South China and Japan the technique has been
introduced only within the last century.

The first animal to be milked was probably the goat,
since man was most evenly matched with it in size and
weight. This is also suggested by the earliest pictures of
milking which have come down to us. These show men
milking cattle from directly behind, a position which
would certainly have discouraged the practice if the first
experiments had been made with cows. Later the milking
technique was extended to take in practically all domestic
animals standing higher than pigs, including such, to us,
improbable species as horses and sheep. The economic
potentialities of milking were enormous. As long as domestic animals were used only for meat, it was impossible
for settled people to raise enough animal food per acre to
dispense with other protein sources. With milking, on the
other hand, herds of a size which could be pastured within
walking distance of the village could provide a steady
increment of necessary food elements and make the villagers independent of other protein sources.

METALLURGY

T H E establishment of grain agriculture and
dairying in the Near East was followed by an exceedingly

rapid advance in culture. Most of the inventions basic to ancient civilization seem to have been made before 3500 B.C. One of the most important of these was the development of metallurgy. Native metals had been known in the Near East since very early times. They may even have been noticed and worked sporadically in the Mesolithic. However, the supplies of native metal were small and the discovery of the new substance had no noticeable effect on the culture. It was treated as an unusually tough and malleable stone and worked cold by hammering and grinding. True metallurgy did not begin until it became possible to reduce metals from their ores. Even then, for two thousand years or more, metal of any sort remained so rare and so valuable that its use was largely limited to weapons and ornaments. Metal tools did not become common until the invention of iron-working.

The reduction of metal from ore began in the Near East somewhere between 4000 and 5000 B.C. Copper seems to have been the first metal to be smelted. The copper carbonate ores, malachite and azurite, were already being mined and ground for paint. They reduce to metallic copper at a relatively low temperature, and one is tempted to refer the beginnings of smelting to the experience of some unfortunate Near Eastern gentleman who dropped his paint bag into the fire on a night when there was a high wind. When the fire had died, he would have discovered in place of his vanity kit a small lump of copper, a material already known and valued much more than its ores. The initial discovery that stone could be turned into metal seems to have been followed by experimentation and by a fairly rapid invention of the basic metal working techniques.

The discovery that metal could be obtained from certain stones must have been an exciting one. Everything indicates that shortly after the first discovery of smelting the metal-workers experimented with every available sort of stone which might be a metallic ore. Most of such ores are readily recognizable by their weight and texture. Silver, lead, antimony, and tin were soon discovered. The ancient metal workers must also have been impressed by the surprising changes in melting temperature, fluidity, and hardness which could be produced by adding a small quantity of another metal to copper. Apparently they experimented with this procedure and finally hit upon the combination of tin and copper which has given its name to the Bronze Age.

Why iron came into use only toward the end of the Second Millennium B.C. must remain a puzzle. Iron ores are much commoner than those of any other metals, and the hematite iron ores in particular are readily recognizable by their weight and texture. It is hard to believe that the Near Eastern metallurgists did not experiment with iron ores as they did with the other ores in their territory. Also, the metal itself was known in Egypt from very early times in the form of meteoric iron. Interestingly enough, the Egyptians seem to have guessed its source, for the hieroglyphic for iron means "star metal." The best explanation for the early neglect of iron lies, I believe, in the sharp contrast between the techniques required for its successful working and those used in dealing with copper and its alloys.

In smelting copper, the molten metal collects in the bottom of the furnace while the slag floats on top. In iron-smelting, at least at the temperatures which could be produced by the ancient furnaces, the iron is never completely liquefied. It forms instead a gray, spongy mass technically known as the *bloom*. The interstices of this mass are filled with molten slag which must be forced out by pounding the metal while still white hot. The process is much like that of squeezing water from a sponge. Molten copper can be run into a mold directly from the smelting furnace. To melt iron requires a very high temperature and involved a second operation for the primitive smith. The more carbon in the iron, the lower the melting temperature and the greater its fluidity, but iron with a high carbon content is exceedingly hard and brittle. Our familiar cast iron is an alloy of this sort and is mainly useful for stoves and ornamental railings. Even in these the metal is so brittle that it can be shattered almost as readily as a glass casting of equal weight. If the early metallurgists had ever succeeded in casting iron they would have faced a further difficulty, since any attempt to soften it by the familiar technique for copper, annealing, would have produced a violent explosion. Even with wrought iron, the copper annealing technique would only result in tempering the metal, making it that much harder and more intractable. It seems exceedingly probable that the early smiths did attempt to smelt iron ores and work iron, but gave the metal up as a bad job.

Whatever the reason, we know that the regular use of iron for tools and weapons appears comparatively late and that it was first used extensively by Barbarians who were marginal to the main area of the Bronze Age cultures. Perhaps it was these Barbarians' lack of skill in the working of other metals which led them to try out new techniques and eventually to develop the methods for smelting and using the new metal.

Iron seems to have been successfully worked first in Turkestan or in northern Asia Minor. It is possible that there was a second center of independent development in southern India; in any case, it was here that steel was invented. While a high carbon content makes iron both hard and brittle, a lower carbon content converts it into steel, hard but also tough. Some groups in southern India still make steel by a method so simple that it may well be the original one.

WRITING

W R I T I N G was also a Near Eastern invention and one whose contribution to civilization has been even greater than that of metal. Without techniques for recording and preserving the results of observations, science never could have come into existence. If the ancient priests who were the first astronomers had had to rely on their memories of the movements of the heavenly bodies, they would never have realized how exact and predictable these movements were over long time intervals. Neither would they have arrived at the concepts of natural laws and of a mechanistic universe which were the foundations of all later scientific research.

Writing appears almost simultaneously some 5000-6000 years ago in Egypt, Mesopotamia, and the Indus Valley. Another equally primitive form of writing appears in China some 2000 years later as part of a complex of culture elements of Southwest Asian origin. Even the earliest written characters from these various areas are quite different, which suggests that there was no single origin point for writing. At the same time all these areas have a common remote cultural ancestry in the Southwest Asian food-raising complex. Probably this ancestral culture had as one of its characteristics a tendency to record events with pictures. This tendency resulted in an independent development of pictographs in several localities within the area and the initial local differences were increased by the use of various materials and techniques. Thus, in Egypt the form of the characters was influenced by their use in painting and low-relief carving, while in Mesopotamia their application to clay led to the development of the highly conventionalized cuneiform symbols. In China, the earliest writing technique seems to have been that of scratching characters on bone or bamboo. Later, they were painted and this in itself modified what had originally been recognizable pictures to the conventional Chinese characters.

In all these areas the first step in the development of writing seems to have been the use of pictographs, i.e., actual pictures of things. However, for these pictures to serve to communicate ideas or to have meaning for anyone except the artist himself, it was necessary for them to be both simplified and conventionalized. Certain characteristics of the thing represented had to be exaggerated in order to make it clearly recognizable. Thus, it would take an exceedingly good artist to draw naturalistic pictures of a dog and a wolf which would be immediately recognizable as different animals. However, if one figure had the tail curled over the back and the other the tail low, there could be no mistake. Dogs' tails curl up, which wolves' tails never do.

In course of time a series of conventional figures of this sort would come to be generally understood and could be used for communication. Some of the North American Indian tribes had reached this stage independently and were able to send simple messages scratched on birch bark. The main difficulties of the system lay in the tremendous number of pictures required for anything except the simplest sort of communication and in the impossibility of making pictures of many things. Thus, no one could draw wind or light, much less such a psychological state as happiness or an abstract concept like energy. At this point, two lines emerged for possible future development. One of them involved the attachment of purely conventional values to signs, as when a scroll represents speech, a series of wavy lines water, or a stone the abstract quality of hardness. Pictures used in this way are known as ideographs. The other was the attachment of phonetic values to pictures of things with monosyllabic names, and the use of these pictures to build up longer words. This technique, known as rebus writing, is sometimes used among ourselves in making puzzles for small children. The real transition from pictographs to true writing came when people speaking different languages took over rebus writing systems. For them each picture would have only one meaning: it would stand for the sound of a particular syllable and nothing else. The number of syllables employed in any language is limited, and most syllabaries, as writing of this sort is called, do not include more than two hundred symbols. Such a syllabary makes it possible for anyone to learn to read and write without devoting a lifetime to the task. However, even the simplest syllabic system is fairly complicated and difficult to learn, and can become the basis of a profitable profession, that of scribe.

Against the advantages of greater simplification and wider distribution of literacy within the society, scribes weighed the possibilities of technological unemployment and were content with the status quo. In Egypt in partic-

ular, although the possibilities of writing were explored
in very early times with the development of a syllabary, of
ideographs, and even of true alphabetic symbols, all three
forms were retained and mingled in the same inscriptions.
Although the characters themselves were simplified for
everyday use, the scribes, who dominated both learning
and government administration, preferred to keep writing
a mystery, and throughout the whole of Egyptian history
the writer was a professional who devoted years to learning his craft. In Mesopotamia, writing was much simpler,
and a knowledge of it seems to have been widespread
among merchants and professionals. Nevertheless, it was
still complicated enough so that most of the population
remained illiterate and the letter-writer was a professional
even as in many Eastern bazaars today.

The development of a true alphabet proletarianized
learning much as the use of iron proletarianized metal.
All alphabets now in use can be traced to a single point of
origin in the Sinai Peninsula. The Egyptians carried on
extensive mining operations here and employed, in addition to criminals and prisoners of war, contingents of pastoral Semites who were forced to work for them when
their regular food supplies failed. The sheiks of the Semites acted as mine foremen and were required to draw up
reports on their output and payroll. Since the regular
Egyptian system of writing was much too complicated for
them to learn, they took the simple symbols representing
single sounds which were a part of the Egyptian system,
and thus developed the first alphabet.

This took place about 1800 B.C. The alphabet spread
from Sinai to other Semitic regions and eventually
reached those great ancient traders and seafarers, the
Phoenicians. As business men engaged in long-range ven-
tures requiring contracts and correspondence, the Phoenicians were quick to realize the advantage of an easily
learned and therefore widely diffusable system of writing.
They carried it west to the Greeks, who, prehensile as
always, promptly accepted it and developed a whole series
of local variations. All of these differed from the original
Phoenician alphabet in the use of vowel signs. Vowel signs

were unnecessary in the guttural Semitic tongues, but were all-important for recording the Indo-European languages. From Greece, the alphabet was carried westward to Italy, where it assumed the Roman form, and, by a much later movement, north into the Slavic countries, where it became the ancestor of the later Cyrillic alphabet, whose characters differ from the Latin ones, thus contributing considerably to the lack of understanding between Russia and the rest of Europe.

Chinese writing followed the same evolutionary pattern as the Western forms up to the point where a syllabary might have emerged, but here, for some reason, it took a divergent course. Instead of developing into a true phonetic system, it evolved in the ideographic direction; i.e., the characters came to represent combinations of ideas rather than combinations of sounds. The reason for this may have been an early extension of political units in China beyond the limits of particular dialects, thus diminishing the value of phonetic writing; or it may have reflected the philosophic and analytical interests of the scholar class who controlled both education and government administration. Whatever the reason, this evolution produced a system of writing which could be learned as a separate language. On the credit side, this writing makes it possible for persons who cannot communicate at all in their spoken languages, Chinese, Japanese, Koreans, and Annamese, for example, to write back and forth freely and with perfect understanding. On the debit side, it requires a vocabulary of characters comparable in numbers to the word vocabulary of any spoken language. Knowledge of several thousand characters is required for ordinary literacy, while the total number is supposed to be in the neighborhood of twenty-five or thirty thousand.

TECHNOLOGICAL INVENTIONS

THE Southwest Asian center also contributed to the development of civilization three mechanical inventions secondary in their importance only to metallurgy and writing. These were the wheel, the plow, and the loom. Until a few years ago it was believed that the wheel was an exclusive Southwest Asian invention. However, it is now known that the ancient Mexicans had discovered the wheel principle, but, curiously enough, used it only for children's toys. It is still safe to say that all wheels put to practical uses, whether for transportation or in mechanics, trace back to Southwest Asia.

The discovery of the wheel principle opened up great areas of technical development. Even today it is basic to most mechanical appliances. In the lathe it made possible the turning of wood and even stone to symmetrical cylindrical shapes. The same principle, applied to clay, became the potter's wheel. The potter's wheel, in its simplest and most universal form, is really an ancient style pair of disk cart wheels with axle attached.

The social effects of the plow and the loom were even more immediate and far-reaching than those of the wheel. In the Southwest Asian Neolithic division of labor, women seem to have carried on the first agriculture, to have made pottery, mats, and baskets, and to have taken care of the cooking and baby-tending much as they do today. The men, on the other hand, hunted, fought, cared for the domestic animals (after animals had been domesticated) and worked in wood and stone. With the development of the plow, which, like the wheel, required animal traction, men passed over into agriculture. This transformation was most complete in connection with crops that were mass produced. The plow is an uneconomic instrument for the small garden which, after the initial breaking of the soil, can be better taken care of with the hoe. Women retained a place in agriculture during the hurried periods of sowing and harvesting the major crops, and in the kitchen garden, which thrives best under close attention and loving care.

The loom made possible a new level of both quantity and quality in clothing. It also may have been responsible for the emergence of the first ideas of personal cleanliness. The older skin clothing could not be washed; cloth, whether woven from wool or vegetable fiber, could be. Cloth could also be mass produced and provided an ideal method for the busy housewife to contribute to the family exchequer in the brief intervals between spells of cooking and baby-tending. The loom could be set up in the house or under some near-by shelter, and the woman could repair to it and weave a few inches whenever there were no pressing demands on her time. The product was sufficiently standardized, useful, and indestructible so that it could serve as currency. Thus, we find in the earliest Egyptian tax rolls that taxes might be collected in either grain or linen, while as late as the 10th century A.D. wadmal, a coarse woolen cloth, useful for many purposes, served as a medium of exchange in Scandinavia.

CITIES

A L L students of culture recognize that there is more than a quantitative difference between the cultures of peasant communities and civilizations, but there is little agreement as to exactly where the line can be drawn. Perhaps the best criterion for differentiation is the presence or absence of cities. Even today there is little realization of how important and unique this form of human aggregate is. It represents a social invention which in its significance for the growth of culture is fully as important as any technological invention with the possible exception of food-raising.

There are certain prerequisites for the establishment of cities. First, a relatively dense population is necessary in order to create the surplus of food required to support the nuclear city group. In early times this was possible only in river valleys where the rich soil gave heavy return for cultivation and made permanent settlement possible. Quite as important as dense population was the presence of effective techniques for the transportation of bulk goods. Luxury objects can be traded over great distances in periods or regions where such techniques are lacking. Thus, in North America, the Hopewell mound builders of Ohio received limited quantities of obsidian from the Yellowstone, copper from Lake Superior, mica from North Carolina, and shells from the Gulf of Mexico. However, the transportation of bulk goods presents a different problem. They can be moved more readily by water than by any other means and, failing this, must rely upon animal transport with or without the aid of wheeled vehicles. Human transport of such bulk goods, especially staple foods, is uneconomic since the human bearer must carry his own food, thus setting strict limits to the distance over which he can carry a payload.

All the great cities of the premechanized era in the Near East, China, and India were on rivers or the coast. In this connection, the presence of irrigation systems is also very important. The irrigated fields support a dense population, while the network of canals provides water transport. In America, where the wheel was completely lacking and pack animals were available only in a limited area in South America, there were very few true cities. Tenochtitlan, the ancient city of Mexico, may well have been the only real city north of the Isthmus. It stood on an island in a large lake surrounded by rich farm lands and could thus be fed by local produce brought by water. Its political dominance made it possible for it to ignore land transport costs and have luxury objects and the more valuable raw materials brought as tribute. Cuzco, the Inca capital, was also a real city, made possible by the use of pack animals and its position as administrative center for a great and highly organized empire.

Wherever cities appeared they posed a whole series of new social problems. Many of these stemmed from the simple biological fact that our species even now has not adapted itself successfully to life in large aggregates. Until some five thousand years ago all human beings lived in relatively small communities which had only infrequent contacts with outsiders. Even today, a large part of the world's population follows this residence pattern. Under such conditions disease outbreaks are localized and communities rarely have to deal with the virulent strains which develop when bacteria pass rapidly through a great number of hosts. In the city there is much greater opportunity for the exchange of diseases and the emergence of virulent mutations. Not only are large numbers of people crowded together, but the far-flung trade on which the city depends for its existence brings constant increments of infection. Nearly all of the great epidemics which have ravaged Europe in historic times can be traced to particular cities into which they were introduced by foreign goods or travelers.

The mortality rate for adults in premechanized cities was bad enough, but that for infants was even worse. It was quite out of the question for such cities to maintain their population by simple reproduction. Even now, when modern sanitary techniques have reduced the death rate to more reasonable size, it is doubtful whether any city maintains its population in this way. As disease diminishes, other factors come in to keep the population down. The city dweller, confronted by the difficulties of rearing children in crowded quarters and by the economic insecurity inseparable from city life, limits his offspring. That there may be a further sterility factor derived from high tension living seems probable, but whatever the complex causes, the results are the same. City populations do not and never have reproduced themselves.

It follows that city populations have always been kept up by a flow of individuals from the villages and farm lands within the city's zone of exploitation—the protoplasm of the city cell. These immigrants were the raw material from which the city shaped its urbanized inhabitants. In colloquial parlance, the village and farm fed

yokels into the city along with other raw materials necessary to its existence and the city transformed the yokel
into a specialized product, the city slicker.

The peasants who went to the premechanized city
were by no means a random sample of the rural population. They were mostly those who did not fit into village
life. At the lower end of the scale were the local ne'er-do-
wells and petty criminals whom the village, when its patience was exhausted, disposed of by the ancient and
world-wide pattern of "running out of town." In the
anonymity of the city such individuals could carry on their
petty depredations with much less danger to themselves.
More valuable material was provided by those peasants
who, having lost their equity in village lands, flowed to the
city in the hope of finding some type of employment.
Such migrants provided the city with a mass of cheap unskilled labor which formed the earliest authentic proletariat. It was also the first labor which could be treated as
a commodity, since it was not linked to the employer by
ties of blood or familiar association.

Lastly, there must have been a fair number of individuals who went to the city of their own free will because
they were conscious of the added opportunities for advancement and employment which the urban environment provided. In other words, the ancient city drew most
heavily from the dregs and, by our standards, from the
cream of the rural dwellers. This gave the city population
a distinctive quality from the start. It was heavily
weighted on the side of the unstable individual, one who
lacked the stolid contentment of the successful peasant.

The city dweller loses the security which comes from
living among neighbors or sharing the activities of an extended kin group, but at the same time, his success is not
hampered by poor relations. The breakdown of extended
kin ties seems to be characteristic of city life in all times
and places. In general, city immigrants seem to find the
possible rewards worth the risk. It may be noted that once
the peasant has moved to the city, he is in almost all cases
unwilling to return to rural life. The leitmotif of the old
song, "How're you gonna keep 'em down on the farm,

after they've seen Paree?" seems to have been as valid in Sumerian times as it is today.

Even today, the population of any city is composed largely of strangers, and of socially difficult strangers. This sets new problems of social control. The informal pressures of public opinion, which are effective in keeping the average individual in line in any small face-to-face community, become largely inoperative. No one in the city cares what you do, nor do you care what strangers think. The behavior of modern conventioneers turned loose on the town might serve as a case in point. It thus becomes necessary to develop new systems of control based on formal patterns of coercion. The police force and the police court appeared exceedingly early in history in forms not very different from those which they still retain.

A significant by-product of the earliest city life of which we have record was the emergence of highly formal patterns of law and legal procedure. The village may or may not recognize the existence of formal laws as distinct from simple taboos and folkways. However, even in those cultures in which formal law exists, it is still possible to achieve a fairly close approximation of justice in small face-to-face communities. Where everyone in the community knows everyone else, the possible number of offenders in any case is so limited that apprehension becomes almost certain, while in interpersonal disputes there can be very little doubt as to who is in the right.

In the city, on the other hand, the number of possible offenders is much greater and the chance of apprehending the wrong man is increased accordingly. In civil cases it is quite impossible for the judge, who can know nothing of the personalities involved in a dispute or their backgrounds of previous interaction, to administer real justice of the sort which emerges more or less automatically in the village. It seems highly probable that, when it first emerged, the whole concept of formal law and legal procedure was actually a by-product of the urban situation. Confronted by the necessity of dealing with persons and disputes en masse and under circumstances where the judge's knowledge of the actual factors involved was minimal, there was an attempt to substitute for authentic knowledge what were, in effect, magical practices. Thus, it was loudly announced that the law was no respecter of persons, a fact which if adhered to would immediately remove its operation from the possibility of achieving justice. The operation of the law and its agents was surrounded by solemn ritual, both to impress the observer and as a part of the magical performance. Proceedings were carried on with rigid formality and in the solemn atmosphere appropriate to an approach to the supernatural. One finds that penalties for contempt of court are practically as old as courts themselves.

The lawyer and judge emerged as technologists who studied the wordings of laws with microscopic care. Precedents were cited, and the more ancient these were and the greater amount of research required to establish them, the greater their magical efficacy. Only in China, a civilization divergent in this as in many other respects, was precedent deliberately ignored in favor of the current situation.

Formal law codes and stereotyped legal procedures may exist in nonurbanized societies, as they do in most African tribes and in Indonesia, with its *adat* law. However, the small face-to-face community can function quite successfully without such patterns. The city definitely cannot. It is significant that, although American Indian cultures were notably lacking in legal concepts, both formal law codes and stereotyped legal procedures were developed in the few localities where city living occurred.

In return for raw materials and population, the city furnished the area which it dominated with specialized services. The most important of these were associated with religion, administration, and trade. The city was normally a religious center for the inhabitants of the surrounding territory, a center to which the peasantry resorted for impressive and therefore presumably hyper-effective appeals to the supernatural powers. The assemblies created by periodic religious ceremonies readily lend themselves to purposes of trade and exchange. The pious pilgrims brought with them surplus produce which they exchanged for goods which their own village could not provide. In this connection, the city also provided a distribution point for foreign products which could be much more economically handled in this way than through small sales to scattered villages.

Temple and market were central features of most ancient cities. Needless to say, the city was a place for the exchange of ideas as well as goods. Cities everywhere functioned as focal points in the diffusion of culture. Not only did travelers and merchants come to them from a distance, but there was also a strong tendency for such strangers to establish foreign quarters within the city itself. This resulted in a close and continuous association between groups of different cultures with greatly increased opportunities for the exchange of ideas. In these ancient cities, as in our modern ones, there was a two-directional acculturation process whereby the settled stranger within the gates both gave and received new things.

The importance of the early city as an administrative center has frequently been overlooked. Every ancient city had its palace, which was not only the ruler's residence but also the site of the various offices required for the administration of the city's territory. In the ancient city the relation between secular and religious rulers was always close, if not always sympathetic, and one often finds the palaces and the administrative offices blending into the temple establishment.

The ancient city also supported a much more varied range of activities and specialists than was possible in the village. Skilled craftsmen, such as jewelers, or armorers, whose services would be needed only intermittently in a small community, could become full-time operators in the city, thanks to the expanded market. The presence of numerous fellow-craftsmen and imports of foreign objects provided both a stimulus to the improvement of techniques and an understanding audience who could appreciate and provide prestige rewards for superior workmanship. The cities were also able to offer continuous employment to doctors, lawyers, scribes, teachers, and so forth. Members of these professions were actually attached to the

temple establishment and aided in maintaining its domination over the intellectual life of the community. Much as
in the case of the skilled craftsman, the presence of numerous workers in the same field had a stimulating effect
on the development of ideas. In the city, for the first time,
it became possible for the philosopher or primitive scientist
to meet others with common interests and to whet his
mind against theirs.

3 SOUTHEAST ASIAN COMPLEX

SOUTHEAST ASIAN NEOLITHIC

T H E history of Southeast Asia during and immediately after the closing phases of the glacial period is still obscure. Technological improvement here seems to have taken the form of an increasing use of wood and bamboo. Since these are perishable materials, the archaeological record gives a false effect of cultural simplicity. Evidence of many sorts suggests that food-raising was developed independently in Southeast Asia and that a distinctive Neolithic complex was developed there. In the absence of archaeological evidence we must turn to that provided by marginal survivals. When a culture complex has been diffused over a considerable area, older forms will tend to survive around the margins and in regions of comparative isolation after they have died out in the original center of diffusion. The fact that Elizabethan English ballads are still sung by some of our southern mountaineers would be a case in point.

The Malayo-Polynesian languages have their center in Southeast Asia and Indonesia and wherever they are found it is safe to assume that they were introduced by migrants from this general region. The ancient Indonesians were excellent sailors and carried their languages and culture eastward to the farthest Pacific Islands and westward to Madagascar. When the same distinctive culture elements are found at the opposite ends of this tremendous area and also among isolated, culturally conservative groups living in remote Indonesian islands and in the mountains of Southeast Asia, it is safe to conclude that such elements are referable to an old stratum of Southeast Asian culture. It is impossible to say with certainty whether such elements are as old as the Neolithic, but they certainly belong to the relatively primitive pattern of life which existed in this region prior to the introduction of Hindu and Chinese culture elements.

The migrations of the Malayo-Polynesian speaking peoples from their homeland in Southeast Asia and the adjoining islands present one of the most amazing phenomena in history. In spite of their atomistic political patterns, which made it impossible for them to organize large communal projects, and their late acquisition of metal, they were able to encircle a full third of the globe in their voyages of exploration and to establish permanent settlements at points as remote as the island of Madagascar, only 250 miles off the East African coast, and Easter Island, only 2200 miles from the coast of South America and nearly due south of Denver, U.S.A.

Migrations from Indonesia certainly began while the Malayo-Polynesians were in the Neolithic stage of culture and continued until recent times. Thus, Malayan trepang fishermen still visit the coast of northern Australia, where they have left mixed blood offspring and have exerted considerable influence on the aboriginal culture. However, the great period of migration seems to have begun around 2000 B.C. and to have ended by 500 A.D., about the time when Southeast Asia and Indonesia came under the dominance of Indian culture.

When the Malayo-Polynesian migrations began, Melanesia was occupied by dark-skinned people of Negroid or Australoid stock who were culturally backward. Lying as it does on the margin of the Malayo-Polynesian home territory, Melanesia was subjected to a constant flow of invaders. By the beginning of the historic period, Malayo-Polynesian languages had been established everywhere except in the interiors of a few of the largest islands. However, in spite of a great many local variations in physical type, the result of social isolation and close in-breeding, even today the population is still predominantly Negroid or Australoid. Proto- or deutero-Malay groups are to be found only on a few small off-shore islands, and even these groups appear to be descendants of Polynesians who drifted back into the region from the east in fairly recent times.

The best explanation for this curious inconsistency in the distribution of language and physical type seems to be that the Malayo-Polynesian migrants found the Melanesian environment much more hostile than the Melanesian natives. Even modern Europeans with modern medicine have found it hard to survive in Melanesia. There are a great many endemic diseases, among which numerous strains of malignant malaria occupy a prominent place. The early Malayo-Polynesian migrants probably made numerous settlements on the Melanesian islands, intermarrying with the local aborigines. Their descendants were hybrids from every point of view. They spoke a variety of languages, in all of which the Malayo-Polynesian elements predominated, and practiced a great variety of local cultures based on various combinations of aboriginal and Malayo-Polynesian traits. However, the aboriginal physical type, with its superior environmental adaptation, gradually replaced that of the invaders. A similar situation can be recognized in some of the older tropical colonies established by Europeans. European languages and much of European culture survive, but present populations show few traces of European blood.

The descendants of the first migrants to enter Polynesia by the southern route survived into historic times in the Marquesas Islands, Mangareva, and Easter Island. They also formed an important element in the great twelfth century migration to New Zealand. Although they showed little or no Melanesian blood, they shared various culture traits with that region. The most important of these were a vigorous head cult, with headhunting and the preservation of the heads of both enemies and ancestors, cannibalism of a gastronomic rather than ceremonial type, extreme political fragmentation and constant intertribal warfare, and a vigorous, predominantly curvilinear representative art in which human figures were the usual subjects.

The migrants who came by the northern route occupied Micronesia and seem to have been the first settlers in Hawaii. A radio carbon date from Saipan in the Carolines gives approximately 1500 B.C. for a settlement there, but sporadic migrations have continued into modern times and the bulk of the Micronesians are of deutero- rather than proto-Malay physical type.

The Malayo-Polynesian occupation of the Philippines and their penetration of Melanesia were only the first steps in their eastward movement. When these were passed, the whole Pacific lay open to them with a multitude of uninhabited islands waiting to be colonized. One migration route seems to have been through Melanesia and along the relatively close-lying Polynesian Islands from Tonga and Samoa eastward to the Society group, the Marquesas, and ultimately Easter Island. Another migration route ran far to the north, taking the migrants into the small and widely scattered Micronesian Islands, from which they eventually reached Hawaii.

The westward migrations of the Malayo-Polynesians are more difficult to reconstruct, but that these migrations were on no inconsiderable scale is proved by the presence in Madagascar of a population not only Malayo-Polynesian in language and culture but also both proto-Malay and deutero-Malay in physical type. The Indian Ocean is the most benevolent of the earth's oceans. Its monsoons make it possible to sail with a steady following wind either east or west, according to the season. It is highly probable that while the Greeks were still harbor-hopping along the barren coasts between the mouth of the Red Sea and India, the seawise Malayo-Polynesians had found their way from Java and Sumatra to East Africa.

The earliest date for the Malayo-Polynesian movement to Africa and Madagascar can only be conjectured, but stone implements of the characteristic Southeast Asian Neolithic types have not been reported from either locality. This does not mean that they may not come to light when intensive archaeological work is undertaken in these areas, but on the basis of present knowledge it seems improbable that the main Malayo-Polynesian migrations took place before the migrants had become acquainted with iron-working. Conversely, the techniques of African iron-working, the shapes of many African tools and weapons, and particularly the use throughout Africa of various modified forms of the piston bellows, an east Asian appliance, suggest that the iron-working of Negro Africa was borrowed from Malayo-Polynesian sources.

OCEANIA

THE marginal Malayo-Polynesian cultures which have survived in Oceania and Madagascar have contributed little to the main streams of cultural evolution. However, they have provided students of society and culture with some of their most interesting comparative material. The relative isolation of many of the islands and the general tendency of the Malayo-Polynesians to live in small endogamous tribes, or even villages which avoid outside contacts, has provided an excellent opportunity for the study of the results of independent cultural growth. One finds every conceivable change rung on a small series of cultural themes which are present almost everywhere. Needless to say, this cultural variety makes generalization difficult. Parallel independent developments seem to have taken place in some regions, while the freedom of movement of the Malayo-Polynesian sea rovers has resulted in a series of broken distributions which defy the neat culture area classification possible in continental regions. Thus, in a general description of Polynesia, a number of the statements true for most Polynesian localities simply do not apply to Samoa. This group was a sort of aristocratic republic whose members paid little attention to genealogy and even less to religion. The regular Polynesian gods appeared as figures in a pleasant and interesting mythology, but there was not a single temple or professional priest in the entire group and the ubiquitous ancestral spirits received scant attention.

The most famous of the "primitive" Malayo-Polynesian areas is Polynesia. Unfortunately it is also one of the areas whose aboriginal cultures are least known, since it received the full impact of late eighteenth and early nineteenth century missionary ardor, epidemic diseases, and commercial exploitation. By the time modern ethnological methods for collecting and analyzing cultural material had been developed, most of the Polynesian cultures were moribund. Early visitors have left valuable records of what they saw but usually misunderstood. They interpreted the Polynesians as a happy combination of the Natural Man, then being idealized by Rousseau and his romantic followers, and the aristocratic, class organized society so dear to all "right thinking" gentlemen of the period. The casualness of Polynesian sex mores and the beauty of the Polynesian women, especially as viewed by sailors many months at sea, also contributed to the picture of an earthly paradise. Unfortunately, the combination of misunderstanding and romanticism led to the development of certain stereotypes regarding Polynesian culture; stereotypes which were followed unquestioningly by later authors of travel books on the area and also by many serious students. Even today there is a tendency to view Polynesian political organization in terms of European monarchy and Polynesian religion in terms of classical mythology and an established church.

It is unfortunate that the early visitors who wrote about Polynesian culture did not include at least one "braw Highlander," who might have recognized how much Polynesian tribes and Scottish clans were alike. In both, the clansmen occupied a particular territory, claimed descent from a remote common ancestor, and normally intermarried among themselves. In both the chief was simply the man who traced his descent from the common ancestor in the most direct line. He could never lack for a successor since, if the tribesmen were taken away one by one beginning with the individual of highest descent, the last survivor could legitimately assume the chiefly title and insignia. The respect and obedience accorded the chief by the clansmen were owed to him less as an individual than as a symbol of the clan. Chief and followers were united by reciprocal obligations springing from their ties as kindred.

To this extent Polynesians and Scots were alike. In New Zealand, the Marquesas Islands, and a few other localities, every tribe stood alone except for temporary alliances, much as in the Highlands. In those Polynesian areas where the later migrants had set up states, notably Hawaii and the Society Islands, the chief of the dominant tribe became a king and received tribute from the other tribes, usually interpreted as an offering in repayment for the use of his supernatural powers in their behalf. The other members of this tribe enjoyed added prestige but they were not transformed into feudal nobles. Unless they reinforced their position by marriage with high ranking families from the subject tribes, they had to work like anyone else.

Polynesian kings surrounded themselves with courts which were supported by forced donations from their subjects. The court was made up partly of royal kindred but mostly of individuals chosen for special abilities without regard to their origin. Visitors from other islands gravitated to the court, where, if they possessed the necessary personal qualifications, they would be made royal body servants. Since they were not descended from the local ancestors, they were nonconductors of the local variety of *mana* and could touch the royal person and belongings without danger to themselves or others. Famous warriors also came to court, where they not only formed a royal guard but also stood ready to enforce royal decrees. Councilors were chosen for their wisdom irrespective of their origin. Lastly, every court included a large number of male and female entertainers. In southeastern Polynesia these entertainers were organized into a society whose members were vowed to celibacy though by no means to chastity. They traveled from court to court in troupes, putting on dances and dramatic performances of an erotic character. It is interesting to note that the natives themselves regarded the royal courts as centers of idleness and profligacy.

There were two points at which the Polynesian social system was unique. Instead of looking back to a great age, the Polynesians looked forward. They conceived of the tribe as an "upward growing, outward pushing tree." Each generation was superior in *mana* to the generation before and the eldest child in a family ranked its own parents. This was carried so far that in many Polynesian localities a chief automatically lost his status as tribal head on the birth of an heir and ruled as regent only, until such time as his son became old enough to take over.

The second distinctive feature of Polynesian social organization, and one which has caused endless confusion to students, was their peculiar system for reckoning descent and establishing rank. The first-born child, whether boy or girl, had highest rank within the family. The second born came next, and so down the line. In recounting genealogies, the line was traced through the ancestor of highest rank in each generation, whether man or woman. Polynesian descent was thus neither matrilineal nor patrilineal but primogenitural, an arrangement found nowhere else in the world. In theory, the social position of the individual was established by both his own birth order and that of his ancestors. Since all a tribe's members were descended from the tribe's founder, the relative ranks of any two individuals within the tribe could be established simply by tracing their genealogies. The more eldest children in such a genealogy, the higher the rank. Since genealogies were also used to establish the individual's rights to land and to other privileges, such as a seat in the tribal sacred place, they were kept with great care. Authentic genealogies running to twenty and thirty generations were not uncommon, while some, probably mythical in the early parts, ran for as much as eighty generations.

The primogenitural method of reckoning descent and rank had important repercussions on Polynesian social and political organization. It meant that many sisters were socially superior to their brothers, wives superior to their husbands, and so forth. This resulted in an unusual degree

of equality between the sexes. Although women were subjected to a few taboos which did not affect men, and each
sex had its own prescribed interests and activities, there is
probably no other "primitive" group in which men and
women stood so nearly on a par socially.

The primogenitural pattern also had important effects
on the political organization. If the eldest child of a chief
was a daughter, she would enjoy the highest social rank in
the tribe and transmit this to her eldest child. At the same
time it was impossible for her to perform the complete
functions of a chief, which included acting as war leader.
In such cases the chieftainship would temporarily pass to
the oldest of her brothers, but if her eldest child was a son,
the chieftainship would revert to him. If the senior line
had first-born daughters for several generations while the
junior lines had first-born sons, the chieftainship would
tend to become fixed in the junior line. At the same time,
the senior line would maintain its higher rank and even
broaden the social gap between itself and the ruling line
generation by generation. Thus in eighteenth century
Tonga, the individual of highest rank was the first-born
daughter of the king's elder sister, also first born. Whenever the king met the lady he had to acknowledge her
superior rank by stooping and removing his upper garment. It is said that the king resented this so intensely that
whenever he knew the lady was in the neighborhood he
kept a screen of scouts out so that he would be warned in
time to avoid meeting her.

When a first-born son appeared in the senior line a
serious problem would arise, since the junior line, understandably, would not want to surrender its powers. The
usual system was to make the representative of the senior
line a sacred chief immobilized by his sanctity. In extreme
cases such a chief rendered everything he touched, even
the ground he walked on or a tree his shadow fell on, *taboo,* so that he could only go out at night and had to be
carried even then. None except the designated servants
could touch his person or handle his clothes, and any vessel from which he ate or drank had to be promptly destroyed to preserve others from injury. One is reminded of

the plight of the equally sacred and impotent Japanese emperors under the Shogunate.

Several of the Polynesian groups had found brother and sister marriage a simple answer to the problems raised by the primogenitural descent system. If the eldest child was a girl, she was married to her younger brother. In this way all conflicting claims to the chieftainship were elmi- nated while the offspring received a double dose of the he- reditary *mana*. In most parts of Polynesia, brother and sis- ter marriage of any other type was as rigidly reprehended as among ourselves. However, in Hawaii, the desire to build up *mana* seems to have led to the marriage even of elder brothers to younger sisters, an arrangement which was regarded as scandalous by the other Polynesians.

It is impossible to understand Polynesian political or- ganization and government without reference to the con- cepts of *mana* and *taboo*. Unfortunately, neither of these terms can be directly translated into English. The nearest equivalent for *mana* would be "power for accomplish- ment." Thus any object or person who was capable of more than ordinary performance, whether the subject was a hook that caught more than the usual number of fish or a chief who was more than usually good in diplomatic ma- neuvering, showed in this way that it had mana. A similar idea is found among many uncivilized people, but no other group had systematized it as thoroughly as the Polynesians. They developed it into a logical philosophic concept by which all manifestations of superior ability were reduced to a common denominator.

Mana was completely inanimate and nonsentient, like our own concepts of force or energy. It was thought of as universally present and available for use, given the correct techniques. One might compare it to radio waves, and the people or things which manifested it to receiving sets. Gods and spirits as well as human beings owed their power to their ability to receive and concentrate mana. The ability varied greatly in degree, so that a living chief might actually possess much more mana than a ghost or even one of the less important gods. Mana was highly in- fectious and anything which had come in contact with an individual or object of high mana was thus rendered dangerous for individuals of lower mana.

While the mana belief was superficially similar to such American Indian concepts as *maniton* power and *orenda,* there was one very fundamental difference which reflected the different attitudes of Polynesians and Indians toward what we call the supernatural. The American Indian recognized the presence of power by a subjective test. He knew it was there because he felt awe, wonder, or what Goldenweiser would call the "religious thrill." The Polynesian had no such subjective test for mana. He could no more recognize its presence before he saw it act than one would recognize that a wire was charged with electricity before he experimented with it. For this reason objects or places which mana rendered dangerous had to be marked. Everywhere in Polynesia *taboo* signs were used to indicate that a place was sacred or that property was under magical protection.

Taboo also has no exact equivalent in English. The word first became familiar to Europeans through the publication of Captain Cook's writings in the late eighteenth century, but it supplied a previous lack in the English language so neatly that it was immediately adopted. To the Polynesians *tapu* meant something forbidden, something involving supernatural danger either to oneself or to others. Tapu did not imply that the thing was immoral or even illegal. The tapu object or act was always associated with mana. Violation of the tapu by one with less mana than the one in whose name it was imposed was automatically followed by calamity.

It was only in the conquest states where the rulers and subjects were not linked by ties of kinsip that the taboo institution was used for exploitation. This reached its maximum in Hawaii where, following the eighteenth century conquest of the entire group by Kamehameha I, successive rulers and a well-organized priesthood imposed more and more taboos until the commoners were reduced to poverty and desperation. Deliverance came as a result of a struggle between church and state. The king himself broke the taboo by eating publicly from the same dish with his queen. When it was seen that nothing happened to either one of them, word spread like wildfire. The entire institution collapsed. The commoners rose, overthrew the priests and destroyed the temples, so that Hawaii was without an official religion when the first missionaries arrived.

Polynesian religion, like Polynesian social organization, has been extensively misinterpreted. The only supernatural beings worshipped everwhere (except Samoa) were the spirits of the tribal ancestors. Each tribe had its own sacred place used for this worship and also in connection with funeral rites. The souls of dead chiefs were especially powerful because of their identification with the tribe as a whole. At a greater emotional distance than the ancestors, but not necessarily more powerful, there were a host of highly specialized deities which took care of every conceivable activity. Thus there were not only gods of canoe makers and fishermen, but also gods of thieves and even of various sexual practices which the natives themselves regarded as perversions. Many of these divine specialists seem to have been the ghosts of especially skillful practitioners of the craft involved, preferably tribe members. Deities whose aid was in demand might have shrines where small sacrifices were made by individuals needing their help.

Lastly, there were a series of great deities who were associated with creation or who supervised whole departments of the cosmos. Thus Tangaloa was God of the Sea and, quite understandably, the special patron of the Polynesian aristocracies which traced their origin to the later invaders from Micronesia. Rongo was God of Vegetation and, by extension, patron of both forests and agriculture. These great deities were sometimes made the subjects of formal state cults in the regions where states existed, but in most of Polynesia they had been "gently relegated to the abyss of first causes." They were literary deities, a fact which most writers on Polynesian religion failed to realize.

Where groups of tribes had been organized into states, as in Hawaii and the Society Islands, there were elaborate temple establishments in which rites were performed on behalf of the state and its rulers. The attendance of the subjects was insisted upon as an expression of political loyalty although they might not be allowed to take part in the actual ceremonies. Thus in Hawaii only members of the chiefly group could enter the temple enclosure. The commoners stood outside and went through the required genuflections and responses when signaled by a priest who stood on the wall. Sacrifices were elaborate, with human sacrifice a feature of most state cults, and rituals were long and complicated. As in ancient Rome, any slip in the performance of a ritual made it necessary to begin again at the beginning, and, in Polynesia, carelessness was usually discouraged by executing the one who made the mistake.

Professional priests were required even for the tribal ancestor cults. They were of two classes, ritual priests and inspirational priests. The ritual priests knew the procedures required in various ceremonies and also were repositories of tribal lore of all sorts. The inspirational priests were hysterics who had the happy ability of becoming possessed by gods or ancestral spirits. While in a trance state they acted as divine mouthpieces, giving oracles, demanding sacrifices, and so forth. Both inspirational priests and images were regarded as media through which the gods and their worshippers could be brought into closer contact. The god was called into his image to receive the sacrifice or hear the prayer, just as he came into the inspirational priest to make known his wants. It is significant of Polynesian attitudes in general that ceremonial priests everywhere ranked inspirational priests so greatly that the two did not conflict.

The Polynesian approach to life was kinetic rather than emotional. One apprehended reality by working with it, and found the universe orderly and comprehensible. If one seeks for a single term to characterize their culture the best one would be *manipulative*. The highest prestige was accorded to the most skilled technicians, no matter what the activity might be. Even in the field of interpersonal relations technique reigned supreme. The rules governing social behavior were elaborate and formal and could never be ignored. Social interaction took on the aspects of a chess game in which the player who made the correct moves in the correct order could compel compliance with his demands. Sex was regarded as an enjoyable physical function on a par with eating. Romantic love was considered an adolescent aberration, and admiration went to the skillful amorist of either sex rather than the faithful one.

Even in its ruins Polynesian culture has maintained these fundamental attitudes. European visitors are usually charmed by the Polynesians, who take as much pride in their skill as hosts as a good Swiss hotelkeeper would, but there is as little emotional involvement in one case as in the other.

SOUTHEAST ASIAN POST-NEOLITHIC

A S W E have observed, Southeast Asia and the adjoining islands, including the Philippines, constitute a single culture area. Although the peoples involved differ widely in cultural complexity, they all have a common background in the old Southeast Asian Neolithic complex and have been exposed to the same influences from the great Indian and Chinese civilizations which are their neighbors. Especially at the village level, their cultural similarities far outweigh their differences. It seems legitimate, therefore, to treat this whole region as a unit, referring to it as the Southeast Asia area and distinguishing between Indonesia and the mainland or between various Indonesian or mainland political units only when these present significant differences.

While the Malayo-Polynesians were establishing their language and culture in the far reaches of the Pacific and off the coast of Africa, conditions in the Southeast Asian area were by no means static. In fact many of the differences between various Malayo-Polynesian outposts are most readily explained by assuming that their founders left the Southeast Asian area at different times and with correspondingly different cultural equipment. Trade relations between Southeast Asia, India, and China must have been established long before the first records of such contacts were written down. By 160 A.D. the Greek geographer, Ptolemy of Alexandria, had heard that the area was rich in mineral resources and mentions it as producing gold and silver. The tin deposits in the Malay Peninsula were certainly known and worked at a much earlier period. Many well-made Neolithic implements have been found in the ancient workings but no metal objects and it seems certain that the local population was mining the tin for export. Since it came in almost pure metallic form it would have found a ready market wherever bronze was made, while its high value relative to its bulk adapted it well to primitive transport.

We do not know where the ancient Malayan tin went but China seems the most probable market. Chinese bronze-casting had reached perfection by the Shang dynasty (1765-1122 B.C.), and bronze was the most important metal in China for the next thousand years. Eastern and southern India, on the other hand, seem to have made little use of bronze and to have acquired iron at this same date. The south Chinese had large, seaworthy vessels since the dawn of history and could easily have visited the Malay Peninsula, while the Southeast Asians were equally capable of reaching south Chinese ports. Lastly, the possibility of overland trade routes between China and Southeast Asia cannot be ignored. In spite of this long contact, the influence of Chinese culture upon southeast Asia has been slight. Although the Chinese readily married native women, they raised their offspring as Chinese and jealously maintained their own culture, while the native peoples maintained theirs. Various objects and techniques of Chinese origin have been incorporated into the native culture, but there seems to have been no transfer of Chinese social, political, or religious patterns.

In sharp contrast to the Chinese situation, Indian culture permeated the entire region and left its mark even on the more primitive tribes. The earliest proof of the presence of Indian rulers in Indonesia is a series of four in-

scriptions from East Borneo. These date from about 400
A.D. If Indians had penetrated to Borneo by this time, they
must have been present in Java and Sumatra considerably
earlier. A statue of Buddha dating from the second century A.D. has been found in southern Sumatra, but this
might have been imported long after its manufacture.

From the time of the first settlement, Java and
Sumatra were the points of maximum Indian influence.
In Sumatra, the state of Shrivijaya was in existence by the
beginning of the seventh century. Its rulers followed the
doctine of Hinayana Buddhism but were converted about
the beginning of the eighth century to the Mahayana doctrine.

The first princes of Java were Hindu and seem to
have been regarded as incarnations of the god Siva. They
instituted a policy of extensive temple building, which was
carried on by subsequent rulers. In the middle of the
eighth century, contemporaneous with the Shrivijaya dynasty, the strong Shailendra dynasty was established in
Sumatra. The rulers of this dynasty were Mahayana Buddhists and seem to have come from Bengal.

From the eleventh century on there seem to have
been no important Hindu or Buddhist increments from
India. The process of fusion between the native and imported culture elements went forward steadily, as did the
fusion of Hindu and Buddhist religious practices. By the
latter part of the thirteenth century it was possible for a
king of Singhasari in Java to build a temple in which the
lower floor was dedicated to Siva and the upper floor to
Buddha, and it was quite customary for kings to have their
ashes divided between a Shivitic and a Buddhist mauso-
leum. This synthesis was assisted by the fact that these
religions were most important to the upper classes. The
villagers accepted the rites as superior magic but did not
try to understand the doctrines.

The next significant event for Southeast Asian culture
was the arrival of Islam. The beginning of this can be
dated quite accurately. When Marco Polo visited the island
of Sumatra in 1292 as an ambassador of the emperor of
China, he found that the little town of Perlak, on the

northern tip of Sumatra, had been converted to Islam. Most of the Muslim who came to Sumatra were not Arabs but Indians, and the doctrines which they taught had already undergone most of the changes needed to adapt a faith created for desert nomads to the needs of peasants living in the monsoon area.

The spread of Islam proceeded with great speed. It offered converts release from a Hindu-derived caste system which must have been uncongenial to Southeast Asians, and its prescription for forcible conversion of the heathen was highly acceptable to ambitious adventurers and to the Malay pirates who infested the Eastern seas. Any leader who was able to muster a small force and convert a hitherto pagan or Hindu district could be sure of reward. The loot provided an immediate incentive, and the heaven promised believers who fell fighting against the infidel was further recompense.

Before the Muslim could consolidate their holdings, European powers took a hand, beginning with the arrival of the Portuguese, who were able to dominate the seaways of the region by 1515. They were followed rapidly by Spaniards, Dutch, and English, who initiated a period of foreign control which is only now coming to an end.

To study Southeast Asian cultures today is like mounting a time machine and going back through successive periods of European, Muslim, and Indian domination to the end of the Neolithic. As one goes eastward from Java to the Philippines or from the coasts to the interiors of the larger islands, one encounters cultures which show less and less foreign influence. However, there are certain features which are common to all or nearly all cultures of the region and others whose distribution points clearly to their origin.

The Southeast Asian mainland, lying as it does between China and India, came into contact with both great cultures very early; with the exception of the land that lay to the east of the mountains of Laos, Indian influence has been much stronger than Chinese throughout the mainland. This seems to be due to the fact that the Indians came as colonizers and missionaries, while the

Chinese were conquerors or traders. Even after conquest they made few permanent settlements in the territory and kept themselves distinct from native people when they did establish colonies. The Chinese have never been a proselytizing group, but the Indians, whether Hindu, Buddhist, or Muslim, included missionary activity in their colonization.

4 SOUTHWEST ASIA AND EUROPE

SOUTHWEST ASIAN NEOLITHIC

T H E most important Old World center of plant and animal domestication lay in Southwest Asia. By 5000 B.C. village life had been established throughout most of this region. The development of food-raising here seems to have been followed by a cultural advance so rapid that the content of various time levels is not readily ascertainable. Even in the earliest period the people lived in villages. There seem to have been no isolated dwellings, which suggests the existence of intervillage warfare. Neighboring settlements no doubt quarreled over grazing land, and domestic animals were a constant temptation to theft. At the same time, the absence of defensive works around villages indicates that the wars were not particularly deadly.

Houses were rectangular, made of adobe or of mats fastened over a wooden frame and plastered with mud. Small fields were cultivated, where the soil was good, preferably close to the village. Poor and distant land was used for grazing and presumably was not individually owned. The principal crops were wheat and barley, with lentils, peas, onions, and cucumbers to vary the diet. Ripe grain was reaped with sickles made from wood or antler, with flint flakes inset along the cutting edge. Each village had its threshing floor, a level platform, of clay usually surrounded by a stone wall. These threshing floors served a dual purpose: they were also used for village assemblies. The threshed grain was stored in pits dug into the hard clay soil or in beehive-shaped mud granaries. To have mice or rats get into the granaries was a major catastrophe. Some of the earliest Egyptian papyri give recipes for the fumigation of granaries and for semimagical methods for keeping rodents out.

The grain was made into meal, which was toasted or served as mush. Leavened bread was still many centuries in the future, but the malting and making of beer had been discovered by at least 4000 B.C.

Domestic animals were cattle, sheep, goats, and, less commonly, pigs. Donkeys were used for transport, but there were few horses. Throughout most of Near Eastern history, horses have been luxury animals used only in war and for display. It may be remembered that one king of Israel was criticized for pride because he rode a horse instead of a donkey. All the village animals were pastured together and herded by the children, with a few armed men as guards. The animals were milked morning and night, and curds and butter were made from earliest times. Butter was more important as a cosmetic than as food, but dried curds made possible the storing of a milk surplus against times of shortage. Domestic animals were too valuable to kill except at ceremonies, so meat was little used.

Women did the cooking and also made pottery, mats, and baskets and wove coarse cloth on handlooms. Clothing was simple, consisting of a kilt for women and a loincloth for men. The main wealth was in herds, but there was unquestionably trade in highly valued objects.

It is improbable that there were any political units larger than the village, yet villages which shared a common language and culture probably recognized certain ties and were able to combine against outsiders. The village chief led in war, directed communal activities, and also, no doubt, exercised his authority to settle disputes and to maintain peace within the community. Chieftainship was probably hereditary within particular families but with the office actually passing to the ablest candidate. Since villages were small face-to-face groups, real power within the community was exercised by family heads and other important men. The operation of this sort of control can be observed in many peasant communities even today and is as informal as it is effective. The men of the village merely converge on some favorite meeting place, often a threshing floor, in the cool of the evening, and there discuss any matters which may be of interest. Any member of the village is privileged to speak his mind on any matter, but the young or socially insignificant are snubbed, while men of importance are listened to respectfully. The decisions finally arrived at are always unanimous, since long practice enables members of the group to sense the direction in which sentiments are moving, and no one is anxious to find himself the sole representative of a dissenting opinion. As in all small communities, every Neolithic village no doubt had a mass of custom which controlled behavior of all sorts. That which had to do with interpersonal relations was ready to crystallize into law but probably had not done so at that period. A tendency to regard law as something imposed from above and not to be invoked in intra-village disputes is as characteristic of the Southwest Asian co-tradition as the constant appeal to *adat* law is of the Southeast Asian one.

Each village had its local shrine, which was usually a high place outside the village, and there probably were also tribal shrines to which members of several villages might repair. Worship was carried on through priestly intermediaries who knew the proper rituals and received a share of the sacrifices as pay. To judge from the earliest written records from this region, many of the rituals were in fact magical formulae designed to compel the god's assistance quite as much as to implore his help. Since the god was regarded as thoroughly anthropomorphic with physical needs for food and shelter, the relations between him and his worshippers was a reciprocal one. If he did not come across, they did not come across.

The grain argiculture and dairying on which village life was based were carried on at first by very simple methods. The invention of the plow, wheel, and loom increased the industrial potential without necessitating any fundamental changes in the earlier way of life. The same may be said for ancient metal-working. The war potential of groups who had bronze was greater than that of groups who had only stone, but bronze was so scarce at first that the actual advantage enjoyed by those who had it was slight.

The introduction of iron was more revolutionary in its consequences, since it led to what V. Gordon Childe has called the proletarianization of metal. Iron ores are abundant and widely distributed, making the new metal cheap and plentiful. It was thus available for tools and even agricultural implements, as well as weapons, and certainly raised the general standard of living. However it had little effect on the already ancient and established patterns of village life. Iron-armed conquerors swept over most of temperate Eurasia, but the villager went on plowing with his oxen, sowing and reaping his grain, wearing the cloth his wife wove, obeying immemorial custom, and placating the supernatural guardian of his fields.

At certain places and times the transition from Neolithic to Bronze Age or from Bronze Age to Iron Age was marked by signficant population movements and abrupt changes in culture. In such cases the terms will be used, but it must always be kept in mind that these phases of the Eurasian culture continuum differed in length in different parts of Eurasia and that the transition from one to another came at very different times in different regions. Thus the use of metal had become common in the Near East by 4500 B.C. but did not reach the British Isles until 2500 B.C. at the earliest. The Iron Age had begun in Anatolia by 18-1600 B.C. but did not become established in western Europe until nearly a thousand years later. The most recent phase of the Eurasian culture continuum, marked by the production of power and the application of the scientific method, originated in western Europe about the middle of the eighteenth century and has not yet reached some outlying parts of the world.

The city was a social invention whose consequences were more far-reaching than those of any technological invention. For this reason its emergence may be set as a terminal point for the period under discussion. The exact point at which a culture became city-centered and took on urban characteristics is sometimes difficult to establish, yet the city as an institution is unmistakable. It appeared first in Southwest Asia and was fully developed in Mesopotamia by 4500 to 4000 B.C. It appeared in Egypt about the same time, although in slightly different form. The peculiar settlement pattern imposed by the Nile Valley made the first Egyptian cities little more than religious and administrative centers within a continuous area of dense population. The Indus Valley cities were of a more familiar type, resembling those in Mesopotamia. Although dating for this region is still uncertain, they probably go back to at least 3500 B.C. In China cities did not appear until about 2000 B.C. at the earliest. Turning to Europe, there were few real cities even in Greece before 900 to 800 B.C., while the pattern was not established in Scandinavia until after 1000 A.D.

The spread of Neolithic village life from Southwest Asia involved both migration and diffusion. The increased food supply resulting from combined agriculture and dairying must have produced an exceedingly rapid growth of population. It is estimated that under optimum conditions a human group can double its numbers every twenty-five years. The methods of primitive grain agriculture, without fertilization or crop rotation, lead to rapid soil exhaustion and provide a strong stimulus to migration. Actually, migrants seem to have poured out of the Southwest Asian region in all directions.

All the regions which were suited to agricultural occupation offered a supply of wild food and were already occupied by hunting, food gathering tribes. However, these tribes were rarely numerous enough to offer serious resistance, and the progressive conversion of their range into grain fields and pasture must have diminished their food supply and reduced their numbers still further. The situation must have been not unlike that of the Indians and white settlers on our own frontier.

EUROPEAN NEOLITHIC

THE first Neolithic migrants to reach Europe apparently came from Anatolia and established a foothold in the region that is now the Balkans. From this point on there were two main lines of migration. One of these followed the Mediterranean coasts with gradual infiltration of the Italian and Iberian Peninsulas and settlement of the various Mediterranean islands as soon as seafaring had been sufficiently developed. Somewhat later this movement was reinforced by direct sea migrations from the lands at the eastern end of the Mediterranean.

The other migration line was into Central Europe by way of the Danube and its tributaries. The descendants of settlers who had come by this route, reinforced by later migrants from the steppe region further to the east, finally reached eastern France, Germany, and Scandinavia. The two routes brought the migrants into markedly different environments and resulted in distinctive cultural developments in each case.

When the movement of agricultural peoples into Europe began, the Mediterranean region was covered with pine forests. Because of the light rainfall this forest could not reconstitute itself. Wherever it had been destroyed it was replaced by dense scrub, the *maquis,* or dry, aromatic heath, the *garrigué.* However, climatic conditions were much like those in the original Southwest Asian center. The rainfall was concentrated in winter so that the ard plow and the dust mulch which it produced were as functional here as in the Near East. All the original crops could be grown without the need for developing new varieties. The main handicap was the lack of level land, as most of the Mediterranean area is mountainous.

The local conditions were set by certain changes in the original economy. The shortage of level land was partially compensated for by terracing, but irrigated terrace agriculture was not employed because, perhaps, of the poor and seasonally fluctuating water supply. Instead there was a development of tree crops. The fig and olive, both natives of the Mediterranean basin, were domesticated and improved, and various nut trees were planted and tended. The vine was added to this inventory during the later Bronze Age. Although it seems to have been introduced from Asia, it found itself completely at home on the stony slopes of the Mediterranean littoral. Olive oil became indispensable to the Mediterranean economy. It served to cook food, to make bread and salads more palatable, to give light, and to protect the skin against cold and salt water. The wine from the Mediterranean vineyards not only cheered the vine growers but also provided them with a valuable export. Well before the end of the Aegean Bronze Age, olive oil and wine were being shipped to less favored areas. The earliest example of fancy packaging was when, by 1500 B.C., the Cretans were putting up their export oil in gaily painted jars. The Classical Greeks carried this trend still farther, and by the time of the Persian wars Athens was getting most of its grain from the settled Scythians north of the Black Sea.

The Mediterranean settlers brought with them the full Southwest Asian series of domestic animals, but here again the environment necessitated changes. The ox remained the only draft animal, but goats replaced both cattle and sheep as the animals of greatest economic importance. Goats could graze on the dry scrub which took over the steep hillsides when the original pine forests had been destroyed. Incidentally, their close cropping and sharp hoofs increased the ravages of soil erosion and were an added factor in preventing reforestation.

To compensate for the relative scarcity of animal products, the sea was always close at hand. The Mediterranean peoples were almost as dependent on fish as the Indonesians. Every coastal village had its fishing fleet, and dried fish was an important article of trade with the interior. Long before the dawn of history the coastal and island tribes had become excellent sailors, and the earliest sea power on record had its center on the island of Crete.

Certain culture patterns may be noted as of Mediterranean origin and common to the entire area. The changes in food economy imposed by the local conditions have already been mentioned. The dependence on fishing, which was a part of this economy, led to the development of the world's first seaworthy ships. These seem to have been evolved first in the eastern Mediterranean, where the numerous islands provided a good training school for deep-sea sailors. The Mediterranean is a sea of long calms and treacherous currents. A vessel which is dependent on sails alone is likely to drift into dangerous waters or lie for days helpless and rolling. The pictures of boats on Neolithic pottery show them with many oars but no masts or sails. Although the latter had been introduced by 2000 B.C., craft, such as war vessels, which required speed and maneuverability, were oar powered until well into the eighteenth century A.D. Incidentally, the technique of rowing instead of paddling, without which the later galleys would have been impossible, also seems to have been a Mediterranean invention.

When the Mediterranean sailors ventured into the Atlantic they had difficulty with the irregular winds and tempestuous seas. Most of their voyaging had to be done in the summer. However, they managed to penetrate as far north as Scandinavia, where the Norse long ships of the Viking period seem to have been simplified and improved copies of early Mediterranean craft. At the same time there was an independent development of shipbuilding along the Atlantic coast. Very large dugouts suitable for short sea voyages and certainly not derived from Mediterranean prototypes have been found in Neolithic and Bronze Age sites. Caesar records in his commentaries that the ships of the Veneti, built to withstand the rough seas of the Bay of Biscay, were massively constructed of oak, with leather sails. He adds that they were so massive that the Roman galleys were unable to ram them successfully but finally overcame them by cutting their rigging and leaving them helpless, an excellent indication that they were sailed, not rowed. We cannot say when this school of shipbuilding came into existence, but we know that it was present in Scandinavia all through the Viking period and that the Norse did most of their traveling and trading in bluff-bowed, slow sailing craft which bore much the same relation to their long ships that a modern freighter bears to a destroyer.

Following the initial settlement of the Mediterranean area two cultural centers emerged, one in the Iberian Peninsula, the other in the Aegean Islands. The Aegean center was marginal to the developing civilizations of Mesopotamia and Egypt and was strongly influenced by them. It reached its flowering in the Cretan and derivative Mycenean cultures which, because of their close relations with the later Classical civilizations, require separate treatment.

Neolithic migrants from the Iberian Peninsula settled in the British Isles, where their physical type survives in much of the present population. They also followed the Atlantic coast to Scandinavia, settling most of France and the low countries and eventually pushing inland to Switzerland, where they met and mixed with other agricultural villagers who had arrived by way of central Europe.

The contact between the Iberian Peninsula and the British Isles was particularly close and was maintained all through the Bronze Age. The peninsula seems to have been the starting point for the so-called Megalithic complex of western Europe. This consisted in the building of tombs and the erection of monuments composed of enormous blocks of rough stone. There is no indication that the diffusion of this pattern was accompanied by any large-scale migration. It seems rather to have represented the spread of a religious cult combined, perhaps, with a new form of tribal exhibitionism. In eastern Polynesia each tribe built its ceremonial structures of the hugest stones possible, since the structure would then stand as an indication of the extent of tribal manpower; one may suspect that the great Megalithic structures of western Europe, which involved the transportation and erection of stones many tons in weight, may have been inspired in part by similar motives.

The introduction of metal-working into the Mediterranean areas increased the economic importance of the Iberian Peninsula, which was rich in copper and other metallic ores. Although the earliest patterns of mining and metal-working were probably imported from the east, the Peninsula seems to have been the origin point for a curious group known as the Beaker Folk. The remains of this culture are scattered over the whole of western Europe, with their maximum concentration in regions where there are evidences of primitive mining. They seem to have established real colonies only in the British Isles, Brittany, and Holland, thus following the Iberian migration routes which had been established in Neolithic times. They have left no extensive remains of settlement elsewhere, but many small cemeteries whose graves contain objects indicative of very wide contacts. They may well have been a group of traders and prospectors who pushed into "barbarous" northern Europe following rumors of mineral deposits, and exploited them with the aid of native labor which they trained. It is interesting to conjecture how they obtained the help of the local aborigines in their mining. They do not seem to have been numerous enough to conquer or enslave local populations. Their grave goods are not very plentiful and no extensive caches of trade objects which might be referred to them have been found. The beakers from which they take their name, actually small tumbler-like clay jars, were probably beer mugs, and one is tempted to guess that, as with the early European traders among many different sorts of aborigines, their main stock may have been alcoholic potables.

One last point should be made with regard to the Mediterranean cultures. None of the Neolithic populations who occupied this region or migrated from this region spoke Indo-European languages. The only clues to what their languages may have been are provided by certain late Bronze Age and Iron Age inscriptions from the eastern Mediterranean and by such historic survivals as the Basque language spoken in the Pyrenees and the Berber languages of North Africa. On the basis of this very scanty information it seems probable that the languages were of several different stocks.

The second line of diffusion of Southwest Asian culture into Europe ran overland from Anatolia to the Balkans and then along the Danube and its tributaries until
the northern watersheds were crossed. The Atlantic river
systems were then followed toward the sea. This brought
the Central European migrants into contact with the
slightly earlier settlements of the Mediterranean migrants
and the two traditions blended to produce a variety of local cultures.

The first Neolithic settlers in Central Europe raised
wheat of several sorts, barley, and various legumes, and
kept a few cattle, although the last were of little economic
importance. Crops were cultivated with stone hoes. There
seems to have been very little hunting or fishing. Villages
were small and had to be moved frequently because of soil
exhaustion. There was some trade from the earliest times.
Shells from the Mediterranean were carried as far as
Czechoslovakia, and stone adzes and even pottery were
transported for considerable distances. The archaeological
record as a whole suggests a hard-working, peaceful peasant society with few differences in wealth or status.

Two important additions to the Central and Northern
European equipment were made during the Bronze Age:
the plow and the horse. The Neolithic Europeans had done
their cultivating with stone hoes, which were well adapted
to grubbing in root-filled soil left after forests had been
burned. The use of the plow indicated not only that
cleared land had been brought under genuine cultivation,
but also that some method permitting continued land use
had been substituted for the old slash and burn agricultural
technique.

The introduction of horses into Europe was an event
of prime cultural importance. A wild forest horse was native to Western Europe, a shaggy, heavy-boned animal
which was hunted like other game. It does not seem to
have been domesticated during Neolithic times, although
it may have been crossed in later time with the imported
type. Some of its blood may survive in the heavy draft
horses of northwestern Europe. The first domestic horses
appeared in Central Europe early in the Bronze Age, and

were of a fast, light boned Central Asian breed. Horses were not particularly profitable animals to raise for either milk or meat, and it was a long time before horse harnesses suitable for heavy traction were developed. There can be little doubt that the horse was brought to Europe as a fighting animal and that it came as a fundamental part of the equipment of invaders from the east. However, these Bronze Age horse drivers must not be confused with the later and much more efficient mounted invaders who came from the same region. The first evidence which we have for the riding of horses in Europe comes from the Hallstatt culture of the early Iron Age.

The light, two-wheeled, two-man war chariot appeared in Central Europe by the last half of the Bronze Age, but riding came still later. Bronze Age tombs show no traces of saddlery. Horses were ridden all through the Iron Age, but efficient cavalry did not appear in Europe until very late. Even in the time of Caesar's wars, the cavalry of the Gauls and Germans was essentially mounted infantry. Horses were used as a means of rapid transportation but riders usually dismounted to fight. Lacking adequate saddles and stirrups, their seat was too precarious for hand-to-hand battle.

During the late Bronze Age important social changes took place throughout most of Europe. Kingdoms and even empires appeared in the eastern Mediterranean, while throughout most of the continent new aristocratic patterns emerged. Scandinavia supported a population of well-to-do, free-holding farmers but elsewhere the peasantry was ruled by chiefs or petty kings. Such rulers concentrated the society's economic surplus in their own hands and used it to employ foreign craftsmen, buy foreign goods, and provide themselves with pretentious equipment for the next world.

In summary, one is forced to conclude that the overland route was more important for the development of European culture than the Mediterranean. Most of the technological and social inventions which reached Europe from Southwest Asia appeared first in Eastern and Central Europe, and the successive waves of migration which laid the foundation for later European civilization all came either from Central Europe or even further east. The priority which has been given to the Mediterranean and coastal route is largely a result of historic accident. The earliest studies of European history were made along the Atlantic coast and the richness of the Central European remains has only become evident within the last fifty years. The Classical civilizations have cast a spell over European scholars, yet one must admit that the modern mechanized civilization of Europe owes more to the north European cultures and their barbarian background than it does to either Greece or Rome.

ARYANS

T H E spread of village culture from Southwest Asia carried its economic and social patterns not only westward into Europe but also northward into the Eurasian steppes. Here settlers encountered conditions not unlike those which confronted our own pioneers when they reached the Great Plains. The western steppes provided excellent pasture, but the soil was difficult to bring under cultivation. There were no forests to serve as a basis for slash and burn cultivation, and the age-old prairie sod could not be broken with primitive plows. To complicate matters still further, the steppes had long climate cycles like those of our own Plains: a run of wet years alternating with a run of drought years. Under these circumstances the immigrants turned more and more from agriculture to stock farming. Since the pasture was good enough to make cattle more profitable than sheep, the emotional and economic focus of this culture was on cattle and cattle products, with horses, apparently first domesticated farther to the east, as a second but less important interest.

Between 1800 and 1500 B.C. cattle-keeping tribes pressed southward from the steppes along a front extending all the way from India to the Balkans. Records left by the civilized groups whom they attacked indicate that these invaders all spoke languages of the Indo-European stock. The tribes who invaded India called themselves *Arya*, hence the much abused term *Aryan*. One may use *Aryan* to designate those tribes who were of cattle culture and Indo-European speech, but the term should not be applied to groups who lacked either of these characteristics.

When the Aryans emerged from the steppes they seem to have been casual agriculturalists as well as dairymen, but they cheerfully relinquished plowing and planting to their subjects. Trade was regarded as a slightly dishonorable substitute for robbery with violence and was employed only as a last resort. Loans with interest were considered on a par with petty larceny. The dominant interests of the society were war and the breeding or theft of cattle and horses. It is suggestive that sheep and goats figure very little in the epics, although they were certainly kept by many of the conquered peasant communities. Horses were important and were both driven and ridden, although there are few mentions even in late epics of fighting on horseback. The favorite conveyance of early chiefs and heroes was the war chariot.

Technology followed the general Southwest Asian pattern, with little or no adaption to nomadic life. The Aryans had no portable shelters comparable to the *yurts* of the Turko-Tatar peoples. Wherever they settled for a few days they built wattle and daub huts, easily made and easily abandoned. Clothing was of loom-woven woolen cloth, draped, not tailored, although trousers soon came into use among the tribes in northern Europe. The wheel and plow were known and pottery was made. All metals except iron were worked at the time of first emergence from the steppes, and the use of iron was soon learned. The weapon inventory was extensive, including spears, swords, and axes of various sorts, the bow and arrow, helmet, and shield. The use of body armor during the early period is uncertain. Wealthy men and women wore many gold ornaments, and the most honorable gift was one of these stripped off and given to the recipient directly. During the early period there were Aryan craftsmen, especially smiths, who occupied a good social position. Later, most manufacturing was relegated to the conquered.

The Aryans were not true nomads, but their attachment to the soil was decidedly loose. On any excuse they would pile their goods in ponderous ox carts, burn their huts, and set out on long treks into unknown territory. Their invasions completely lacked the lightning speed and mobility of the much later Hunnish and Mongol attacks. The whole tribe moved as a ponderous unit, complete with its cattle. Victory meant new pasture lands to be occupied, defeat annihilation.

All the epics picture a three-class society, consisting of nobles and commoners, who together formed the Aryans proper, and serfs, who represented the conquered local population. There were no kings, in the ordinarily accepted meaning of the term, although able chiefs might become the leaders of alliances of tribes. Families which had produced leaders over several generations formed the highest aristocracy, and their members would be considered first when a high chief was needed. Chattel slaves seem to have been very rare in the early period. Few if any male prisoners were taken in war between Aryan groups, while women became the concubines of the victors, and were eventually assimilated into their tribe. Commoners and nobles were frequently related, the difference being mainly one of wealth and prestige. Serfs, when they appear at all in the epics, figure as socially inferior to the nobles' horses and dogs. The Aryans felt strong affection for these animals, and their names and individual qualities often appear in the epics beside those of their masters.

An Aryan tribe consisted of a series of households, each composed of a household head, his wife, or wives, and children, younger brothers and their families. Life in these households was enlivened with feuds and cattle raids. Wandering bards came to stay and remained as long as the host's generosity warranted. Gambling was usual and heavy drinking the rule. The early Aryan attitude toward sex and marriage can best be described as casual. Although there was no recognized period of premarital experimentation, as in Southeast Asia, little value was attached to virginity. There was no formal bride price, although an exchange of gifts usually accompanied marriage. Lacking economic stabilization, marriages tended to be brittle.

Aryan attitudes toward the supernatural were also rather casual. In the earliest period family heads acted as priests, a practice which continued in Scandinavia until the introduction of Christianity. Elsewhere, specialists in dealing with the supernatural emerged, but their social status was low. They were kept in noble households to insure the proper performance of rituals but were treated like family chaplains.

Perhaps the most important contribution of the Aryans to later civilization was the establishment of the aristocratic pattern which survived in Europe until recent times. Any culture of national scope is inevitably composed of numerous subcultures. While the peasant and bourgeois subcultures of various European countries have been distinctive, their aristocratic subcultures have been so similar that an aristocrat from one nation could understand the attitudes and values of an aristocrat from another nation better than he could understand those of his own lower classes. The outdoor hunting life has been an aristocratic prerogative since the dawn of European history. When it was no longer required to supplement the food supply, it continued as a sport and as a symbol of membership in the aristocratic group. The nobleman had to be a good horseman, and in fact, such terms as *ritter* and *chevalier* reduce to this. It has been said that even in nineteenth century England any young man of the aristocratic class would much rather have his morals aspersed than his horsemanship.

The European nobleman was strictly limited in his occupations. He could not work on the land himself without losing caste, nor could he engage in trade. The one gainful pursuit which was open to him was horse and cattle breeding. It is interesting to note that now that the horse has lost its economic importance, young Englishmen of the upper class can, by a transfer of the sort familiar to anthropologists, become automobile salesmen without violating the taboo on trade. Intellectual and artistic pursuits were regarded with some contempt, once more following the original Aryan pattern. The aristocrat might act as a patron of the arts and science, but he was not supposed to engage in either himself. Until very recent times most European aristocrats have been poorly educated, and the schools designed for them have been more interested in "character building" than in providing the student with useful knowledge or practical skills. It has been said that the battle of Waterloo was won on the playing fields of Eton, and one might add that Singapore was lost in its classrooms.

The aristocrat might go into the church, especially if he was a younger son, but religiosity was frowned upon and Christian taboos more honored in the breach than in the observance. Sex mores retained the old Aryan casualness. Aristocrats were expected to marry within their own caste to insure the legitimacy of their descendants, but no high degree of chastity was required either before or after marriage and the use of lower-class women in casual liaisons was taken for granted. In this connection it should be noted that in spite of the formal monogamy demanded of Christians, European royalty has been polygymous until quite recent times. It was expected that a king or great noble would have a number of concubines, usually drawn from various aristocratic families who hoped in this way to obtain additional political influence. The offspring of such concubines, although excluded from the succession, nevertheless had a recognized social position within the aristocratic hierarchy. Since they were debarred from the succession and their fortunes depended upon the good will of the royal parent, they were in general more trustworthy than legitimate heirs and could be placed in positions where a legitimate heir might foment revolt. Thus the "Grand Bastard of Burgundy," a title as specific as that of "Prince of Wales," was by custom commander-in-chief of the Burgundian armies.

Gambling and heavy drinking could also be indulged in by the aristocrat without loss of caste. The only requirement was that he gamble honestly and give his gambling debts precedence over all others, perhaps because these were debts normally owed to equals. To cheat at cards was an unforgivable sin, only one degree less deadly than physical cowardice. From the time of the first Aryan invasions, chiefs had been expected to lead their followers in battle and to risk their own persons recklessly as an example to the rest. Since the supremacy of the aristocratic group rested upon the tradition of their superior courage and pugnacity, anyone who showed himself lacking in these was regarded as a traitor to his class.

TURKO TATARS

T H E horse culture of the steppes was the most perfect example of a nomadic domestic animal economy which the world has ever seen. The tribes who followed it were thoroughly adverse to agriculture. Sometimes they sowed millet, which would grow untended, but they did this mainly as a reserve against famine. Under normal conditions they made no use of agriculturally produced foods or materials. Their domestic animals were sheep, horses, Bactrian camels, and cattle, in order of their economic importance. Sheep were raised in enormous numbers. The historic Kazaks of the region counted their flocks, not by individual animals, but by the number of dogs required to herd them. Sheep were sometimes milked, but their main importance lay in meat and wool. Mutton was the staple everyday diet and was eaten in tremendous quantities. One sheep per man per day was regarded as a standard ration. Wool was used for felt.

The great importance of the horse lay in its use as a fighting animal. It was ridden or used as a pack animal, never for draft. Horse meat was regularly eaten, and the flesh of a young mare was regarded as a special delicacy, usually reserved for feasts. When food ran short, soldiers drank blood drawn from their mounts. Mares were milked and their milk fermented to make *kumiss*. Mare's milk was much richer in sugar than cow's milk, and by proper fermentation it was possible to produce an alcoholic beverage with considerable authority. The horse people in general were heavy drinkers, and the end of a successful banquet saw all the guests unconscious. Genghis Khan is reported to have said: "A man who is drunk is like one struck on the head; his wisdom and skill avail him not at all. Get drunk only three times a month. It would be better not to get drunk at all. But who can abstain altogether?"

Camels were used both as pack animals and to draw baggage carts. They were rarely milked or eaten. Cattle were of minor importance in the Mongolian plateau but became more significant as the horse culture expanded westward. Cattle were both milked and eaten, and oxen were used for draft.

It is interesting to note that the attitudes of the horse people toward their domestic animals seems to have been a highly utilitarian one. There are no famous individual horses or dogs described in their epics. Animals were mass produced and mass consumed. The Mongol warrior took with him a string of anonymous mounts to be abandoned or slaughtered for food when they gave out. Perhaps life in the plateau was too hard to allow for sentimental attachments to pets. The horse people seem to have carried over into the pastoral stage the attitude of hunters who looked upon animals simply as potential meat. Even in the days of the Mongol conquests, hunting remained more of a business than a sport in this region. Great surrounds were organized from time to time, and all animals caught in the circle were shot down and eaten.

Hunting and herding produced not only food but also clothing. The normal costume consisted of trousers, boots with upturned toes, a sleeved, shirt-like upper garment, short skirted for men and long skirted for women, and a cap or hood. Over this a cloak was worn in bitter weather. All clothing was made of skins or felt, the only exception being occasional festive garments of cloth obtained through trade or loot. The favorite material was sheepskin worn with the wool inside.

Horses were probably used as pack animals in the Mongolian plateau even before the introduction of the wheel, and it may be conjectured that the first saddles were pack-saddles and the first riders small children settled among the bundles when camp moved. Even when the successors of the cattle people unhitched their horses from their chariots and began to ride them, they employed only pad saddles, and their cavalry was correspondingly inefficient.

The conquest-empires created by the horse people were in general short-lived. They passed like a scourge, taking for themselves whatever they could understand and use and destroying the rest. It is said that after the Mongol conquest of China they seriously considered exterminating the Chinese and turning their territory back into pasture land. Where they settled among conquered populations, they maintained their clan and tribal organization, living in concentrated groups and adhering to their old nomadic life as far as possible. They had in their own culture few patterns which could be applied to the rule of subject peoples, and the high organization of such units as the Liau empire in China or the later and much more extensive Mongol empire was due to the adoption of Chinese models and was actually operated largely by Chinese officials.

In sharp contrast to the Aryans, the horse people seem never to have developed a successful adjustment to conquest. Perhaps the values of their nomadic culture were fundamentally incompatible with the role of rulers over settled communities. In any case, wherever they abandoned their nomadic life they were rapidly assimilated by the conquered groups, and became Chinese in China, Muslim and Persian in middle Asia, and in the case of the last significant westward movement of horse people, that of the Turks, essentially Muslim and Byzantine.

Perhaps a last word should be said regarding the fate of the horse people after the Mongol conquests. As has already been said, these conquests swept the last remnants of the original cattle people out of the western steppes and established Mongol and Turkish groups throughout their entire extent. One division of the Mongols, the Golden Horde, was drafted by Ivan the Terrible and deprived of its political power. The men remained in southern Russia, on sufferance, until the time of Catherine the Great. Under the increasing pressure of the Russian government, they finally made a fighting retreat eastward to their original home in Mongolia, where they arrived greatly reduced in numbers. The central steppes, which were occupied by nomadic tribes of Turkish stock both before and after the Mongol sweep, remained for centuries a breeding ground for tough fighters and, even more, for able generals. Individually or in small groups, these Turks infiltrated the higher cultures to the south and finally seized control of the Near East, but after the Mongol conquests the steppe peoples launched no more major offensives.

Some writers have seen the cause for this in the conversion of the Mongols to Buddhism, but most of the steppe peoples to the west of Mongol territory were converted to Islam, hardly a pacifist religion. The real answer probably lies in the increasing mechanization of warfare that came with the introduction of gunpowder and with the development of disciplined troops and skilled tacticians outside the steppe area. The steppe people, with their atomistic settlement patterns and their relatively crude hand industries, were incapable of producing the weapons which the new situation required. The influences which brought about their downfall were beginning to exert themselves even in the time of Genghis Khan, whose armies were accompanied in their later campaigns by contingents of Chinese engineers whose appliances included flame throwers and probably gunpowder bombs. As long as the steppe peoples had superior discipline they could compensate somewhat for their technological deficiencies, but when other armies became as well disciplined as their own, their fate was sealed. The last European appearance of the mounted bowmen who were once the "Scourge of God" came during the Napoleonic wars, when a Khirgiz contingent was included in the Russian forces. The French soldiers were vastly amused and dubbed them "cupids." *Sic transit gloria mundi.*

SEMITES

T H E people of the Southwest Asian arid lands once more illustrate the thesis that, within a region having few natural barriers and a uniform ecology, languages and cultures will also tend toward uniformity. Practically all the occupants of the Southwest Asian arid lands spoke Semitic languages and adhered to the same patterns of symbiotic interdependence between villagers and nomads. The Southwest Asian ecology continued across most of northern Africa and so did the linguistic and cultural similarities. Although the historic importance of two of its languages, Hebrew and Arabic, has led Western scholars to treat Semitic as a distinct linguistic stock, modern research has shown that it is actually only one division of a larger family of languages which are spoken throughout Africa north of the Sahara as well as in Southwest Asia. There is probably no other example of such a close linkage between a particular linguistic family and a particular environment. The wide distribution of specifically Semitic languages in Africa seems to be a relatively recent phenomenon linked in part to the rise of Islam, but the other divisions of the African-Asian linguistic family have certainly been established in the African arid lands since very ancient times.

The shift of certain Semitic tribes to complete nomadism was no doubt accelerated by the domestication of the Dromedary camel, an animal which is adapted to hot desert conditions very much as its two-humped Bactrian relative is adapted to cold desert conditions. Camels can live in territory which cannot support even goats and, particularly in Arabia and later in Africa, their domestication opened wide stretches of real desert to human occupation. The camel's mouth and alimentary tract seem to be copper lined. He can chew up and digest camel thorn, which is about as tender and succulent as barbed wire, and can grow fat where a mule would starve to death. His hump provides him with a mechanism for fat storage, so that he can go for weeks on very scanty rations, while his multiple stomachs provide a parallel arrangement for water storage. The camel is thus invaluable to desert dwellers, but anyone who has made the acquaintance of the animal must marvel at its ever having been domesticated. Even the finest modern breeds seem to a European to be phenomenally bad-tempered, stubborn, and malodorous. It must be admitted that the Arab does not agree with the European on this point. He regards the camel as a paragon of virtue and an epitome of loveliness. Pre-Islamic Arabian literature is full of poems extolling the beauties of the beast.

The shrinkage of the agricultural area and the development of camel nomadism produced a distinctive pattern of life which was almost ideally suited to the local conditions. The towns, with their associated agricultural areas, were the centers of population and also of manufacturing and trade. Many of them specialized in particular products for export. The regions between the towns were occupied by nomadic tribes who represented the pastoral half of the original dual culture. While the patterns of town life were typically Southwest Asian, the patterns of pastoral life were distinctively Semitic. The main animals raised by the nomads were sheep, goats, and camels, all adapted to poor pasture. Very few cattle were kept outside the agricultural areas, and even then their main value was as draft animals. The only important baggage animals were camels. These were infrequently milked and still less frequently eaten.

The famous Arabian horses were reserved entirely for fighting and parade. They were never used for draft and were not even ridden when the tribe was on the march. Since the pasture was usually inadequate, horses were fed on grain purchased from the agricultural areas. They were frequently stabled in the owner's tent. An unusual feature of Arab usage was the preference for mares as fighting animals. The pure Arab horse had only two gaits, a walk and a gallop. Although the nomads became excellent horsemen, they never learned to use drilled cavalry or developed any great skill as mounted archers. Their horses were used as transport on fast long-distance raids rather than for line of battle combat.

The complete dependence of the nomads upon the townsmen becomes obvious when one examines their culture. Although their women weave the coarse, black, goat-hair cloth which is used for tents and the men know how to repair their saddlery and other gear, the nomad tribes have practically no manufactures. The entire equipment of the modern nomad dwelling is obtained by either trade or loot, and this seems to have been the case since time immemorial. Even the standard food is an unleavened bread made from wheat grown in the agricultural settlements. This bread is simply a thin batter of flour and water spread on hot stones or sand. A sanitary version of it is familiar to many Americans as the Passover *matzoh*.

The social and political organization of the nomads was based upon tribes, patrilineal endogamous groups occupying particular territories. Larger political groupings were ephemeral, breaking down when the dominant tribe lost control. All tribe members were related, and it was unthinkable that a family should try to change its tribal affiliations. Control of the tribe was vested in a sheik, whose post was normally hereditary in a particular family line. Preference was given to the eldest son by the first wife, but there was no absolute rule, since under nomad conditions the post was far from a sinecure and had to be filled by the best man available. The relation of the sheik to his tribesmen was modeled on that of a Semitic father to his family. He directed tribal activities and administered justice. It is impossible to say how far formal law codes were recognized by the nomads in pre-Islamic times, but in the administration of the law the sheik was expected to show wisdom in determining who was the real offender and to make the punishment fit the crime.

The judgments of Solomon as recorded in Near Eastern folklore are in the best pattern of both nomads and settled people. Although in practice the sheik was influenced by the opinion of tribal members and did his best to function by persuasion rather than force, his powers were autocratic and, in theory, absolute. Needless to say, these patterns had their effect on the development of Islamic patterns of government.

The Arabian nomads not only practiced tribal endogamy but also approved of the marriage of certain close relatives. They were one of the few groups in the world in which marriage with a father's brother's daughter was not only permitted but preferred. This pattern was incorporated into Islam and still survives in many Islamic countries. Marriage among the nomads seems to have been normally monogamous, but with polygyny permitted for those who could afford it. Certainly this was the rule of the early Hebrews.

A striking aspect of all the Semitic cultures seems to have been extreme insistence on virginity at marriage. The exhibition of tokens of virginity is still a part of the regular wedding ceremony in most Islamic countries, and the values which this reflects certainly go back to pre-Islamic times. This insistence was only one aspect of a cultural preoccupation with sex and the sexual organs which found one expression in the practice of circumcision. This was shared by practically all Semitic peoples. Corresponding mutilation of the female organs was also widespread, reaching its greatest development in parts of the Sudan, where all the external female sexual parts were cut away and the vaginal opening so nearly closed with scar tissue as to make intercourse impossible. The bridegroom was thus insured of a virgin bride, but had to win her consent to a further operation before the marriage could be consummated.

The exigencies of nomadic life made the seclusion of women impossible for all but a few of the richest families, but death was inflicted upon both the unchaste girl or the unfaithful wife and her lover. Since unchastity in men was not disapproved, they made the most of their visits to the town, where the sexual vigor of the Bedouin was as famous as that of sailors among ourselves. In pagan times these masculine needs were taken care of in part by a regular institution of temple prostitutes. A further corollary of the situation was a high development of male homosexuality, which even today is widespread in Islamic countries. It is mainly carried on by unmarried men and boys and later gives place to normal heterosexual relations.

The family control was rigidly patriarchal. The father had complete control over his wives and sons throughout his life and even beyond. A father's blessing was an important asset, while a father's curse could ruin his son's future. Note the story of Jacob and Esau. Daughters were under the father's control until marriage but thereafter passed to the control of their husbands. The average Semitic father seems to have taken more pride in his sternness than in his justice. The son's attitude toward him was one of fear and respect. Especially in polygynous families the strongest emotional tie was between mother and son. There was real affection in this relationship and very commonly the two formed an amiable conspiracy to circumvent the father.

The whole situation was such as might be expected to develop a strong and censorious superego in the individual. The Hebrew picture of an all-powerful deity who could only be placated by complete submission and protestations of devotion, no matter how unjust his acts might appear, was a direct outgrowth of this general Semitic family situation. Another product of the exaggerated superego to which it gave rise was the elaborate system of taboos relating to every aspect of behavior. One system of this sort has been recorded and codified in the Laws of Moses, but these laws were by no means an isolated phenomenon. All Semitic tribes had similar series of regulations differing only in content. Such codes provided those who kept them with a sense of security, comparable to that of the good child who is able to remember everything that his father ever told him not to do and carefully abstains from doing it. The Hebrew

Iaveh was a portrait of the Semitic father with his patriarchal authoritarian qualities abstracted and exaggerated.
The combination of patriarchal suppression and sexual
deprivation has left its mark on the Semitic basic personality. From Moses to Freud, Semites have been preoccupied with sin and sex.

The position of the Asian Semites was particularly
favorable for cultural advance. They were in close and
continuous contact with the world's two oldest centers of civilization, Mespotamia and Egypt, and by
2300 B.C. had conquered the Mesopotamian center and
assimilated its culture. Their addiction to trade brought
them into contact with a wide range of peoples and made
them keenly conscious of cultural differences. They were
always ready to borrow new appliances or art styles
when this was advantageous. At the same time the Semitic cultures have shown a fundamental continuity perhaps unequaled by those of any other group. Whatever
they borrowed was reinterpreted in terms of their own
values and interests, which survived with little change.

The most important Semitic contributions to civilization have been in the fields of mathematics and astronomy on the one hand, and religion on the other. It is a
curious fact that we owe to them both the concept of a
mechanistic universe and that of one completely subject
to the will of a single all-powerful deity. The first was
evolved from the Mesopotamian priests' age-long observation of the wheeling heavens. The second grew out of
an ecstatic devotion to the tribal deity, a devotion so intense that all other Beings and forces ceased to exist for
the worshipper. The Semitic quest was always for absolutes, and it has been the bad fortune of their cultural
heirs that they should have found two of them and that
the two were polar. All monotheistic faiths of which we
have records can be traced to Semitic sources, and all of
them are confronted by the same enigma of an all-powerful deity in a universe governed by law.

5 EARLIEST
CIVILIZATIONS

MESOPOTAMIA

EVERYTHING indicates that the pattern
of village life developed in Southwest Asia spread over
the rest of Eurasia and into northern Africa with considerable rapidity. The modifications which it underwent
as adjustments to various environmental conditions have
been discussed in previous chapters. The rise of the earliest civilizations can hardly be interpreted in similar
terms. They were not necessary for existence in the regions in which they arose, but conditions in these regions made them possible. The results of the spread of
Southwest Asian village culture over the temperate Old
World were comparable in certain ways to the results one
gets when one draws a loop which has been dipped in a
bacterial solution across a gelatin plate. In due course of
time, isolated dense colonies of bacteria will appear at
various spots. In the same way, spots of dense population
appeared at various points in the territory the village
culture had reached. The civilizations sprang up at those
points where a combination of dense population and
certain cultural and environmental factors made city life
possible.

The significance of the city as a new and distinctive
type of social grouping has been discussed in Chapter II,
along with the conditions under which cities can exist.
They require not only a dense settled population but also
the technological equipment needed to transport food
and other bulky raw materials to the city site and to dis-

tribute the goods produced by the city's skilled craftsmen. City living seems to have arisen spontaneously in several localities in the Old and New Worlds where these conditions were met. In others the diffusion of patterns for city life which had been developed elsewhere created the necessary local conditions.

In the Old World the earliest centers of civilization, which may be taken as synonymous with city life, were all in the valleys of great rivers. Here the rich soil could support a numerous peasantry, while water transport made the supplying of cities easy. After urban organization had been established in these centers it was diffused outward from each center over wider and wider areas. Its spread was encouraged by the need for raw materials and by application of irrigation techniques developed in the great river valleys to smaller local areas. It cannot be emphasized too strongly that the first centers seem to have arisen independently. Their resemblances were due to their common derivation from the Southwest Asian village culture and to the similar problems which the new type of social grouping presented to all of them.

The first cities were built beside the Nile, the Tigris-Euphrates, the Indus, and the Hwang Ho. City life came to Europe exceedingly late. The early Greek and Italian cities were really small towns, economically self-sufficient. The first European culture complicated enough to be classed as a civilization, that of Crete, also was not a city culture. The island population although relatively dense, was distributed in many small towns, thus minimizing the need for transport of goods in bulk. The skilled craftsmen who produced the goods which the Cretans exported were concentrated at a few places on the coast, where ships could bring the raw materials and carry away the finished product. True cities did not appear in Greece until after the first Olympiad (776 B.C.) or in Italy until the Greek (sixth-seventh century B.C.) or possibly the Etruscan (eighth century B.C.) settlements. They were even later in the rest of Europe and did not appear in Scandinavia until almost the end of the Middle Ages.

Egypt and Mesopotamia were probably the first

centers of city life. Its beginnings in these two regions
seem to have been independent and practically simulta-
neous (about 4000 B.C.). Although there were occasional
contacts between Egypt and Mesopotamia as early as
3500 B.C., real interaction between the two civilizations
did not begin until Egypt became a military power with
Asian commitments (1500 B.C.). The beginnings of the
Indus Valley civilization are more difficult to determine,
since we have no way of establishing a local chronology.
However, this center lay so close to the origin point of
the Southwest Asian village culture that settled life must
have been established there at a very early time. Trade
objects prove contact with Mesopotamia by 3000 B.C.,
and the beginnings of the civilization are undoubtedly
older. The Hwang Ho Valley civilization in northern
China was established much later than the others. Even
if one accords the status of a civilization to the Black Pottery culture which preceded the Shang Dynasty in this
region, the earliest date for its development cannot be
much before 2000 B.C.

Mesopotamia has influenced our own civilization
more than have any of the other earliest centers. We are
only beginning to recognize how heavy a debt Classical
Greek culture owed to this region. The debt of the Hellenistic cultures was still heavier, since the economic and
political patterns which they incorporated came directly
from this region with the Assyrian and Persian civilizations as intermediaries. Through the Hellenistic cultures,
these patterns were transmitted to Imperial Rome and
became a part of the western European tradition.

The Egyptian contributions to our civilization have
been next in importance but are much less numerous.
They have been mainly in the fields of technology and
theology and were filtered through the Hellenistic civilization before they reached the West. Egyptian culture followed a divergent line of development based on values
and interests which we find hard to appreciate. Its preoccupation with the future life, and its enthusiastic acceptance of the Pharaoh as a God upon whose well being

that of the nation depended are incomprehensible to Europeans.

Mesopotamia was the earliest example of a civilization of the sort which we know and can understand. Many of the economic and social patterns which still operate in modern Western society can be traced to this region. It has been said that if George Washington had been transported back to the court of Hammurabi of Babylon, about 2067–2025 B.C., he would have felt vastly more at home there than he would in the modern capital city which bears his name. Apart from language difficulties, he would have encountered very few things in Hammurabi's empire which were not familiar and understandable, while in Washington he would have been baffled and confused by the tremendous technological changes of the past two hundred years and the fumbling efforts which our society is making to bring the other aspects of its culture into adjustment with these.

The Sumerian technology was essentially that of the Southwest Asian Neolithic center with a few additions and a marked increase in technological skills. The Sumerians knew and worked practically all the metals except iron, which was found only in meteorologic form and was therefore too rare for ordinary use. They cast by the lost wax method, drew wire, and were able to solder pieces together. Their jewelry shows filigree and grain work. During the early Sumerian period the difference in value between metals was slight. Copper and bronze were so scarce that they were almost as valuable as gold and silver. Spears, daggers, and battle axes, actual weapons, not ceremonial objects, were made from alloys of gold and copper or gold and silver. These alloys were practical working metals, hard and resistant to corrosion. Pottery was made on the wheel and was turned out in great quantities by potters who were obviously professionals. Their product was standardized and strictly utilitarian. Luxury utensils were made from metal, stone, or shell.

The Sumerians were always threatened by the Semitic-speaking villagers and nomads on their borders and finally succumbed to a Semitic conquest in roughly 2000 B.C. The invading Semites rapidly took over much of the Sumerian culture, and the relations of the two groups are perhaps best illustrated by the numerous carvings in which a Semitic king with embroidered robe and tiara and long, formally curled hair and beard is attended by a Sumerian scribe with shaven head, cloak, and kilt. After a few generations the two groups fused. The Semitic language triumphed but the Sumerian culture, already well stabilized at the time of the conquest, was continued with little change. Not a single item of the later technology was introduced by the invading Semites.

The Sumerian city was surrounded by a tremendous wall built of mud brick, faced with a few layers of burned brick. Each walled city was dominated by a temple enclosure, also walled, which covered several acres and included living quarters for the entire temple entourage, as well as storerooms and workrooms. In the center of the enclosure would be an artificial hill known as the *ziggurat,* on top of which stood the shrine of the city god. The shrines of several minor gods would also be built inside the enclosure but at ground level.

The principal god of the city was usually provided with living quarters furnished like those of a ruler but even more richly. He was also provided with priestly servitors of various ranks and with a harem modeled upon royal lines. At the head of the harem stood the *entu,* who was the god's head wife. This woman was supposed to be faithful to her divine husband and was well chaperoned. She also was, as a rule, the sister or daughter of the ruler of the city. In some cases she regularly slept in the living quarters of the god. She always slept there on the night before some important political decision with the idea that her divine husband would visit her and give her the answer. The ruler might also sleep in the shrine when he was confronted by a difficult problem. The god would come to him in a dream and tell him what to do. Since the god's head wife was always a close relative of the ruler of the city, the god's orders and the ruler's will were rarely in conflict.

Below the head wife in the social scale were the god's other wives, knows as *Sal-me*. These women seem to have been regularly married to the deity and to have brought with them a dowry. They usually lived in the temple grounds but could come and go freely and even keep a house outside the precincts. They could own property and engage in trade. The only business which was out of bounds for them was that of tavern keeper. The conflict between religion and alcohol, still familiar to us, apparently goes back to at least 2000 B.C., for the code of Hammurabi specifies that a *Sal-me* who keeps a wine shop shall be burned. These secondary wives were under no pledge of chastity. Any children they bore were considered the children of the god, which accounted for the frequency with which the heroes of ancient legends were able to claim divine paternity. A rather curious provision was that which allowed *Sal-me* to marry but not to have children by their human husbands. This was regarded as an infringement of the rights of the god, and if a married *Sal-me* had a child she was executed. Apparently *Sal-me* wives usually bought their husband a concubine to take over the child-bearing function. One suspects that such marriages were usually contracted by older women who entered them for business purposes or to gain congenial companionship.

The temple dominated the intellectual and economic life of the city as the *ziggurat* dominated its buildings. It was a huge corporation which, as time went on, drew more and more of the wealth of the community into its hands. The city god was owner of all the land and ten per cent of the produce was paid to him as ground rent. Peasants and artisans paid their tithes in kind. The raw materials obtained in this way were worked up in the temple factories and the finished goods were exported and sold through agents in other communities. This temple trade required a great corps of clerks and accountants, all of whom were officially classed as priests of lower grades. The higher level priests formed a self-perpetuating board of directors for the temple corporation, which continued in operation for as long as a dynasty lasted. Money and goods which once found their way into the temple coffers were never redistributed, while the temple's custom of lending money at rates which we would consider exorbitant hastened the concentration of wealth. This tendency for wealth to accumulate in the hands of religious organizations can be observed in many cultures. At the time of the Protestant Reformation, the Church owned about a third of the total area of Europe and was rapidly creeping up on the rest.

The temples were the only educational centers and maintained schools which were theoretically co-educational, although few girls attended. These schools trained students for the professions of scribe, doctor, and lawyer, as well as for the priesthood. All professional men were rated as priests, although most of them were in independent practice with only a formal connection with the establishment of one or another god. There were two orders of priests: the ceremonial priests, who saw that the rituals, including sacrifices, were performed properly, and the diviners, who answered questions and made prophecies based on various methods of divination.

The most important contribution of these Mesopotamian diviners to later civilization came from their study of the stars. Although the Egyptians also studied the heavens, learned the true length of the year, and discovered the cycle of more than a thousand years intervening between the time that the star Sirius rose at a certain point on the horizon and returned to the same point, the Mesopotamians elaborated the science much further. It is to them that we owe the concept of the zodiac and the recognition of the difference between planets and fixed stars. It is interesting to note that they included the earth and the moon among the planets. The Mesopotamian star watchers kept records over the centuries of planetary movements and of the eclipses of the sun and moon. In due course of time they learned to predict at least lunar eclipses with great accuracy and were able to put this knowledge to good use in their prophecies. Although their astronomical knowledge has come down to us through the Greeks and the Arabs, they were unquestionably the originators of the still flourishing pseudo-science of astrology. Even more important than their astronomical discoveries was the concept of a mechanistic universe resulting from these. A world in which planetary movements and eclipses can be accurately predicted centuries ahead is no longer a world ruled by the casual whims of deities. Upon this recognition is based the search for regularities and natural laws which is the fundamental activity of the scientist.

The Sumerians seem to have been the first people to make slavery a formal institution, and the patterns which they originated have persisted in the Near East until very recent times. Slaves were chiefly prisoners of war, with a few criminals and debt slaves. Earlier peoples had killed off war prisoners, but the Sumerians, living in a settled community where there was much rough work to be done, realized that even an enemy was worth more alive than dead. Slavery for crime and debt are often misinterpreted. Enslavement of criminals was designed less as a punishment than as a means of insuring good behavior of troublesome individuals. It was used mainly in the case of persistent petty offenders. The master who bought such a slave was responsible for any offense which he committed and could be counted on to watch him and to give him a thrashing when he misbehaved.

Debt slavery was merely the end-product of a system under which a man could borrow beyond the amount of his assets. He put himself up for security, and, if he was unable to repay his borrowings within an agreed length of time, became a slave of his creditor and by his labor reimbursed the creditor for the loss of the loan.

Sumerian slavery was not particularly onerous. Since the slaves were captured from nearby cities or had been members of the community, there was no difference in physical type between slave and free. The slave could own property, could borrow money if he could offer security, and could buy his freedom. The slave could also protest his own sale in court, that is, he could show that the man who wished to buy him had a grudge against him and was likely to mistreat him. Runaway slaves were severely punished, as were those who aided them in their flight. Slave women were automatically concubines to their owners. However, at the master's death the concubine and her children were free. The owner of a slave was recompensed if the slave was injured, just as in cases of other property damage. Any damage done by a slave had to be made good by the slave's owner.

The Sumerians were the first people in history to organize and drill their armed forces. The early wars were local affairs, quarrels between city states over fields or water rights. Later, as the city states expanded, long-range campaigns of conquest were inaugurated. By 3000 B.C. we find Sumerian cities fighting for the control of trade routes. The earliest monuments show four-wheeled battle wagons drawn by teams of donkeys. However, it must have been extremely difficult to maneuver with these or even to drive them into the thick of an attacking force. Donkeys, unlike horses, are inclined to use their own best judgment on these occasions. By Akkadian times horses were present in Mesopotamia and the superior two-wheeled chariot was known, but there are no indications of the use of effective chariot tactics.

The strength of the Sumerian army lay in its drilled infantry. The Sumerians were the first people to develop the phalanx, ascribed by most historians to Epaminondos of Thebes some two thousand years later. Monuments of 2500 to 3000 B.C. show these phalanxes marching to battle with the king gallantly striding in front wearing a gold helmet and carrying a scimitar or mace. He must have skipped to the flank before the phalanxes met. The opposing phalanxes operated somewhat like the flying wedge formation familiar to night club waiters. The two phalanxes would advance at the double, gathering speed until they crashed front to front.

The Semitic conquerors of Sumer found themselves confronted with the problems that have plagued conquerors ever since. They were themselves villagers and nomad tribesmen, and as soon as they had taken over the civilized Sumerians they discovered that running an empire was no sinecure. It is easy for nomads to loot a country, but when they try to move in to collect taxes and to keep up production and really profit by their conquest, they are forced to turn to those who already know something about government administration. Within a few years after the Akkadian conquest, the conquerors were using the old Sumerian bureaucracy to keep the system going. Within a few generations the shaven-headed Sumerian scribes, who are shown humbly following the gorgeous Akkadian kings, had gotten most of the real power back into their own hands. In the long run the pen is a deadlier weapon than the sword.

Mesopotamia was the first civilization to have business as one of its major interests. Trade was necessary to any sort of civilized life, since the only raw materials which the valley provided in adequate quantity were clay, reeds, and grain. Even the beams needed in house construction and the stone from which the images of the gods were made had to be imported. As the Sumerians made increasing use of metal their trade routes extended farther and farther. Trading posts staffed by Sumerian merchants were established as far afield as Asia Minor and Palestine. They also seem to have carried on a fairly extensive sea trade by way of the Persian Gulf, since we have one record of a trading expedition which was gone for over three years and came back loaded, no doubt, with "ivory, apes, and peacocks." Goods from the upper river districts, which were the principal sources of lumber and animal products, were brought to the Sumerian cities by a method still in use. A bull boat, which was simply a large circular basket woven of osiers and covered with hides, was loaded with produce and floated downstream. The bull boats were large enough to carry two or three men and one or two donkeys in addition to their payload. When the boat reached the city it was broken up and sold together with the cargo. The crew stowed their personal possessions and purchases on the donkeys and walked home.

All the appliances for effective business were established by 3000 B.C. Standard weights and measures were developed. Those of the various cities probably differed at first as they did in Medieval Europe, but the spread of empire resulted in increasing standardization. The earliest medium of exchange was a fixed measure of barley, the measure being, in many cases, carved in stone and set up in the market place so that if a farmer thought he was being short-changed he could measure out the grain. By 3000 B.C. metal currency was beginning to replace barley currency, and the government was beginning to worry about the shortage of money. The code of Hammurabi attempted to stabilize the relative value of barley and metal, with serious penalties for abuse of the standard. A merchant who refused to take barley in payment for his wares forfeited his life, as did anyone who refused to exchange metal money for barley at the current rate.

Metal was cut and weighed at each exchange. The Sumerians did not have coins. The difficulty was, of course, in assessing the purity of the metal, and in later times private banking houses stamped metal ingots with their seals as a guarantee against adulteration. These "stamped shekels" were the ancestors of our own coins. In the Sumerian-Akkadian period the ratio of silver to gold was 12 to 1.

We have cuneiform records of elaborate financial transactions, loans with fixed rates of interest running up as high as two or three hundred per cent in cases in which the individual had no security. The lowest rate was twenty-five per cent per annum. There were principals and agents and also joint projects, corresponding to our stock companies and corporations. It is interesting that, in the laws governing principals and agents, an agent who defrauded his employer was punished only half as severely as the employer who defrauded his agents. Apparently the financial forces were already operating to squeeze the little fellow, and the law was attempting to protect him from the big operators, particularly the temple corporations.

Because of the Sumerian habit of making contracts for all important transactions we have an amazingly complete picture of the life of these people. Not only documents and contracts but a good deal of private correspondence have been preserved. One tablet from before 2000 B.C. contains the familiar lament of an old man about the degeneracy of the younger generation. Another personal document which shows a high continuity of pattern is a letter written to his parents by a boy at school complaining about the food.

From the legal documents and private correspondence we gain an excellent picture of Sumerian home life. The Sumerian family was much like our own. There were no clans or extended kin groups. This was probably a reflection of city living, since it is very difficult to maintain extended family patterns in a city population which is constantly shifting and being recruited from the outside. Any city population tends to be made up of isolated individuals, and consequently the small family with only the parent-child tie is the strongest social unit.

Marriage was monogamous, except that a rich and important man might have several concubines. Family capital was held and used jointly. Women could run businesses, lend money, make legal contracts in the absence of their husbands, and, in short, held positions of economic equality. As a matter of fact their legal position was much better than that of the English woman prior to the Married Women's Property Act of 1926. A wife was not responsible for debts that her husband had contracted before marriage, and vice-versa; but, after marriage, debts contracted by either party were family debts and either party could be held for them. A husband could sell his wife under certain circumstances but only with her consent. If she preferred being a concubine in a rich man's house to being a hard-working wife in a poor family, she could ask her husband to sell her.

Sumer was the first place in history to have a fully developed concept of law and written and published law codes. The Indonesian development of *adat* law cannot be dated, but must be ascribed to a later time. The first complete Mesopotamian law code which has been preserved is the Code of Hammurabi, which was drawn up in 1940 B.C. However, fragments of a number of older codes have survived, and their compilation must be regarded as a sort of Code Napoleon, intended to simplify and unify the preexisting legal system of a whole series of cities. This was made necessary by the spread of the Sumerian-Akkadian empire of which Hammurabi was ruler.

Hammurabi was a Semite and, to judge from the fragments of earlier codes, the Semitic conquest led to a considerable stiffening of penalties and a worsening of the status of women. Incidentally, according to his own statement, the infant Hammurabi was found floating in a reed basket in a drainage ditch and adopted by a gardener, thus antedating Moses by some five hundred years.

Hammurabi had his code inscribed on pillars which were set up in the market places of the various cities in his empire. The laws were stated with a brevity and conciseness which is rarely found in our own. The king had important judicial powers and represented the court of last appeal. This pattern has been continued by some Near Eastern rulers down to the present day and seems to be a characteristic Semitic pattern. It provided a method by which the king could make himself accessible to his subjects and gain their favor. A king who made wise judgments, was able to evaluate conflicting evidence and detect false witnesses gained tremendously in prestige. Solomon, who held court in good Sumerian fashion, was such a king, and his judgments are still famous.

The higher officials whom the king had appointed to outlying districts performed his judicial functions there. There were both ecclesiastical and civil lower courts, but the jurisdiction of each type was not too clearly defined. Presumably the system had originally been weighted on the ecclesiastical side like the rest of Sumerian culture, but the civil courts had arrogated additional power to themselves. By the time of Hammurabi the ecclesiastical courts could pronounce judgments in affairs pertaining to the temple, but even these decisions were subject to royal review. Ordinary civil suits were heard in civil courts by judges appointed by the king.

The principals and witnesses gave testimony under oath, documents were produced and examined by the court, and the decision was handed down on the basis of precedents. In important cases the accused would be represented by counsel. A judge who reversed his decision could be fined and disbarred, as it was assumed that he had been bribed to do so. However, a case could be appealed to a higher court if the judgment was unsatisfactory, or new evidence could be brought in. Court stenographers recorded all cases on cuneiform tablets, which were put down in sand in large jars. There were heavy penalties for perjury and contempt of court. In fact, the whole courtroom procedure would be entirely familiar to a modern lawyer.

Some of the most interesting sections of the code are those dealing with economic matters. Prices were rising steadily, and the poor land-owner was being progressively squeezed out. There was legislation directed at the redistribution of agricultural land which was not kept in use. In these codes we can observe the first attempts to control wages, rents, working hours, etc. In fact, there is a recently translated tablet from the Sumerian period in which there is a dispute over portal to portal pay. This controversy was brought to court and decided in favor of labor, a not infrequent result in Sumerian courts. However, in spite of the effort to fix prices and wages throughout Mesopotamian history we can trace a steady rise in the cost of things, comparable to that which has been going on ever since.

Sumer even had its New Deal and social reform instituted from the top down, which was undertaken by Urukagina of Lagash in 2630 B.C. In his inscriptions Urukagina is exceedingly vague as to his ancestry, which suggests that he was a commoner who had risen to power. One of his first acts was to reduce taxes and to cut the excessive charges which the priests were making for necessary services such as funerals and divination. In fact he tried to introduce socialized divination, putting the diviners on a straight government salary and forbidding them to receive extra fees. He also tried to institute agrarian reforms, breaking down the large estates and redistributing the land to the peasants. This naturally earned

him the enmity of all the better people, who called upon
the ruler of a neighboring city for help. In the resulting
rightist revolution Urukagina was killed and everything
returned to normalcy. One of the most personal of ancient documents which has come down to us deals with
this event. An unbaked clay tablet was found buried in a
rubbish heap outside the city wall of Lagash. Upon this
tablet a minor priest, who must have been a friend and
partisan of Urukagina, had listed the shrines destroyed
and looted by the foreign allies of the conservative fac-
tion and had eased his mind by calling down a comprehensive curse upon the traitors.

EGYPT

         A L T H O U G H Egyptian culture had its
foundation in the same Southwest Asian Neolithic that
fathered the civilizations of Eurasia, it developed into
something profoundly alien. Egypt is the ideal territory
for the historic archaeologist. There are endless inscriptions and numerous manuscripts. The dry climate has
preserved delicate and perishable materials intact and the
Egyptian's unquestioning belief in a future life much like
the present, and his attempts to equip the dead for living
in it, have resulted in the preservation of an almost complete inventory of objects of daily use. The situation of
the prehistoric archaeologist is much less satisfactory,
since the annual deposition of the Nile mud has buried
even Neolithic settlements under many feet of accumulated silt.

         In about 6000 B.C. Asian immigrants to Egypt
brought in domestic plants and animals and Neolithic
technology. In the delta the Merimdeans cultivated
wheat and barley and kept cattle, sheep, and goats. In
upper Egypt a different and less advanced type of Neolithic culture (*Tasian*) appeared slightly later. These
Tasians seem to have been seminomadic.

         Lower Egypt was united under a single ruler by

4500 B.C. and conquered Upper Egypt about two hundred and fifty years later. The northern conquest was short-lived and by 400 B.C. the two regions were once more independent. It was during the following seven hundred years of independence that the foundations of the later Egyptian civilization were laid.

By 3300 B.C. each of the two Egypts had its king and court, its royal symbols, and its national gods. Upper Egypt had the white crown, was under the guardianship of the vulture goddess, *Nekhebet,* and had as its emblem the sedge. Lower Egypt had the red crown, was under the protection of the cobra goddess, *Buto,* and had as its emblem the bee. The differences between north and south survived throughout the whole period of Egyptian history and went deeper than mere political organization. One can see certain parallels in the case of the Scots and the English. The up-river Egyptians were hardy, quarrelsome, suspicious of refinements, forthright and, from the Egyptian point of view, puritanical. The delta Egyptians were gay, clever, pleasure-loving, and eager for novelties, but preferred battles of wits to those of arms. They regarded the Upper Egyptians as barbarians and poked fun at their harsh dialect and crude ways.

Even when the two kingdoms were united under Menes, the Upper Egyptian conqueror, he found it politic not to try to consolidate their governments completely. Instead he ruled as king of Lower Egypt and again as king of Upper Egypt, much as in Europe the same individual was emperor of Austria and king of Hungary. Pharaoh had a palace and an independent bureaucracy in Lower and in Upper Egypt, and functioned sometimes as king of one and sometimes as king of the other, his status at the moment being shown by his wearing of either the red or the white crown.

The period immediately following the unification of the two Egypts was one of tremendously rapid cultural advance. From 3300 to 2563 B.C. Egypt was the scene of one of those culture mutations whose causes are one of the main problems still to be solved by the investigators of culture dynamics. During the first five hundred years of this period Egyptian technology achieved its final form in everything but architecture. Specialized craftsmen supported by the ruling group were producing vases carved from the hardest decorative stone, a wealth of beautifully wrought copper vessels, and ornaments of gold, lapis lazuli, and turquoise. More practically, the beginning of the dynastic era saw the introduction of the plow.

Hieroglyphic writing was perfected and so firmly integrated into religious and governmental practice that it underwent no significant changes after this time. There seems to have been an outburst of all sorts of intellectual activity. The first scientifically conceived treatises on the diagnosis and treatment of disease and injuries date from this time. Religion was organized and the elaborate rituals of temple and court were crystallized. Lastly, the ruling group developed one of the most thoroughly organized and politically centralized systems of government that the world has seen.

Toward the close of this period the great pyramids of Giza were built. How extraordinary these structures were can be appreciated if one realizes that they were erected less than two hundred years after the Egyptians first essayed to use stone in any sort of construction. The pyramids were built with the simplest appliances: ramps, rollers, and levers. Even the pulley was unknown. To organize and supply the tremendous labor force for this construction was an administrative achievement of the first magnitude.

The last two dynasties of the Old Kingdom period became obsessed with the desire to conquer Nubia and waged constant war with the Negroes there. This, and the unproductive labor expended in pyramid and temple building, finally overtaxed the patience of the peasants and exhausted the land's resources. The Old Kingdom period ended, about 2300 B.C., in political breakdown and confusion. When effective central government once more emerged in 2065 B.C., the common people had won their freedom from serfdom, and, although they were still subject to royal tax collectors, and more often than not tenants upon the royal or temple lands, they possessed and thereafter retained much greater freedom. Above all, it was possible for individuals to rise in the world. Many a high official boasted in his funeral inscriptions that he was a self-made man, son of a middle-class or even peasant family.

Egypt's most significant contributions to the growth of world civilization were in the two fields of technology and religion. Its governmental forms were too rigid and too permeated with theocratic patterns to be acceptable outside the Nile Valley. A peasantry which is accustomed to defending itself against outside attacks cannot be expected to grovel before innumerable priests and officials. The relative safety of Egypt, fortified by its deserts, made possible a degree of absolutism which could not be enforced elsewhere.

The Egyptians were by far the cleverest craftsmen of the preclassical world. Their best skills were expended on luxury objects, and the great demand for these, created by the custom of burying them with the dead, had a curious by-product. The tombs of the Pharaohs and their nobles were filled with treasures of gold and precious stones, and, although tomb robbers returned much of this to circulation, the supply could not keep up with the demand. The dead are not hard to deceive, and the Egyptian craftsmen soon began to produce imitation goldwork in which the metal was simulated either by gilding or by surface finishes which made base metal look like gold. It was in these efforts to imitate precious materials and to find substitutes for them that the science of alchemy, ancestor of our own chemistry, originated. The earliest alchemic texts, which come from Ptolemaic Egypt but probably embody much older material, are, with few exceptions, recipes for making alloys or giving surface finishes which will look like gold. It is significant that the same texts include recipes for making a dye which would imitate the costly Tyrian purple. Alchemy thus began in a search for cheap substitutes, and became confused and transformed into a mystic search for the philosopher's stone only after the Neo-Platonic philosophers had captured it from the craftsmen.

To the modern Westerner, reared in the tradition of Greek logic and of constant sequences of cause and effect, Egyptian religion appears quite incomprehensible. The names of two thousand Egyptian gods are known to us. None of these could be categorized as good or bad; their aid could be invoked for ethical or unethical purposes. Their worshippers did not regard them with affection nor feel powerless before them. Every deity could be circumvented and controlled if one knew the proper formulas. The elaborate rituals of the temples were as much incantations for the purpose of manipulating the gods as acts of worship.

The importance of deities rose and fell with that of their cities or districts. However, there were certain centers whose gods retained their influence throughout Egyptian history. Thus the oldest of the great principal gods was *Ra, Atum,* or *Ra-Atum,* god of Heliopolis. He was a sun god, a world creator always depicted in human form. Below him in the doctrine of Heliopolis were a series of eight other gods, including *Osiris* and *Isis.* Their son, *Horus,* headed another ninefold group of deities, but in good Egyptian fashion he was specifically identified with Ra-Atum under the name of *Harakhte* and was known as the son of Ra. More concretely, Horus was personified as the rising sun, Ra as the midday sun, and Atum as the setting sun, represented as a tired old man. The legend of Osiris falls into two parts which seem only incidentally related. In the first, he ruled in Egypt together with his queen-sister Isis. His brother Set desired her and, by a trick, murdered Osiris and set the body afloat in a chest which drifted to Byblus in Syria. Isis followed and brought it back to Egypt, where the god *Anubis* mummified it under her direction. The soul of Osiris then descended to the underworld, where he became ruler of the dead. Isis took the mummy to a hiding place in the marshes of Lower Egypt, where she contrived to get herself impregnated by it. (The inconsistency might be resolved by the *Ka* belief, but the Egyptians themselves probably were not troubled by it.) In due course of time she gave birth to a son, Horus. Set also had been searching for his brother's body. He discovered it in Isis' absence, carried it off, dismembered it, and scattered the pieces throughout the length of Egypt. Isis sought them out and reassembled them. When Horus grew to manhood he set out to avenge his father's murder on Set. An epic but inconclusive battle ensued. In the end the quarrel was submitted to the arbitration of the earth god, *Geb,* who first awarded Lower Egypt to Horus and Upper Egypt to Set but later placed both kingdoms beneath the sway of Horus.

In the first half of this legend Osiris appears as a typical Near Eastern vegetation god. Many of the incidents resemble those told of *Adonis* of Byblus and *Tammuz* of Mesopotamia. Like them, Osiris was killed, dismembered, buried, and resurrected, a cycle annually reenacted in the reaping and threshing of the grain, and the planting and growth of the new crop.

The second part of the legend is an allegory of Egyptian history providing divine sanction for the rule of Pharaoh. Isis was the ideal queen-sister and loyal wife, and Horus the perfect son who defended his father and avenged his death upon his murderers. The initial division of Egypt between Horus and Set is a folk memory of the actual division of Egypt in prehistoric times, while the final assignment of the whole of Egypt to Horus commemorated the first unification of Egypt, which took place under Lower Egyptian rule.

Osiris, as benevolent Pharaoh and a ruler in the land of the dead who was willing to share his immortality with all his subjects, became the most popular deity in Egypt. Where the gods of the other doctrines were worshipped mainly by the upper classes, the Osirian trinity was worshipped by all classes, from Pharaoh to the peasants. At his great shrine at Abydos, the incidents of his life, death, and resurrection were reenacted in a sort of passion play which continued for many days. The important roles were assigned by the king to high officers of state, the part of Horus, the ideal son, being regarded as a special honor. The local population and the thousands of pilgrims who came to the celebration joined in the proceedings as extras. The ceremony culminated in an epic battle between forces representing the armies of Horus and those of Set, Osiris' murderer, during which no one was killed but many eyes were blacked and heads were broken.

Last but by no means least among the Egyptian deities was Pharaoh himself. At his coronation Pharaoh *became* the god Horus and at his death was transformed into Osiris. His spiritual potency, on which the well-being of the land depended, was increased by the purity of his royal blood, and for this reason the Pharaoh was married in childhood to the most suitable of his small sisters or half-sisters. When he became a man he was permitted to take as many additional wives and mistresses as he desired, but it was desirable for his heir to possess the strongest possible strain of royal blood. To insure this, Pharaohs not infrequently married their own daughters.

There were hundreds of other gods of which we know little more than the names and the shapes in which they were represented. The Egyptians had a penchant for showing their gods in part animal, part human form and, in later days, worshipped animals as divine incarnations. Many of the nomes also had as their symbols particular animals which they were forbidden to kill or use. The whole arrangement is very suggestive of totemism. There are two curious aspects of these animal gods and symbols. Although the predynastic Egyptians' culture was largely Asian in its origins, the wild animals represented are all African; at the same time, two most impressive African animals, the elephant and the rhinoceros, are conspicuous by their absence.

The Egyptian concepts of the spiritual element in man and its fate after death were as disorganized and nonlogical as the rest of their religious beliefs. Description is made even more difficult by the transformations which some of these concepts underwent in the course of Egyptian history. The predynastic Egyptians certainly believed in individual survival for all classes, for they provided all their dead with tomb furniture, varying in amount and quality with the resources of the family. The

Old Kingdom centralization of power deprived the common people not only of freedom but even of the hope of immortality. For a time at least the only individuals to enjoy life after death were the Pharaoh and the nobles to whom he communicated certain magical formulae, and whom he allowed to be buried near him, thus sharing a portion of his divine life-force. We do not know whether the commoners concurred in this opinion or not, but that they never lost their desire for immortality is proved by the rapid development of the cult of Osiris, Isis, and Horus after the Old Kingdom collapsed.

The Egyptians believed in the existence of at least two and possibly more spiritual entities connected with the individual. The most clearly defined of these was the *Ka,* the individual's double. There is some reason to believe that in the earliest times this was equated with the placenta. The Ka was born with the individual, maintained a separate existence during his lifetime, and was reunited with his body at the instant of death. If the body was seriously damaged or destroyed, the Ka would perish, hence the practice of mummification and the custom of placing in the tomb an image of the deceased which the Ka could occupy if the body was destroyed. The Ka lived in the tomb, feeding upon the offerings, and the elaborate tomb furnishings and wall carvings were for its benefit. Every Egyptian attempted to assure his Ka not only of shelter but of a steadily renewed food supply. The worship of the dead by their descendants was obligatory, since the dead were able to control the destinies of the living. The sacrifices in connection with the ancestor cult were much more numerous than those given to the gods and included animals and libations of blood, milk, and wine. Certain passages in the pyramid texts may indicate that human sacrifices were made before the individual's death to assure him proper service in the next world.

In historic times Egyptian society was class-organized, but with considerable opportunity for vertical mobility. In the Old Kingdom there were actually only two classes, royalty and commoners, all important offices in both the governmental bureaucracy and the priesthood being filled by royal relatives. The large harems maintained by men of the royal group insured an extensive supply of these. As time went on, the society was differentiated into a peasantry, a middle-class of craftsmen and professional soldiers, and an aristocratic group of nobles, administrators, and priests. Above them all towered the Pharaoh, whose divinity set him beyond classification as a mere human.

The Egyptians were never interested in fighting, and in the Old Kingdom days there were few professional soldiers. When the military establishment became more important and permanent, foreigners made up a large part of the Egyptian forces. Some were volunteers, but many were slaves. They made good soldiers because they could be subjected to the strictest discipline, and from the slave's point of view war was vastly preferable to labor in a quarry or on public works. The pattern of slave-soldiers thus established survived in Islamic countries until late times. Outstanding examples are the Janissaries in Turkey and the Mamelukes of later Egypt.

On the borderline between the middle and upper classes stood the scribes. The old saying that knowledge is power was nowhere truer than in Egypt. It required years of assiduous study to master the intricacies of the hieroglyphic writing, but the scribe's training by no means ended there. He was expected to know the ancient literature and also to have mastered enough mathematics and engineering to be able to cast accounts, design buildings, and supervise public works. His royal master might even call upon him to lead a military expedition. The biographies which some successful scribes have left in their funeral inscriptions suggest a versatility equal to that of Leonardo da Vinci.

The Egyptian upper class consisted of government officials, hereditary nobility, and the priesthood. As just noted, officials might be of either common or noble origin, but the higher positions in the priesthood were normally held by nobles. The situation was not unlike that of the medieval church in Europe. The officials were divided into the administrators and the court group, who were particularly concerned with the care of the Pharaoh's person and establishment.

At the head of the administrative hierarchy stood the Vizier, who took over all the routine secular duties pertaining to Pharaoh's office. These duties were heavy. The Vizier acted as a supreme court and had to hear all cases referred to him from lower courts. Great stress was laid on his expeditious handling of cases. He superintended public works and, three times a year, received reports on conditions in the various nomes. Tax authorities sent their accounts to him and he issued receipts from the royal storehouses. He also recruited the Pharaoh's bodyguard and took care of all the arrangements when he traveled. Every morning the Vizier went to the palace, met the Pharaoh, inquired after his health, and then reported to him on the state of the nation.

Closely associated with the Vizier was a second great minister known as the Director of the Seal. He was in charge of the financial affairs of the kingdom. It was he who assessed taxes and saw to their collection. Since the taxes were paid in kind, not cash, he was further responsible for the distribution of the goods turned in and, in later times, for their conversion into money. He also managed the incredibly complicated affairs of the funerary foundation and temple estates. Lastly, he had to fix wage scales for labor on the royal and temple estates, which thus set a general standard for the kingdom. During most of Egyptian history, there were a single Vizier and a single Director of the Seal, but, by the New Kingdom, administration had become too complex to be handled in this way, and there were separate Viziers and Keepers of the Seal for Upper and Lower Egypt.

The palace officials were exceedingly numerous. Closest to the king's person were a group of intimate advisors known as the Honored Ones. This group automatically included members of the royal family but was primarily made up of men who had proved their worth by many years of administrative service. The Honored Ones were maintained at court at the king's expense, but their most prized privileges were the provision which the king made for their splendid burials and his permission to be laid out to rest near his own person. Individual Honored Ones were also assigned posts connected with the operation of the court and the care of Pharaoh's person. These posts carried honorary titles such as "Lordship of the Secret of the Royal House," i.e., custodian of the crown jewels. Court protocol was exceedingly elaborate. The king's person was attended by a Director of the King's Dress, under whom were a Valet of the Hands, a Director of the Oils and Unguents, a Keeper of the King's Wigs, and many others. The queen and ladies of the royal harem had even more elaborate personal staffs. Even the staff of the royal kitchen was organized in a rising order of precedence. The three royal meat-carvers preceded the cake maker, who in turn preceded the soufflé maker, who in turn preceded the jam maker.

The most important group in the hereditary nobility was composed of the nomarchs and their relatives. These were the descendants of the kings who had ruled over the various nomes before the unification of Egypt. Although every strong dynasty tried to limit their power and minimize their importance, they retained the devotion of the nome members and, whenever the central power weakened, functioned as petty kings. The nomarch was really a sort of viceroy in his province, combining administrative duties with religious functions as high priest of the nome god. The hereditary nobility were in general supported by estates which had been granted to the family in the past by Pharaoh. Although many of the noble families boasted long descent, able commoners might be promoted through Pharaoh's favor and become the founders of noble houses. It is interesting to note that the Egyptian nobility was not primarily a warrior caste. Although a few of the great families produced able generals through several generations, many others concerned themselves mainly with religious or administrative activities or were simply courtiers.

The priesthood was one of the most important elements in Egyptian society. In addition to the observance of the daily rites and the annual festival of the god, which often lasted for weeks, the priests gave oracles and presented individual requests to the god in return for suitable fees. Unfortunately, our knowledge of the staffing of the temples is limited to the names of the various officials. The priests as a whole were divided into two classes, consisting of prophets and ordinary priests. No matter what the duties of these two groups may have been in historic times, this division is highly suggestive of the well-nigh universal one between the inspirational priest, who goes into a trance state and permits the deity to speak through his mouth, and the ritual priest, who takes charge of the proper performance of the formal rites. Every temple was staffed with a Chief Prophet, Deputy Prophet, Priest, Deputy Priest, and so forth. Priestesses were ranged in a hierarchy of their own, but were much less significant in religious exercises than the priests. Their principal duties consisted in providing music and dancing on religious occasions. Sacred concubines and sacred prostitutes were attached to the temples of most gods. A separate group of priests supervised the worship and offerings in the royal mortuary temples.

Lastly, most of the schools in which advanced education was given were associated with temples, and it was customary for Egyptian professional men, doctors, and lawyers to take orders and to be nominally connected with some temple establishment. A similar arrangement was common in Europe during the Middle Ages.

The study of Egyptian culture leaves one with the feeling that the Egyptians were a clever and ingenious people whose progress was stultified by the development of one of the most rigid and highly centralized governmental systems which the world has seen. There was a complete union of church and state, with a correspondingly complete control of the subjects' bodies and minds. Such systems can function successfully only through a rigid maintenance of the status quo. The Egyptian inventions which eventually became incorporated into the general stream of developing Eurasian civilization were almost all made during the first five hundred years of Egyptian history. It is

even doubtful whether the Egyptian contributions outside
the field of technology were not a result of the classical
misinterpretation of Egyptian beliefs and rituals rather
than an authentic diffusion of Egyptian elements.

6 MEDITERRANEAN COMPLEX

CRETE

THE Cretan civilization was derived from the same Southwest Asian Neolithic center which was ancestral to the other ancient cultures just discussed. However, it seems to have been more strongly influenced by Egyptian civilization than by Asia. Crete lies about halfway between Egypt and the Greek mainland, a position which proved highly advantageous, since it made it possible for the Cretans to dominate the carrying trade between these two centers in later times. The first Cretan settlement seems to have been made about 5000 B.C., probably by migrants from the Greek mainland. Their culture was a simple Neolithic one, but they could reach Crete by island-hopping without having to cross more than fifty or sixty miles of open sea at any point. This would be quite possible in dugout canoes in calm weather. Racially, the settlers were long-headed, dark-haired, slender Mediterraneans. Even in Classical times the back country Cretans did not speak Greek, and from this and the Minoan (early Cretan) inscriptions, we feel sure that the original language of the island was not Indo-European.

Contact with Egypt seems to have been established before the end of the pre-Dynastic period there, roughly 4000 B.C. So many Egyptian elements appear in Crete during the next thousand years that some authorities believe there was an actual migration from Egypt. In the classical period the Cretans were famous for two things: their archery and their mendacity. They seem to have used the composite bow, even in Minoan times, having presumably acquired it through trade contacts with Asia Minor. The mendacity was presumably a local development. There was a Classical Greek phrase, "to lie like a Cretan," which acknowledged their supremacy in an art at which the Greeks themselves were no novices.

Even in Neolithic times Crete must have been a relatively poor region for agriculture. However, the island was well forested, providing timber for ships, and the olive tree was well adapted to the stony slopes which were left when the forests had been cut off. The Cretans seem to have been one of the first peoples to domesticate this tree. Olive groves are profitable only for a thoroughly settled population, since it takes them about thirty years to come into full bearing, after which they will keep on bearing for about one hundred years. Throughout Cretan history olive oil was one of the island's main exports. Their use of the fine pottery which was produced locally for the fancy packaging of this product has already been mentioned.

The main Cretan domestic animal seems to have been the goat. Horses reached the island before the Minoan culture was overthrown, but they were of little importance. Cattle were also kept and bulls had very definite ceremonial and religious connotations. However, the Cretans must have got most of their protein food from fish. The poverty of the Cretan soil and the proximity of the sea led them to seafaring and commerce. They were the first people in history to develop a civilization of the modern commercial type. Throughout the period when Crete was a great power, the Cretans lived much as the English have lived in recent centuries, by their control of the ocean-carrying trade and by the sale of manufactured products. Much of their food must have been imported. Crete was densely populated even in Homeric times, when the civilization was in a state of relative collapse. The Homeric poems constantly speak of the "many-peopled Crete," and the Greeks of this period were greatly impressed by the number of towns and the crowded streets of the island.

By 3000 B.C. copper was being obtained in trade from the island of Cyprus. Our own word for copper, passed down through many languages, really means "metal of Cyprus." Bronze, silver, and gold were in use by 2400 B.C., and since there were no rich ore deposits on the island, all of these must have been obtained through trade. Iron did not reach Crete until after the collapse of the Minoan civilization. The Cretan artists of the late Minoan period, 1600-1200 B.C., developed a skill in alloying which has rarely been equaled. They tried out all sorts of metallic mixtures and finishes, until they were able to literally paint in different colored metals. Relatively few examples of this work have been found in Crete itself, and one wonders whether its products were intended primarily for the non-Cretan mainland princes for whom the Cretan artists produced luxury objects. Perhaps the metal painting was too flamboyant for the highly refined Cretan taste.

Pottery was known from the first Cretan settlements. Although they had frequent contacts with Egypt, where the technique of making faience was well developed, most of their vessels were unglazed. Nevertheless, the forms are excellent and the decoration not only beautiful but painted with a freedom and skill which marks the professional. Not until the great age of the Greek vase painters do we find pottery of equal artistic quality.

The Minoans also must have been excellent woodworkers, although no examples of their craft have survived. We know that they built chariots and seagoing ships, both of which require careful preliminary design and expert joinery. It is interesting in this connection that the few Minoan tools which have survived include a fragment of what seems to be a large bronze crosscut saw, probably used in sawing out planks for shipwrights. Other Minoan tools are much more like modern European hand tools than are those of the Mesopotamians or Egyptians. A modern craftsman could use them with little change in his muscular habits.

The ingenuity and technical skill of the Cretans was recognized by the later Greeks in their legend of Daedalus, the master craftsman who contrived numerous machines for the use of his royal master. At least one of the devices with which he is credited, the ball-and-socket joint permitting universal motion, may well be a Cretan invention. According to the legend, when he fell from favor he escaped with his son Icarus by means of artificial wings. The fate of Icarus, who ventured too near the sun, is still familiar as an example of disastrous pride.

Minoan art represented an early flowering of that keen observation of nature and attempt to reproduce it, while maintaining balance and harmony of design, which was so characteristic of the later Greeks. Like the Greek art of the later Classical period, Minoan art was instinct with life. Its artists did not represent remote and awful deities or divine kings, but proud and happy humans. Minoan pottery was decorated with floral and marine forms of surprising naturalism, and similar forms, particularly dolphins, were used as repeat designs in the frescoes with which the Minoan palaces were decorated.

Thanks to frescoes and figurines it is possible for us to reconstruct various details of Cretan equipment. The usual costume of young men was a scanty loin cloth and a broad belt designed to produce a wasp waist. Older men wore a long gown, and apparently cloaks were worn for warmth or on solemn occasions. The women's costume gives a curious feeling of modernity. The upper garment was a short-sleeved bolero jacket worn with or without a blouse of thin white material. With this was worn a flounced bell-bottomed skirt or wide-bottomed lounging pajamas gaily decorated with ruffles. Color was extensively used. The footgear for both men and women was completely modern. Men are sometimes shown wearing sandals but more commonly wearing a solid shoe much like the army field shoe. Women wore high-heeled, open-strap slippers almost identical with those shown in the summer displays of Fifth Avenue shops. Women also wore large, gaily decorated hats which might well have come from the workroom of Lily Daché. Both sexes were addicted to elaborate ornaments of gold and gems, and the variety of costume details shown in paintings and figurines suggest that the Minoan ladies, like our own, followed the dictates of frequently changing fashions.

The Cretans were the first people to develop large

seaworthy vessels. To judge from engravings on gems and occasional representations on pottery, these ships were galleys with single banks of oars. They seem to have been decked over for their entire length and to have had one to three masts with square sails. The bow and stern were high and sharply upcurved and, at the bow, the keel projected for some distance beyond the cutwater. This arrangement must have been designed for ramming, and we know that by the end of the Minoan period fighting ships had rams which were shod with bronze. They were thus the originators of what was to be the main naval tactic throughout the Classical period. It may also be noted that the Minoans were the first people to develop the type of anchor still in use, complete with flukes and rig.

If they were able to ram successfully, the Minoan galleys must have been fast and maneuverable. They enabled the Minoans to establish the first sea empire in history. In order to maintain this, they set up naval bases around the eastern Mediterranean. Their bases in the Nile delta were leased from Egypt. Those in less civilized areas were probably established by force. Such bases were the earliest examples of the deliberate colonization brought to such a high point by the later Greek cities. While these bases were mainly useful for trade, the Minoans also no doubt indulged in piracy. It may be remembered that in the *Odyssey* King Nestor politely asks Odysseus' son Telemachus whether he is a trader or a pirate. Both occupations were regarded as perfectly respectable at this period and were obviously merely alternate ways of getting what the voyager wanted.

Although the island of Crete apparently was not politically unified until about a century before the final collapse of the Minoan culture, the Cretan villages were all open towns. The Minoan control of the sea made defense against foreign invasion unnecessary. There seem to have been no fortifications on the island, which suggests that the various districts must have had some sort of confederate organization. Apparently the Cretans lived at peace with each other, aside from the usual family feuds. This was in sharp contrast to the mainland settlements.

The Cretan communities seem to have been more prosperous than any of the early city civilizations. Certainly the economic surplus was more evenly distributed. The Egyptian cities consisted of a few great temples and palaces surrounded by extensive slums. There was a larger middle class in Mesopotamia than in Egypt, but even there the proportion of middle-class families seems to have been much smaller than in Crete. The Minoan towns suggest a predominantly bourgeois population.

The largest establishment on Crete was the great building at Knossos, usually referred to as the palace of the Minos. Minos was the title of the Cretan priest-kings, as Pharaoh was of the Egyptian divine kings. The palace was a vast complex which had apparently grown over several hundred years until it had come to include over a thousand rooms. None of the rooms was very large and the construction was of a sort easily accomplished without the use of mass labor. The building contained a throne room and living quarters for what must have been a ruling family, but most of the complex was taken up with storehouses and workshops. It seems to have been more a community center and factory than a palace. In the throne room there was a gypsum throne with guardian griffins painted on the walls on either side. In the royal living quarters were bathrooms and toilets much more modern than anything in most of the villages on the island of Crete today. There was a good sewage system, with drains arranged in such a way that, when it rained, the water from the roof would flush the sewers and keep them clean. The sewers also had manholes so that workmen could go down into them for cleaning and repairs. The Cretans were the first sanitary engineers in history.

A combination of palace and factory such as the great building at Knossos was quite in line with the importance of trade and manufactures in the Cretan economy. Trade between Crete and Egypt began as early as 4000 b.c., and by 2000 b.c. the contact was close and continuous. Cretan art objects were thought worthy of inclusion in the tombs of the Egyptian Pharaohs, and Egyptian frescoes show the arrival of Cretan merchants with characteristic costumes and wares. Even the Minos of Crete traded with the Egyptian Pharaoh, although their business transactions were phrased in the lofty terms of a gift exchange. Thus, we have a copy of a letter from a Pharaoh complaining to the Minos that the last shipment of olive oil had not been up to specifications. There must have been many other traders, and the finding of what can only be described as country villas suggests a class of wealthy merchant princes.

Cretan trade and manufacturing seems to have left the local population with plenty of time for spectator sports. As part of the Knossos complex there was an open-air theater which, to judge from the frescoes, was used mainly for bull baiting. The bulls were the wild aurochs of Europe. These looked much like the modern Spanish fighting bulls but were considerably larger and more ferocious. From a slightly later period we have some marvelous gold cups showing how wild bulls were caught with nets. The frescoes show young men and women dressed only in loin cloths and shoes baiting these dangerous animals. Apparently the trick was to meet the charge of the bull between his spreading horns, catch them, swing up and vault over the bull's back when he tossed his head. The trick must have demanded perfect timing and acrobatic skill. Since the bull baiters were unarmed, the bulls were unhurt, but the actors must have suffered numerous casualties. Apparently bulls were in some way associated with the Cthonic deities of the old Mediterranean religion, and the sport, if one can call it such, probably had religious connotations.

The end of the Minoan period came with startling suddenness. We are not sure who the invaders were, but they were unexpected, as there are no indications that any preparation for defense had been made before the blow fell. A new section of the palace at Knossos was under construction and the workmen's tools and materials were found where they left them, ready for the next day's work. The attack seems to have coincided with an earthquake which shook down sections of the palace, but this did not prevent the attackers from doing a singularly complete job of looting. After the fall of Knossos, Crete rapidly sank into cultural and political insignificance. However, by this time, its culture had taken root on the mainland.

One last contribution of Cretan culture may be suggested. It seems highly probable that Crete gave us one of our own most fascinating myths, that of the lost Atlantis. This myth, as related by Plato, may well have been elaborated for his own symbolic purposes, but it seems improbable that he invented it out of whole cloth. According to the legend, the Egyptians told Solon of Athens (sixth century B.C.) that there had once been an island, Atlantis, whose fleets controlled the Mediterranean, held Athens to tribute, and traded on equal terms with Egypt. A great earthquake had destroyed the island almost overnight. By the time that the Greeks emerged from the Dark Ages, the Minoan civilization had been completely forgotten. When confronted by the necessity for finding a site for Atlantis they were in much the situation that we would be if we had no written records, but were told by the Abyssinians that a few centuries before there had been a great power which held the whole of the East African coast to tribute, captured cities in India, conquered the spice islands, and fought England on equal terms. It would scarcely occur to the modern American to equate such a power with present-day Portugal, and similarly, it did not occur to the Greeks that Atlantis might be Crete. Since they knew the Mediterranean geography quite well by this time and nothing seemed to fit the story, they placed the island beyond the pillars of Hercules in the wastes of the unexplored Atlantic. Actually the few bits of information which the legend gives us about the habits of the Atlantians are not inconsistent with the Cretan ascription, while even the last catastrophe might be a folk memory of the earthquake which seems to have overthrown the palace at Knossos.

GREECE

WITH the emergence of Greek civilization
Europe passes from the prehistoric to the historic period.
It is salutary for us, as Europeans, to remember that
Mesopotamia and Egypt had made this transition almost
two thousand years before. After the seventh century B.C.
we have increasingly complete written records covering
wider and wider areas within Europe until the whole continent is included. Where these records are available it becomes possible to apply the historian's techniques for determining their authenticity and for fixing the dates of
particular events. I have no intention of trespassing upon
this well-cultivated field. I also feel considerable hesitation
in approaching the Classical cultures from an anthropological viewpoint. The study of these cultures has occupied
many of the best minds of Europe for centuries. There are
innumerable works dealing with the philosophies and
value systems of the Greeks and Romans and, more recently, with their economics and social and political patterns. The most that I will attempt is to give a brief description of certain features of Classical culture which, it seems
to me, have not been sufficiently emphasized in the literature but which exerted considerable influence on later
cultural developments in Europe.

The first fact of which the average reader needs to be
reminded is that the great periods of Greek and Roman
civilization were by no means contemporaneous. The Age
of Pericles was separated from the Age of Augustus by an
interval nearly as long as that from the discovery of
America to the present. At the time of the Athenian
ascendancy, Rome was little more than a village, and the
Romans were vastly inferior culturally to those Asians
whom the Greeks were accustomed to call barbarians. By
the time the Romans had completed the subjugation of
their Etruscan and Italic neighbors and were making war
on the Greek cities in Sicily, Alexander had made his

conquest of Persia, and the hybrid Greco-Asian culture which we call Hellenistic was rapidly taking form. When Rome suddenly and quite unpredictably became a world power, this culture was well established throughout most of the civilized world, and it was this culture which the Romans assumed in their own transformation from barbarism to civilization. Classical Greek culture bore about as much and as little similarity to Hellenistic culture as the culture of our eighteenth century ancestors bears to our own. It was in the Hellenistic culture that Greeks and Romans were able to unite with Asians and Egyptians in an *oikouméne,* which had become for the first time something more than a geographic division.

The influence of the Hellenistic culture was so far-reaching that it must be dealt with separately. Similarly, the Greeks and Romans of the pre-Hellenistic period differed in so many respects that any attempt to deal with them simultaneously can only result in confusion. Grecian culture is the obvious starting point for any study of the development of European civilization within the historic period. However, the influence of Classical Greece runs through that civilization as a bright colored thread rather than a broad skein. Its heavy strands were drawn from Rome and, even more, from the northern barbarians whose culture stemmed, in turn, from Central Europe.

As always, Greek culture cannot be understood without reference to its background. We have already discussed the Aegean peoples, the Cretans, and the Indo-European-speaking invaders whose blood and cultures blended to produce the Greeks. Still another element contributed to this mixture, although its importance is difficult to evaluate. After the destruction of the Minoan sea power a Semitic people, the Phoenicians we have previously discussed, dominated the Mediterranean. Their earliest cities were on the Syrian coast but, like their Minoan predecessors, they soon felt the need of naval bases and founded colonies at various points in the west. One of these colonies, Carthage, was destined to play a significant part in later history. In the eastern Mediterranean they were always in competition with Greeks and

Egyptians, but they made the seas beyond Sicily their own and profited greatly from their exploitation of the mineral wealth in Spain. They also explored north and south along the Atlantic coast and reached the British Isles.

The Phoenicians were mainly interested in trade and profit, and cared little about political affiliations as long as commerce was not interfered with. They were quite willing to become a part of the great empires which emerged successively in Western Asia. They have left few records, and the accounts of Carthaginian culture given by the Romans can be largely discounted as war propaganda. Their main role in the development of the Greek and other Mediterranean cultures was as intermediaries between Asia and Europe. Their most significant contribution to Greek culture was the alphabet, a Semitic invention. As good businessmen they had been quick to appreciate the advantages of a system of writing so simple that professional scribes became unnecessary. The Minoan system of writing had completely died out in Greece during the Dark Ages following the fall of Crete and, according to Greek tradition, it was Cadmus, a Phoenician, who reintroduced the art. This much is certain: the Greek alphabet was taken from the Phoenician one.

In Greece alphabetic writing encountered a particularly favorable milieu. As traders the Greeks could appreciate the immediate advantages of the system, but they combined with their business interests a range and variety of other interests and lively curiosity which the Phoenicians lacked. The Greeks liked to find out new things and to tell as many people as possible about them. Moreover, their religion was simple and relatively unorganized, with no strong priestly class which might have pre-empted the new skill. In Greece, writing escaped at last from both the counting house and the temple and became a medium for the exchange and preservation of ideas.

Greek culture not only was of mixed origin but also demonstrated what the biologists would call hybrid vigor. It gave to and borrowed from every culture with which the Greeks came in contact. All cultures owe much of their content to borrowing, and it is no disgrace to the

Greeks that they took advantage of the unusual opportunities offered by the time and place. The rise of the Asian empires had broken down the old patterns of tribal isolation over wide areas and created an insatiable demand for mercenary soldiers. During their Dark Ages Greeks wandered all over the Near East and served in the armies of Egypt, Assyria, and lesser states. By the Classical period they were traveling simply to satisfy their curiosity, like modern tourists, while their philosophers, who were also their scientists, were eagerly contacting people with similar interests in all the places they visited. One can recognize in these early Greek travelers an attitude much like that of the nineteenth and early twentieth century Japanese. While their belief in their own fundamental superiority was never lost, they were keenly conscious of their inferiority in certain directions and had an overwhelming eagerness to learn. They borrowed shamelessly, and there were few items in Classical Greek culture which could not be traced to outside origins. The distinctive element in the Greek situation was the catalytic quality of the Greek mind. Ideas brought together in its presence combined to produce new and unexpected results.

Each of the older civilizations contributed its quota. The Egyptians impressed the Greeks by the magnitude of their structures and, above all, by their claims for the immemorial antiquity of their civilization. They regarded the Greeks as amusing parvenus and the Greeks, who had forgotten their Minoan ancestry, shamefacedly concurred in this opinion. At the same time the animal gods and essential confusion and illogic of Egyptian religion had little appeal for the highly logical Greeks. They were not greatly impressed by the Egyptian priests' claims that these things only concealed deep mysteries. The Egyptian political system, with its god-king, was equally incompatible with Greek values. Although they learned what they could from Egyptian astronomers and mathematicians, time showed that these were inferior to the Mesopotamians, while the technological knowledge, in which the Egyptians excelled, was ignored as beneath the notice of gentlemen. On the other hand, Egyptian art, with its vigorous if conventionalized use of men and animals and its success in depicting motion, struck a responsive chord and strong Egyptian influence can be traced in the development of Greek art, especially sculpture.

In Mesopotamia the Greeks found a science which they could appreciate and a mechanistic view of the universe which was quite in line with their own skepticism regarding the extent and nature of divine interference in human affairs. They brought back from their Mesopotamian contacts a much improved knowledge of astronomy and a better mathematics, both freed from the shackles of priestly control. These led to a great expansion of the Greek mental horizon. When wedded with the keen Greek interest in natural phenomena and vital behavior, they produced Greek philosophy, with its essentially agnostic approach to the universe, and also the much-overrated Greek contribution to later science.

The ascription of high scientific ability to the Greeks rests mainly upon the fact that a study of the Greek philosophers reveals in one place or another conjectures which foreshadow most of the discoveries of modern science. However, it must be remembered that these were conjectures. They were developed as parts of logical systems and were completely unsupported by what we would regard as scientific evidence. If one takes the collection of "scientific" theories which the various philosophers found it necessary to include in what each of them attempted to make a comprehensive interpretation of the universe, one finds that the Greek score was relatively low. For every suggestion which later science has shown to be correct, there were at least a dozen which were later proved to be wrong.

A disconcerting by-product of these Greek philosophies was the need felt by the early Christian fathers for a cosmology as well as a theology and an ethic. Without some explanation of the universe, the Christians found themselves at a disadvantage in their competition with the philosophies which were their most dangerous rivals in their struggle to win over the educated minority. Modern fundamentalism thus owes its existence to a pattern based on pagan pseudo science.

In Alexandria at the close of the Classical period the Greeks seem to have made some feeble gestures in the direction of real science based on experiments and observation. However the entire Greek system of thought suffered from one incurable defect. The average Greek always preferred talking to working, and the Greek philosopher believed that ultimate truth in any situation could be arrived at through verbal manipulation. The Greeks never seem to have been able to appreciate the distinction, difficult enough for ourselves, between the external reality and its verbal symbol. The Greeks were the originators of the analytic method, by which configurations of phenomena were broken down so that particular items or sequences within the configuration could be conceptually isolated for independent study. They never were able to realize the importance of configurations *per se* or to understand that, in the presence of multiple factors, the logical extrapolation of assumptions based on a few of these may, in the long run, lead the logician further and further from reality. The modern scientist accumulates as much data as possible, develops his theories logically on the basis of this data, and then checks them by the experimental method or whatever technique it may be necessary for him to substitute for it. The Greek philosopher began with little data, developed his theories by the application of logic, and then stopped.

The influence of this attitude was reflected in Greek technology. Until well into the Hellenistic period it was characterized by an increasing perfection of manual dexterity and an almost complete lack of new basic inventions, or even of borrowings which might have fundamentally altered the existing technical patterns. Thus the arch and dome, which had been known for millennia in the Near East, were not adopted by the Greeks in spite of their obvious practical advantages for many purposes. The most revolutionary change which took place in their architecture, from the late Mycenean on, was the substitution of stone for wood in their public buildings, and even here the forms developed in the older material were almost slavishly preserved. At the same time their skill in manipulating the existing techniques reached an amazingly high point. The essentially primitive architectural forms were refined until they showed perfectly balanced proportions and such subtleties as those of the Parthenon columns, in which the sides are slightly bowed outward in order to give the visual illusion of a continuous straight line from top to bottom.

The Greek political systems should be of particular interest to us, since the Greek city-states were confronted with certain problems not unlike those of our own municipal governments today. In both cases a culture, which had been developed under essentially rural and village conditions, and which had inherited patterns of attaching extreme value to personal independence and individual initiative, found itself confronted with the problems of city living and of far-reaching changes in the economic structure. True cities did not appear in Greece much before the Classical period. It has already been mentioned that the Classical Greeks lived largely by exporting both manufactures and their specialized agricultural products of olive oil and wine. The replacement of subsistence farming by staple crops raised for export is always hard on the small landowner, who finds himself at the mercy of the middleman. Although the Classical Greeks did not develop great plantations worked by slave labor, as the later Romans did, many peasants lost their holdings. There was an increasing concentration of population in the cities, with the breakdown of the older extended groups, and a developing potentiality for individual anonymity such as we have today.

The Greeks met this situation in part by their rigid rules of citizenship, which limited the electorate to individuals either born of citizen parents or, more rarely, those upon whom citizenship had been conferred. Every city contained a large number of aliens who might be respected and affluent members of the community but who were not allowed to participate in government. While the num-

ber of individuals was too large for the citizens to function
as a face-to-face unit, even in cities the size of Athens or
Corinth, any candidate for office would be personally
known to a great many of the electorate, while the candidate's record would be well known to all. The limitation
of the electorate made the problem of representative government simpler, but this was counterbalanced by the low
level of education in much of the electorate and by the
Greek basic personality, which combined individualism
with high emotionalism and intense jealousy.

The culture pattern established political participation
as not only a privilege but a duty of citizenship. The Greek
citizen seems to have spent a large part of his time and
energy in discussing politics and in the intrigues which
were inseparable from it. Coupled with this there was a
survival into urban life of the loyalty and strong in-group
sentiment characteristic of the primitive tribe. It would
have been quite unthinkable for a Greek dramatist to open
a new play in any city other than his own. Even artists
and authors felt obligated to give their own cities the first
fruits of their genius, and only moved on to greener fields
when their own cities had rejected them or when their
genius had been generally recognized and added to their
city's fame.

The development of most Greek city governments
began with the old Indo-European pattern of a king and a
tribal council dominated by the heads of noble families,
but with free discussion and any tribesman allowed to
speak his mind. The king was primarily a war leader and
executive instrumenting the council decisions. He had no
hint of personal divinity and even his priestly functions
were unimportant. With the rise of the new commercial
urban culture the power of the king and the nobles evap-
orated, giving place to an oligarchy dominated by the
nouveau riche. The oligarchies were followed in turn by
democracies, which soon came to be dominated by dema-
gogues. Finally a strong man would seize power and rule
like a king, but usually with careful avoidance of royal
symbols. The position of such a man would correspond
roughly to that of the boss of a well-entrenched political

machine in one of our own cities. Although the outward symbols of democracy would usually be preserved, all power would be gathered into his hands. The Greeks applied to such city bosses the term *tyrannos* (master), which was the origin of our own word *tyrant,* although in its original uses it lacked most of the connotations of cruelty and oppression which that word carries for us. The first "tyrant" in any city was often an able and benevolent ruler, but in due course of time one of his successors would become cruel and oppressive. The "better element" would then oust him and establish an oligarchy. This in due course of time would give place to a democracy and the democracy to another tyranny. The Greeks recognized this cycle and regarded it as a sort of natural phenomenon which could be postponed but not averted.

With this as a starting point the Greeks developed various constitutions, none of which seem to have worked successfully for very long. The drawing up of a constitution was part of the advanced planning which went into the founding of a new city, and these constitutions represent the highest points reached by Greek political theory. Unfortunately, they very rarely remained in force for any length of time. None of them provided for a successful civil service which might have had a stabilizing effect, and, in politics as elsewhere, the Greeks were poor losers. Defeated candidates for office were likely to stir up revolt, and this was the basis for the institution of ostracism, by which the losing candidate was exiled from the city for a period of years.

In one respect at least the Greek cities were more fortunate than the later Roman cities. They did not have an idle, pauperized proletariat which would be at the beck and call of any politician who wanted to create a disturbance. During the Classical period the exclusion of noncitizens from political life and the relatively small size of the citizen body prevented this. There must have been a fair number of impoverished citizens, but there were not enough to require a regular and continuous dole of the Roman sort. During the late pre-Classical and much of the Classical period, the poor and the surplus population drawn cityward from the surrounding countryside were taken care of by the founding of new cities. Most of them were in the western Mediterranean, especially in southern Italy, which later came to be known as *Magna Graecea,* "Greater Greece."

The ability to establish planned colonies at favorable locations was no mean cultural accomplishment in itself. Apparently the Delphic oracle operated as a clearing house for news of available sites. A city aiming to found a new colony consulted the oracle, and the priests, drawing upon the pooled knowledge which they had acquired from other clients, suggested the best place. The colonists were selected from among those citizens who volunteered to go. They were provided with necessary equipment and food to tide them over until they could plant and harvest their own crops, and the mother city helped them until they could take care of themselves. Although there was no continuing tie between the daughter city and the mother city, there was a strong emotional attachment and, as a symbol of the continuity, sacred fire was usually carried from the mother city and used to kindle the first fires in the new settlement. Many of these new cities came to have greater wealth and larger populations than their parents on the Greek mainland, but in artistic and intellectual matters they were regarded, and regarded themselves, as provincials. Any famous Greek who took a colonial tour was as sure of profit as an English literary light visiting the United States.

The development of the Greek pattern of colonization is difficult to trace. No doubt it was greatly stimulated by the presence of uncivilized but not unfriendly tribes to the west who offered high profits to the Greek traders. However, the resettlement of several hundred people involved in the founding of a new city is a very different matter from the mere establishment of trading posts and requires careful planning, as the failure of many of the American colonizing attempts shows. The Phoenicians also were establishing colonial outposts in the period from 1000 to 700 B.C., although they seem to have been less systematic about it than were the Greeks, and the Greeks may have used them as models. More probably, both Greeks and Phoenicians learned the necessary techniques from their contact with the Minoans, whose widespread naval bases have already been mentioned. The Assyrians also had been carrying on extensive resettlement programs for a long period as part of their imperial policy, and the Greeks may have borrowed some techniques from them.

One other result of Greek urbanization should be mentioned, since it has exerted an important influence on certain aspects of our own culture. Although each Greek city of the period had its temples to the Olympian gods and had selected some one of them as its guardian and the recipient of its special devotions, the worship of these deities became more and more an excuse for pageantry and ritual from which the participants and observers derived aesthetic satisfaction rather than spiritual refreshment. It has been said, probably truthfully, that after Salamis the Olympian deities were dead.

The pre-Indo-European religious practices, on the other hand, now reasserted themselves and acquired new meaning in the urban context. What had been before local rites carried on with the orgiastic accompaniments characteristic of many of the old Mediterranean cults were now reorganized and extended beyond their original local contexts to become the mystery religions. The urban populations, especially the many individuals who were living in cities of which they were not citizens, felt a strong need for some system by which they could establish ties with others in the same position. Human beings seem to have a deep seated need for social contacts and for membership in-groups. Viewed from this angle, the rise of the mystery religions can be seen as a result of the same frustrations which have led to the tremendous multiplication of organizations of all sorts in our own society. Wherever patterns of spatial and social mobility break down kin and local groups, substitutes will develop.

The rise of the mystery religions cannot be explained entirely on these grounds. The lack of opportunity for unconscious identification with a larger social group increased the tendency toward individualism, already strong among the Greeks. The unattached, anonymous individual could no longer satisfy his desire for posthumous survival by contemplating the continuity of his kin group or tribe. He began to yearn for assurances of his own immortality, and with this came the natural desire for a pleasant and satisfying future life. The Greek Hades must have appeared even duller to an urban slum dweller than it did to a villager. Lastly, the informal social controls which enforced ethical behavior upon the villager were no longer operative in the city, and to those who had been born and reared in smaller communities, always the majority of an adult urban population, this must have been felt as a tremendous loss. In the absence of personally applicable public opinion there was a need for some effective substitute. The old gods had been essentialy amoral in their outlook. The new ones became a source of supernatural sanctions, rewarding good behavior and punishing evil, even when these remained unnoticed by the individual's contemporaries.

Out of this combination of factors there developed a series of sects which had certain features in common. Entry into all of them involved some preliminary instruction and a ceremony of initiation, in which the individual was prepared for his later psychological identification with both the deity and the cult by repeating, in company with others, certain experiences of the deity. All the cults promised their initiates survival and a happy after-life, and all involved certain obligations of ethical behavior, at least toward other members of the cult. A mystery religion was thus not only a religion but also a secret society with obligations of mutual help among the members, and with ethical precepts which made it possible for these members to feel secure in dealing with each other.

As the Classical period in Greece passed into the Hellenistic period, with its much greater urban concentrations and increased spatial mobility, these mystery religions increased in number and took on added significance. Local chapters included not only citizens and resident aliens but also slaves. In view of the common Greek pattern of selling whole city populations as part of the spoils of war, there were inevitably many slaves who had been initiated into the mysteries before they were enslaved and who therefore had to be accepted as brothers if the secrecy was to be maintained. The various cults emphasized their autonomous existence by having their own status-systems based on different degrees of initiation, and a man who was a slave outside the lodge might occupy the highest position inside it.

The trend toward mystery religions which began in Classical Greece increased rapidly during the Hellenistic period, since all the conditions to which these religions were a response were then intensified. Not only were pre-Indo-European deities and rites revived, but foreign gods were accepted and their worship internationalized and reorganized on the mystery pattern. Thus, in later Hellenistic times, we have the mysteries of the Egyptian Isis and the Persian Mithras, and only slightly later the emergence of Christianity which, beginning as a minor Jewish sect, was opened to Gentile converts through the ministry of Saint Paul, and was then reorganized by these converts upon the familiar mystery pattern.

The total Greek contribution to our own culture has been so extensive and is so well known that this brief summary of some of the less-emphasized aspects of the contribution must suffice. The most important thing to remember is that the Classical Greek culture, like all other cultures for which we have records, borrowed widely. At the same time it reintegrated and reinterpreted its borrowings to an unusual degree and gave the resulting culture complex a distinctive quality. One who digs into the background of Greek culture finds its roots extending far into the past and branching and rebranching to draw upon many different sources, but the keen curiosity and the analytical attitude which characterized the Greeks were their own contribution.

BARBARIANS

A T T H E foundation of all European history
has lain the *drang nach Westen,* the steady pressure of peoples forcing their way into the continent from the east.
The steppes have been an inexhaustible breeding ground
for warriors, and barbarian tribes have flowed out of them
in successive waves. We do not know what has been responsible for these movements. Some of them may have
been due, as Elsworth Huntington has suggested in *The
Pulse of Asia,* to an alteration of long periods of abundant
rainfall and good pasture, causing population increase,
with drought periods which squeezed out the surplus. We
also know that shortly before the beginning of the
Christian era the development of superior military equipment and techniques among the peoples of Mongolia resulted in the displacement westward of a whole series of
tribes who were less effective fighters. However, we need
not seek for any single cause. For a nomadic or seminomadic tribe, migration is the simplest answer to pressure
of any sort, including cupidity. When the steppe people
discovered how much loot was to be obtained in the more
civilized areas beyond their borders, no local calamity was
required to set them moving.

Throughout most of the prehistoric period the movements from the east seem to have been carried out by
small groups. They were in the nature of a gradual infiltration rather than a massive conquest. The newcomers
spread themselves over the pre-existing populations and
became assimilated in them. From the Bronze Age until
the arrival of the Mongolian Huns and Avars after the
Roman collapse, the cultures of all the barbarian invaders
seem to have been of the general type already described
for the early Aryans. The patterns by which a hunting,
cattle-keeping aristocracy dominated a much larger peasant population were transmitted from one conquering
group to another with little change. The differences which

existed among the conquerors were mainly a matter of sophistication, based on the amount of their contact with the more civilized peoples of the south, plus, in the case of the Germans, a few borrowings from their Circumpolar neighbors.

The first Classical accounts of the barbarians reveal the presence of two groups in western Europe north of the Mediterranean basin, the Celts and the Germans. The Gauls, who figure so largely in Roman literature, were a division of the Celtic group who had their center in what is now France. The Germans were mainly east and north of the Rhine at that time and were the more barbarous, since they were the more distant from the southern centers of civilization. The description of the Germans given by Tacitus, a Roman contemporary, shows that they were a cattle people, and he notes that, like the modern cattle tribes of Africa, they rated their wealth by the number of their animals, paying little attention to their quality. They raised only grain and cultivated new fields each year, facts which, since most of their country was heavily forested, probably mean that they followed the cutting and burning technique.

The Germans attached little value to the utensils of gold and silver sent to them as gifts by the Romans. They were indifferent metal workers and even iron was in poor supply. Their weapons were long, straight, double-edged swords, light spears with small heads, and shields. A few men wore helmets, usually of leather, but body armor was infrequent. A young man was given the right to carry arms at a solemn ceremony which no doubt marked his assumption of full adult status. Such an investiture is reminiscent of the Medieval ceremonies by which a squire was raised to knighthood and given for the first time the right to carry a sword.

The one road to advancement was war, just as, in the absence of trade and manufacture, looting was the one road to wealth. A commoner who was a successful warrior was honored almost as highly as a man of chiefly family. At the same time great importance was attached to high descent, and anyone who aspired to chieftainship without it would be regarded as a usurper. Tacitus says that the Germans chose their chiefs by inheritance and their generals by ability.

The men of the tribe met in council once a month at the time of either the new or full moon, the tribal priest presiding. Such councils combined the functions of a legislature and a court of justice. The chief was an executive carrying out the mandates of the council and was bound by its decisions. There were law codes which distinguished between offenses against the community and against individuals. The former were treated as crimes, and the offender was punished in his person, usually by death. The latter could be compensated by payment of danages. Murder was regarded as an offense of the second class and could be atoned for by payment to the murdered man's kin group.

The Gauls occupied the territory south and west of the Germans, and closely related Celtic groups were in possession of Britain and Ireland. The Gauls had been in contact with the Mediterranean civilizations for centuries, alternately trading with and raiding them, and had absorbed much of Mediterranean culture. Remains from the region immediately west of the Alps show that, by the fifth century B.C., the Gauls had achieved extraordinary skill in working iron, bronze, silver, and gold. The metal objects were decorated with elaborate and beautiful scroll designs embellished with colored enamels, coral, and gems. Many of the objects produced by this so-called La Tene culture were technically equal to any made in the Mediterranean basin at this time. It is significant that even after the Roman conquest of Gaul native craftsmen continued working in their own style for the Roman trade.

The main southern influence on the culture of the Gauls came from the Greeks. By 400 B.C. there was a Greek settlement at what is now Marseilles, and Greek traders were penetrating the hinterland. In the third century B.C. a Greek geographer and explorer, Pythias, even sailed northward along the Atlantic coast until he reached Scandinavia and heard rumors of an island to the northwest, which may have been Iceland. Among other things the Greeks introduced the use of money, and coins struck in Gaul by local chiefs show a fascinating series of simplifications of original Greek patterns.

The Gauls also came in contact with the Etruscans, who had established themselves at the head of the Adriatic by 800 B.C. The light chariot, extensively used by the early Gauls, may well have been developed from Etruscan prototypes. Its use had died out on the European mainland by Caesar's time, but he found the Celtic Britains still using scythe-armed chariots. In Ireland chariots survived even later.

The accounts of the Gauls which have been left by Classical writers have to do mainly with their fighting ability and the ravages which they inflicted on their southern neighbors. They invaded Italy repeatedly, and when Caesar finally "pacified" Gaul, the Romans rejoiced less at the addition to their territory than at the removal of what they had come to regard as an ever-present threat. The Gauls also raided into Greece and Asia Minor, and the famous statue from Pergamum which we know as the dying gladiator actually represented a dying Gaul, a monument to the defeat of one of these expeditions.

The Roman conquest of Gaul resulted in the collapse of the local culture and the Latinization of the survivors. The conquest of Britain was later and less thorough, but here also the Roman overlay obscures the features of the earlier culture. The best picture of early Celtic life is provided by Ireland. Here the Celts succeeded in maintaining their independence through the Roman period and did not succumb completely to foreign control until the time of Cromwell. Even Christianity, which the Irish accepted with enthusiasm, was revised in Celtic terms.

The Irish economy was based primarily on domestic animals: cattle, horses, and pigs. Cattle were not only milked but also bled periodically and the blood boiled and eaten. Horses were neither milked nor eaten. They were driven in chariots or, later, ridden. Cavalry played little part in the Irish forces, perhaps because they never acquired the tree saddle. In the fourteenth century A.D. the English authorities passed a law fining any Irish-born Englishman who rode without a saddle "in the Irish fashion." Pigs, then as later, were the mainstay of the small householder. Ham and bacon seem to have been Celtic inventions, and even the Romans spoke with admiration of the hams prepared by the Gauls.

The Irish social organization throws much light upon that of the mainland Celts. The basic unit was an extended kin group made up of several related families who shared in the ownership of farmland but leased cattle from their noble patrons independently. Most families were monogamous, but a man was permitted to have concubines.

There were no villages, but a group of related families usually lived in the same neighborhood and shared in the cultivation of plowland held in common. The political unit was the *tuath,* sometimes mistermed a clan.

At the head of the tauth was a king, the post being filled in each generation from a particular family line, all of whose members ranked as royal. This, coupled with the fact that many of the Irish "kingdoms" were little larger than a New England township, explains the frequency with which the "king of Ireland's son" occurs not only in Irish but in continental romances. Below the king came the nobles; then the "worthies," freemen with the right to keep cattle and share in plowland; and lastly, the serfs. At the bottom of the scale were chattel slaves who were bought and sold freely, slave women being ranked with cattle as units of value. Nobles and "worthies" were further divided into numerous subgroups based on wealth and descent.

Side by side with the secular organization just described there was a hierarchy of learned men: bards, priests, and those skilled in the law, who gave Ireland cultural unity. In spite of the apparent fragmentation and the almost constant raiding between kingdoms, every individual and social unit had its place in a single, all-embracing system and every person held the same rank everywhere. For legal purposes this rank was indicated by his *dīre* or honor price, which determined the amount of damages which he could collect in case of injury to his property or person and, conversely, the size of the fines which could be assessed against him.

Under the honor price system, rank and wealth were inseparably linked, and a family rose or fell according to the establishment which it could maintain. Thus a "worthy" family which acquired wealth equivalent to that of a noble and retained it for three generations was accounted noble. Conversely, a family which could not maintain "noble" economic status after three generations dropped to the "worthy" class. The three-generation rule, when applied to kingship, became one of the most perfect systems ever developed for maintaining constant turmoil. A family line whose head had not actually ruled within three generations was demoted to noble level and lost the right to rule in the future. Since all of a king's sons and grandsons were accounted royal, but only one of them could be king at any given time and transmit royal rank to his descendents, there were always numerous pretenders to every throne and fratricide was the commonest road to succession. After the Irish became Christian the situation was mitigated somewhat, the king being allowed to nominate his successor and share rule with him, but assassination and invasion by claimants who had been ignored were still rife.

The basic uniformity of culture was maintained by the fairs and councils and, above all, by the professional bards, priests, and law-men. All the Celts accorded these great respect. In Ireland the bard was entitled to the seat on the king's left, while the law-man sat across from him on the queen's right. Under the sumptuary law bards could wear five colors and the king only seven. Famous bards wandered from court to court and through their control of publicity were able to operate rackets not unlike those of the modern columnist. Failure to entertain them properly would be punished by a satire, which seems to have been feared as a form of malevolent magic over and above the resulting ridicule. Lesser bards were attached to the courts of various kings. Both verse and versifiers were robust. The royal bard was expected to take his place beside the king in the line of battle so that he could contribute the magical efficacy of his satires, as well as be able to observe the royal deeds and celebrate them properly in his verse.

The Irish records all come from a time considerably after the period when the mainland Celts were making themselves a terror to their Mediterranean neighbors, and it is probable that the Irish social system had become considerably more elaborate than that of the Gauls of Caesar's day. However, partly hereditary, partly local groupings of the *tuath* type; the organization of local chiefs under a paramount chief; the grading of individuals even within the threefold division of chiefs, nobles, and commoners; a system of vassalage by which men received cattle from the chief and paid him rental for these rather than for the use of land; a well-developed legal system with law-men; an extensive literature transmitted verbally; and an exaggerated respect for learned men: all these seem to have been present among the Gauls.

One is forced to conclude that, aside from the lack of writing and the rarity of cities, the Gauls were little inferior culturally to the Romans of the Republican period. How much of this culture was able to survive the Roman conquest is a problem deserving further study. In the new society which emerged in western Europe after the fall of the Roman Empire, German and Latin elements were predominant, but the Celtic social institutions must have survived in rural districts long after the Roman conquest and prepared the population for the feudal system.

THE ROMAN PENINSULA

R O M A N culture has been even more thoroughly studied and described by scholars than Greek culture. The extent of the Roman contribution to later European civilization is evident to anyone who is familiar with the languages spoken over nearly half of the European continent; the letters of the alphabet, the solemn and massive architecture of our governmental buildings, our devotion to the letter of the law and to legal procedure, and our crippling system of checks and balances in government are only a few of the things which we have inherited from them. In addition there is the legend of Rome as the world state, the bringer of universal peace. All this has served to overshadow the fact that until well after Rome had become a world power, the Romans were themselves barbarians. Even Pyrrhus, the Epirote, who encountered them almost a hundred years after the time of Alexander the Great, regarded them as such and noted with surprise that there was nothing barbarous in the way they handled their troops. Their conquest of the Greek cities of southern Italy, and the amazingly rapid expansion which established their power over the eastern Mediterranean in the short space of fifty years, must have been regarded by the civilized populations of the regions as very much on a par with a Gaulish invasion.

Culturally, Italy lagged behind the Aegean countries throughout most of its history. This was merely a reflection of the well-known fact that it takes time for any culture pattern to spread from the point of its origin and that, other things being equal, the greater the distance from the origin point to a particular region, the longer the culture lag. The first Neolithic settlers of Italy came from the east, either by sea or following the coast, and were a part of the Mediterranean wing of the Neolithic colonization of Europe. The culture of these first settlers was relatively simple and there were no significant new developments after they reached Italy. The Neolithic period in Italy was also shorter than it was in northern Europe, since Italy in particular contained considerable mineral wealth which lured in foreign miners and merchants. Both traders from the Aegean and Beaker Folk from Spain had reached Italy by 1200 B.C., but seem to have had no great influence on the local cultures.

About 1500 B.C. bronze-using invaders established themselves in the Po Valley. These Terramare people apparently came from Central Europe, possibly Hungary, and spoke an Indo-European language. They established fortified villages from which they dominated and finally

absorbed the older Neolithic population. From the Terramare period on, there were repeated incursions into
northern Italy, first by representatives of the Hallstatt culture and later by Celtic tribes. The Romans themselves
first emerge in history as a group of traders and farmers
who settled on a group of low hills on the left bank of the
Tiber River. The settlement became a thriving trading
center, and by 753 B.C. it was a small city-state governed
by a king. The Roman feeling for republican rule was apparently inculcated early, for in 509 B.C. they deposed the
king, who was an Etrurian from across the Tiber, and
wiped out the dynasty. They spent the next hundred and
fifty years warring with their neighbors, subduing them,
and bringing them into the Roman orbit. In 390 B.C.
Rome was invaded by the Gauls, who plundered and
sacked the city before they were driven off. However, by
338 B.C. Rome had made herself mistress of all Latium.
Roman power grew rapidly after this. A series of successful campaigns subdued the Samnites, the sturdy highland
tribes of central Italy. Etruria was brought under Roman
domination, which gave Rome access to Adriatic ports
and increased trade. By 270 B.C. Rome had succeeded in
doing what no Greek city-state had ever done: she had
welded the whole southern peninsula into a single confed-
eracy completely under her domination. The Gauls continued to harass Rome from the north, however, until
Caesar reversed the usual direction of movement by invading Gaul and pacifying the Gauls.

There was one group of invaders who came to stay
and left a deep and enduring stamp on Roman culture.
The Etruscans were the first really civilized people to reach
Italy. They left few inscriptions, and even these were
mainly brief epitaphs which throw little light upon their
culture or origins. The most that can be learned from
these inscriptions is that they wrote with an alphabet obviously derived from a Semitic rather than a Greek proto-
type, and that the Etruscan language was neither Indo-
European nor Semitic. Scholars have surrounded their origin with mystery, but the Romans, who both conquered
them and incorporated much of Etruscan culture into their

own, had no doubt as to where they came from. They believed that the Tyrrheni, as the Etruscans called themselves, came from Asia Minor, and until quite late in Roman history the anniversary of one of the earliest Roman victories over the Etruscans was celebrated by leading mummers dressed in Asian fashion through the streets, while criers shouted, "Sardinians for sale!"

The Etruscans seem to have arrived in Italy between 800 and 900 B.C. Their movement may have been a last act in the diffusion of the "People of the Isles" from Asia Minor. Apparently the Etruscan movement was neither a mass migration nor a planned colonization. They seem to have come a few shiploads at a time, settling first along the coast and establishing themselves as an aristocratic class ruling over the native population. Each Etruscan city seems to have been founded by a different kin group, and the remains show significant cultural differences. The relations between conquerors and conquered followed much the same pattern as the Aryan conquests elsewhere, although the organization of the noble group itself was quite different.

The social organization of the Etruscans was an aristocratic one. At the top were the *lucumones,* the nobles of Etruscan blood; below them, the bourgeois middle class who were attached to them as clients, in the Roman usage of the term, and who were probably of mixed origin. These included skilled craftsmen and merchants. At the bottom of the scale were the peasants and ordinary artisans, who were largely of aboriginal stock. Class membership seems to have been strictly hereditary. There was no way in which a bourgeois or peasant could become a noble. The nobles were temendously proud of pure blood and kept extensive genealogies. After the fall of the Etruscan power, many of the noble families were incorporated into the Roman state, and many of the Roman patrician families boasted of their Etruscan origin.

All wealth seems to have been concentrated in the hands of the patrician families, and their great rock-cut tombs and the wealth of objects placed in them contrast sharply with the simple cremations of the lower classes.

Their tombs are filled with pictures of banquets and decorous revelries in which both men and women participated. The Romans, who were an exceedingly puritanical people, especially in their earlier period, had a great deal to say about the general profligacy and degeneracy of the Etruscans, but there is little real evidence for this. Roman men were not supposed to strip in each other's presence, while the Etruscans followed the Greek tradition and used nude figures in their art. They evidently knew how to enjoy themselves and how to live luxuriously. Thus, Etruscan goldwork was the best in the ancient world, and the frescoes show them wearing mantles bordered with the purple which later became the mark of Roman senatorial rank.

The tomb materials show extensive contacts, and it seems highly probable that the Etruscan nobles, like the later Italian ones, themselves engaged in trade. They certainly lacked the Greek contempt for technology. They were good farmers who introduced the grape and olive into Italy, and they probably were responsible for the use of the plow and crop rotation. The later Roman interest in agriculture and its practice by patricians probably stems from Etruscan origins. The Etruscans were also the best bronze workers of their times, their superiority being acknowledged even by the Greeks.

The Romans finally succeeded in breaking the power of the Etruscans and incorporating their fragments and those of various conquered Italic tribes into a single state. It may be noted that in this incorporation they did not show their reputed genius for statecraft. The conquered groups were given no share in government, and, although they were expected to furnish levees for the Roman armies, they were so thoroughly exploited both militarily and economically that most of them were ready to side with any enemy of Rome. Having consolidated the north, the Romans gradually extended their power southward through their progressive conquest of the Greek cities in southern Italy and Sicily. These Italian Greeks were vastly more civilized than the Romans, who regarded them with envious contempt. The city fathers at this time made numerous attempts to prevent the younger generation in

Rome from accepting Greek culture, but its attraction proved too strong for censorship and repressive legislation.

The subjugation of the Greek cities brought the Romans face to face with the Carthaginians, a Phoenician group who at that time dominated the western Mediterranean from their bases in North Africa, Sicily, and Spain. The final destruction of Carthage after the Punic wars created a vacancy in the Mediterranean power alignment, and the Romans were swept into this. In reading the records, one feels that the Roman overseas empire originally came into being more by chance than by intention. Roman isolationists, not unlike our own, protested every step in the early growth of the empire, and, when Rome finally found herself a world power deeply involved in world affairs, she had no constructive plan for meeting the situation. Within fifty years she had passed from an insignificant barbarian state on the outer edge of civilization to control of the whole Mediterranean basin, including its Asian coasts. The only previous parallel for such expansion had been the conquests of Alexander the Great, and, in these, power was already centralized in the person of the conqueror.

The Roman republican system, with its paralyzing elaboration of checks and balances, proved quite inadequate to the new conditions. The Roman virtues were the parochial virtues of poor, hard-working peasants. Republican Rome had had no educated or leisure class, and its poor patricians, laboring as cultivators on their own lands, could not afford most of the vices they condemned. When wealth began to flow into the city from the East, their virtues proved to have no solid basis. The last days of the Republic were marked by a wild scramble for money, the sort of ostentatious waste to be expected from *parvenues,* and a callous indifference to all human values. The commanders of the conquering armies and the governors whom the Senate sent out in their wake devoted themselves to looting on an unprecedented scale. Determined revolts in the East, where the population had been abused beyond the endurance of even Asian peasants, and the struggles for power between various generals, completed the collapse of most of the old Roman republican institutions.

The one institution which was able to survive and perform its original functions effectively under these circumstances was the Roman military establishment. The old army tradition of loyalty to the state was increasingly replaced by loyalty to the commander, but discipline remained firm and the Roman military techniques were superior to those of any of their antagonists except the Parthians, whose mailed and mounted archers were more than a match for the legions. Except on the Parthian front, the limits to Roman conquest were set only by the increasing poverty and cultural backwardness of the tribes whom they encountered. Good businessmen as always, the Romans established their frontiers at the point where the anticipated income from new territories would not pay the cost of conquest and administration.

The evils of the period of conquest reached a climax in the wars of Marius and Sylla, which paved the way for the creation of the Roman empire under Augustus. In this the Roman Senate and the old forms of the Roman Republic were maintained for their psychological effect but were carefully shorn of real power. The state which emerged was a Hellenistic monarchy of the type which had already been developed in the Near East through centuries of trial and error. The worship of the emperor, which was an integral part of the Hellenistic system, was accepted reluctantly by the early emperors, who found it rather ridiculous. Augustus himself carefully avoided any of the old titles which bore connotations offensive to Republican ears; nevertheless, he was in complete control. The empire was treated as the personal estate of the emperor, and no distinction was made between the national treasury and his private fortune. Since he was also commander-in-chief of the army, he was able to attach to his person both such loyalty to the state as had survived and the devotion of the soldier to his commander.

The Roman imperial organization called for the creation of an honest and devoted professional civil service. The peculations of Roman officials in the provinces, which under the Republic had been taken as much for granted as the grafting of American politicians, now became embezzlement of the imperial property. It is interesting to note that the secretaries of Augustus, who would correspond to our own presidential cabinet, were, with few exceptions, Greeks, and several of them were Greek freedmen who had been reared in the Near East and were thus familiar with the Hellenistic patterns both for government and for the management of great estates. With their aid Augustus organized the empire on such a sound basis that it was able to carry on for centuries in spite of vicious and incompetent emperors and even the wars of rival aspirants to the purple. After the initial period of conquest had come to an end, and during the long periods when contests for the purple did not reach the dimension of civil wars, the Roman Empire conferred genuine benefits upon its members. It maintained peace among its subjects and protected them from barbarian inroads. It established new trade routes and improved old ones. It gave the most civilized part of the ancient western world a common system of laws and a common language, the latter increasingly Greek rather than Latin.

Lastly, the Romans were the first to make constant use of the device of awarding citizenship, with all its accompanying rights and privileges, to a selected group of individuals among the subjects. This arrangement not only gave the subjects the hope of final social equality, but performed the more immediate function of detaching many of their ablest potential leaders and affiliating them with the dominant group.

In spite of these advantages, the Romans never developed an adequate fiscal policy, and from the time of the establishment of the Empire on there was a gradual decline in the extent of Roman resources. Even under good emperors it became increasingly difficult to finance the defensive wars against barbarians. It should be pointed out that the Hellenistic patterns of government which the Romans had made their own had been developed in the Near East, in a territory in which a dense rural and urban population had been supported from time immemorial by irrigation, the practice of crop rotation, and a high development of trade and manufactures. Europe, even Italy, was by contrast a backward region with a sparse and dwindling rural population whose lands were becoming increasingly impoverished, and with few and insignificant cities. In the long view of history, one must think of the Roman Empire as a westward extension of the Hellenistic civilization which had its origin and continuing center in the Near East. As with many other advances of culture into regions to which they were ecologically unadapted, the Hellenistic civilization never really took roots in the West. In due course of time the Celtic and Germanic cultures reasserted themselves, and the Hellenistic civilization retreated eastward, where it survived in Byzantium, the so-called Eastern Roman Empire, until the fifteenth century A.D. Its retreat left the control of Europe to the barbarian tribes whose culture had been enriched but certainly not transformed by contact with Hellenistic Rome. These tribes had found many elements of the Hellenistic culture incompatible with their own long-established institutions, and, while the great legend of Rome predisposed them to accept the outward forms of the Roman state, they reinterpreted these in terms of their own values.

In western Europe the chaos, following the Roman collapse, crystallized into the feudal system, which, as H. G. Wells remarked, was not a system but "confusion roughly organized." With the breakdown of authority the prevailing need of early medieval society was for protection. Governmental control, which normally guards the rights of citizens, was lacking. The peasants and small landowners were easy prey for any roving band of invaders who descended upon them. They were therefore obliged to seek protection where they could find it and pay whatever was demanded. Thus the powerful landowner with a retinue of fighting men could force his weaker neighbors to become his dependents in return for his protection. This resulted in a system of nobles holding the manors, with the peasants working for him as serfs and fighting for him when necessary.

Feudalism was essentially a rural society, with the nobles established on the manors. In the towns was a small group of burghers who produced the few specialized things which could not be made by the peasants. With the rise of the cities, feudalism collapsed. In fact, in the region around the Mediterranean, where city patterns survived the fall of Rome, feudalism never became strong as it did in the north.

Feudalism presented a rigidly stratified society in which, theoretically at least, no man could rise above the position into which he was born. However, as in most integrated social systems, a safety valve was provided to draw off the energies of able and aggressive members of the lower class who might otherwise have revolted. The one outlet for social advancement was through the Church. The villeins were chained to the soil and could be sold along with a plot of land, but the son of a serf, if he were able and ambitious, could go into the Church. In this organization it was theoretically possible for him to rise to the position of Pope and to stand on a par with the emperor, who was the secular head of the heirarchy. In this way the Church succeeded generation after generation in drawing off the best brains of the society and also in providing an outlet for the restless and aggressive ones who were potential troublemakers in this rigid system.

The Church shrewdly prevented the priesthood from becoming an hereditary aristocracy by passing two basic regulations: first, the clergy were forbidden to marry, and second, no illegitimate son could take orders in the Church. Consequently the road to advancement in the Church was always open, and new blood was constantly being drawn from all levels in society.

The Church, which had modeled its organization on that of the Empire and even taken over many of the Empire's secular functions at the time of the Roman collapse, had remained the last Hellenistic stronghold in western Europe. Its incompatibility with the barbarian cultures led to innumerable clashes between Church and State which finally culminated in the Protestant Reformation.

ISLAM

W H E N the Roman Empire went into a decline in the West, the eastern Empire carried on. Two great powers emerged from the Near East. One was called the Byzantine Empire, which is a much better term for it than the Eastern Roman Empire, since its official language was Greek and its cultural background was predominantly Greek and Syrian. The other power, lying farther to the east, was the Persian Empire. The Romans were never able to conquer the Parthians, the people living in what is now Persia, but who at one period extended their boundaries as far as the Tigris and Euphrates. Here, in the early centuries of the Christian era, a strong and highly civilized power emerged.

The Sassanian kingdom was the direct descendant of the Persian Empire with which the Greeks had fought. In the course of time, the dynasties had changed, yet the general patterns had carried over. It was highly organized and civilized. Zoroastrianism, the state religion, was for a time the great opponent of Christianity. The Persian religion was a fundamental dualism. It was based on the idea that the universe was controlled by two contesting forces, darkness and light, or evil and good. Ormuz was the God of Light; Orimon, the God of Darkness. The struggle between them was an equal one, so that the outcome was constantly in doubt. Neither of them was all-powerful, as the Christian God is supposed to be. It was the duty of the good man to align himself with Ormuz, and to take an active part in the struggle. Christianity borrowed one very important thing from it: the idea of the Devil, and of the evenly balanced struggle between God and the Devil, which left the outcome in doubt.

To the west of the Persians the Byzantine Empire was developing, becoming more and more rigid and formalized, but accomplishing one thing which was exceedingly important. It managed to incorporate people of many different cultures into itself and to do it successfully. Its lists of officials, emperors, and generals name men of the most diverse origins. For instance, Belesarius, the great Byzantine general, was the son of a Slavic peasant from the Balkans. Several emperors were Arabs; some of the others were Slavs, Greeks, and Syrians.

Byzantium was constantly being exhausted, on the one hand by its wars with the Sassanian Persians, on the other, by successive raids from the north by Bulgars, Slavs, and the like. In the seventh century A.D. Byzantium and Persia had just about fought each other to a standstill, and had reduced the peasantry in the fought-over territory to a condition of complete despair and indifference. The rulers' technique for getting taxes was to make the richest man of each district the tax collector. If, given a free hand as to methods, he could not raise the required taxes, he had to supply the difference out of his own pocket. This hardly engendered enthusiasm toward the central government.

It was upon this scene that the conquering Arabs of Mohammed's immediate successors appeared. This background has been described because the usual and far more dramatic picture suggests that small Arab armies came from the desert and overthrew the forces of the two mightiest empires in the world. But great empires are not easily conquered unless they have rotted from within. Here we find a situation which slightly parallels the invasions of the barbaric tribes. But the significant difference, which facilitated the Arab conquest, was the fact that while the earlier barbarian invaders of the Roman Empire had a tribal organization, which meant a certain amount of resistance to outsiders becoming part of the tribe, the Arabs were united by a common faith which was a vigorous, proselytizing religion, and were eager for converts.

Mohammedanism, or more properly, Islam, began with the teachings of Mohammed. He was an historical figure whose life is amply documented. He was born in Mecca in 570 A.D. of a good family, but his father died before his birth and his mother when he was six. His childhood was insecure and difficult, for the orphan was handed around to various foster-mothers and relatives. During his early adolescence he served as a shepherd, which gave him much time for contemplation. At seventeen he went to Syria with an uncle and fought in a local religious war. When he was twenty-four he became commercial representative for a caravan owned by a wealthy widow. A year later, in 595, he married the widow, who was then forty, had been married twice before, and had borne her former husbands two sons and a daughter. She bore Mohammed two sons, who died in childhood, and four daughters. From 595 to 610 Mohammed was a respected businessman in the city of Mecca. He was given the surname Al Amin, The Just, because of the wisdom of his decisions. At the age of forty, however, he began to feel dissatisfaction with his tranquil and prosperous existence and retired for meditation to a cave outside the city. Revelations in the form of dreams came to him, and he was convinced that he had been chosen by Allah as a vehicle of enlightenment.

As well as being an important town in the caravan trade, Mecca was a center for religious pilgrimages, for it was the shrine of an important deity of the old Arabic religion. Because of this, the Meccans were highly attuned to religion; also their contact with traders had exposed them to the Jewish and Christian ideas. Mohammed's revelations attracted a number of followers and he began to preach and make further converts. Like all Arab towns, Mecca was split into various factions. A powerful group who disliked Mohammed's clan, and saw in his new teaching a threat to the old pilgrim trade, made an unsuccessful attempt to assassinate him. Mohammed and his small group of loyal disciples fled to Medina on July 16, 622. This is a very important date, for it is the year of the Hejira, or flight, from which all Mohammedans reckon, just as Christians date their calendar from the time which is assumed to be the birth of Christ.

The people of Medina, a town lying north of Mecca, welcomed Mohammed, chiefly because they were old rivals of the Meccans. Towns frequently followed the policy of taking in an exile and helping him to become a distinguished citizen in order to make trouble for the town from which he had fled.

Mohammed returned to Mecca in 630. He destroyed the idols of the old religion and forbade any pilgrims except the Faithful of Islam to enter the city. He ruled that the idol-worshippers must be either converted or slain, but the "People of the Book," meaning Christians, Zoroastrians, and Jews, were allowed to worship in their own way, although they were assessed a special tax.

Two years after his return to Mecca, Mohammed died at the age of sixty-two, a ripe age for a prophet. Most of the great religious leaders died long before the religious ideologies which they inspired were formulated. The doctrine of the Trinity, the nature of the Holy Ghost, and other theological concepts which arose subsequent to the original doctrine of Christianity, and which have been the concern of divines for centuries, would probably also have puzzled Jesus of Nazareth. But Mohammed, as a religious leader in Medina and then in Mecca, coped with immediate questions of doctrine. Following the tradition of Arab sheiks, he administered justice and handed down decisions.

Mohammed died a successful and prosperous citizen, which is also outside the pattern for prophets. He was a man of experience, having been a herdsman, a warrior, and a trader. He had a thorough understanding of Arab culture and his teachings were adapted to the needs of the people and made no demands which would disrupt their patterns of life. He worked for unity and a funneling of the old tribal loyalties into a new religious allegiance. Certainly Mohammed's teachings were more direct and comprehensible than those of Zoroastrianism or Christianity, the religions with which Islam had to compete at the time of its origin.

The Arabs, who were familiar with Jewish and Christian ideas, had felt themselves at a disadvantage because they had no scriptures nor any written tradition. The desert Arabs were just beginning to learn to write at this time and had the awe and respect, characteristic of all illiterate people, for written records and their apparently magical effects. Out of the pronouncements of Mohammed came the Koran, which filled a long-felt need in Arab life. Much of the Koran was dictated by Mohammed while in a state of possession and is phrased in Arabic poetry, a mixture of mystic prayers and exhortations to the faithful. Other sections are pronouncements of all kinds. Although this book abounds in obscure illusions which are dull and confusing to the modern reader, these referred at the time when it was written to contemporaneous events with which the community was thoroughly familiar. Mohammed's pronouncements were occasionally inspired by momentary irritations. For instance, after a difficult session with a strong-willed, old lady litigant, he made the statement that no old woman would be accepted in Heaven, since Heaven was designed as a peaceful place. He later relented on this dictum, but the question as to whether or not women have souls is still a point of doctrinal disagreement among various sects of Islam.

Although Mohammed did not live long enough to answer all the questions that arose, he laid the foundation of a creed and a legal system which were later supplemented by his followers. The *Koran* contains innumerable laws governing all phases of behavior. Supplementing the *Koran* proper, which contains the actual words of Mohammed, is the *Hadith,* which contains the traditional sayings and decisions of Mohammed as these were recalled by his followers after his death. Some were reported by those who had known Mohammed, others were based on hearsay evidence. After Mohammed's death all the scribes of Islam began a frantic collection of all the sayings and episodes which could be recalled at first or second hand. This went on as long as there was anyone alive who had been alive in Mohammed's time. From these sacred works developed the peculiar pattern of Islamic sacred history which is still the background of Islam.

The legal content of the Koran was derived, for the most part, from the pre-Islamic customary law, with only minor variations by Mohammed himself. These in every

case were ameliorations of earlier laws, for Mohammed
was a social reformer. Thus, there is a statement in the
Koran to the effect that a master must be kind to his
slaves. Another specification on which Islamic peoples
laid great stress was that all true believers were brothers
and social equals. Coupled with this was an extraordinary
degree of vertical mobility. A man born into any position
in society, even that of slave, could rise to any heights.
This was logically consistent for, since Allah controlled
the universe, he could make a man a beggar one day and
a sultan the next if that were his will. Islam has represented throughout its history an unusually flexible social
system.

Although the intellectual life of Islam is at present
perhaps old-fashioned, Mohammedanism is still a strong
and alive religion which is a force in the lives of its followers. In Islamic countries the mosque services and the
reading of the Koran are always in Arabic. This means
that all educated people in the widespread Islamic countries have a common language, much as all educated people in the Middle Ages in Europe understood Latin, which
was the language of the Church. Thus, behind all the political divisions of Islam there is a solid core of common
learning and common understanding. Islam rises superior
to international political lines, an important point to consider when attempting to predict the reactions of the Islamic world in any world crisis.

7 AFRICA

STUDENTS of cultural history find the Dark Continent well named. Although it was one of the first continents to be occupied by man, its past is shrouded in obscurity. Outside the narrow limits of Egypt, Abyssinia, and the northern littoral, there are no written records earlier than those of the medieval Arab travelers. The great Negro kingdoms which are ranged across the continent south of the Sahara have oral traditions which carry the record two or three centuries further back, but as history they are subject to the limitations imposed on all records handed down by word of mouth.

Remains of human occupation are to be found everywhere in Africa, yet vast areas are still, for all practical purposes, archaeological *terra incognita*. The earliest African blade-industries resemble those of Europe and the Near East in so many respects that there can be little doubt that they were introduced into Africa in developed form. The skeletal material coming from Upper Paleolithic and Mesolithic sites is of special interest because of the light it throws on African racial history. Although the remains are not numerous, they indicate two things: that a number of different human breeds and types were present on the continent at this time, and that Negroid physical characteristics were less pronounced and less widely distributed at this period than they became later. The North African population associated with Upper Paleolithic industries was predominantly Caucasic and showed many of the characteristics of the modern inhabitants of the same region. Scattered finds made in the African plateau from the eastern Sudan to South Africa indicate that the Bushman-Hottentot type once extended much farther north than it has in the historic period, while Caucasic elements extended farther south. Lacking any clues as to pigmentation, hair form, and so forth, some of the east African remains would probably be classed as Caucasic if found anywhere else.

That the African Neolithic cultures stem from the Southwest Asian center can hardly be doubted. Their technologies are basically similar and everywhere north of the Sahara the African Neolithic economy seems to have been based on Southwest Asian plants and animals. Although there may have been some mixture between these imports and closely related native fauna, no economically important animal was domesticated on the African continent. The Egyptians did domesticate the cat, but this animal has contributed more to man's psychological than to his physical satisfactions.

Most of the crops grown in west Africa and the Sudan today are of either American or Southeast Asian origin. The remainder seem to have been domesticated for the most part in Abyssinia. Those which seem most likely to have been grown south of the Sahara in Neolithic times are various sorts of millet and ground nuts.

The main migration route of Neolithic settlers coming into Africa was apparently by way of the Sinai Peninsula and across the Red Sea. When the techniques necessary for a pastoral economy had been developed, there were numerous migrations from Arabia into the Horn of Africa. These went on all through the later prehistoric period, which in this region extended until after the beginning of the Christian era. Still later, the development of Islam was responsible for an extensive movement which carried Arabian pastoral tribes over much of semi-arid North Africa.

In this connection it should be noted that the horse and the camel were both comparatively late arrivals in Africa. The first appearance of horses anywhere on the continent seems to have been with the Hyksos invasion of Egypt about 1500 B.C. The Egyptians took over the animal from their temporary conquerors, but used it only for fighting. Horses were driven in light one-man chariots. The driver's main weapon was the bow. In action he freed his hands by fastening the reins about his waist. Egyptian ingenuity and craftsmanship made their chariots the lightest and strongest in the ancient world. The camel was not used in Egypt until the Ptolemaic period, although there is at least one unmistakable carving of a camel which goes back to early dynastic times.

There was no Bronze Age in Africa, a fact which is often attributed to an early and independent discovery of iron. It now seems more probable that stone tools continued in use in Africa until after iron had replaced bronze in the adjoining parts of Eurasia. Techniques and tool and weapon forms strongly suggest that Negro Africa derived its iron-working from India or Indonesia rather than from Europe or the Near East.

HISTORIC AFRICAN PEOPLES

T H R O U G H O U T the entire historic period Africa has been divided racially and culturally by the Sahara Desert. North of this tremendous waste the African population has been predominantly Caucasic, and the African cultures essentially Eurasian. North Africa has been a part, first of the classic Ecumene and, from the eighth century to the present, of the far-flung Islamic civilization. South of the Sahara the population has been predominantly Negroid and its cultures, in spite of occasional accretions from outside sources, have remained distinctive. It will not be necessary to record the cultures of the North African peasants and city dwellers. Apparently the local populations have conformed readily enough to the patterns set by their successive rulers, Phoenicians, Greeks, Romans, Byzantines, and Arabs. In the Atlas and at those points in the Sahara where a scanty rainfall permitted pastoral occupation, elements of the older culture survived through all these vicissitudes, but the information which we have on these from either archaeological or classical sources is negligible.

With the Islamic conquest most of the distinctive North African culture survivals were eliminated. The North African environment was so similar to that of the Arabian regions in which Islam had its source that the Islamic culture patterns could be introduced almost *in toto*. In addition, whole tribes of pastoral Arabs moved into the North African interior and, backed by the prestige of Islam, were able to establish a cultural ascendancy over the local population.

Northeast Africa east and south of Egypt forms a distinct province both racially and culturally. The local population, generally referred to as the People of the Horn, have physical characteristics which place them in an intermediate position between the Negroid and Caucasoid stocks. They combine exceedingly dark pigmentation with Caucasic features. Their hair is quite different from that of typical Negroes, being coarse and closely crimped, so that when allowed to grow long it stands out from the head in a bush.

Three distinct cultures were represented in the region, two in the lowlands and one in the Abyssinian highlands. Both of the lowland cultures were based on animal economies. One, that of the Somali, followed in most respects the familiar Semitic pastoral pattern. Its economic emphasis was on camels, sheep, and goats, with cattle few and incidental. The other domestic animal culture, characteristic of the Galla, was a dairying culture of distinctively African type with cattle as the most important animals. The Abyssinian culture was based on a mixed agricultural and domestic animal economy but with agriculture paramount. Since the Abyssinians had been Christianized in the third century and had maintained contact with other Christian and later Muslim societies all through the historic period, this civilization was less African than Near Eastern. It showed strong Byzantine and Arab influence, and the governmental institutions were essentially of Semitic type.

Negro Africa extended from the southern borders of the Sahara and eastern Sudan to far South Africa, where one encountered the somewhat divergent Khoisan, i.e., Bushman-Hottentot physical type and cultures. In spite of numerous local variations, certain features were present throughout this entire region, making it appear probable that the various cultures shared a remote common origin. The diversity was most marked in the fields of technology and economic organization, aspects of culture which are most readily affected by differences in natural environment and by foreign contacts. There were also marked differences in the size and patterns of organization of political groups.

Certain social patterns were present everywhere in Negro Africa. Polygyny was universal and was correlated with an equally universal surplus of women, due partly to the more dangerous activities of men and partly to a strong tendency for females to exceed males in both birth and survival ratios. Payment of a bride price was practically universal. This payment was construed primarily as reimbursement to the woman's family for the loss of her services and those of her potential children. It did not make the woman one of her husband's chattels, and it did not prevent her from dissolving the union under sufficient provocation.

The basic, universal religion of Negro Africa was ancestor worship. This was directed primarily toward founders of kin groups and heroes whose exploits were remembered. It was firmly believed that the dead took a lively interest in the doings of their descendants, that they were able to help or harm them, and that they could be influenced by prayers and, especially, sacrifices. Upon these basic assumptions numerous local beliefs and practices had been developed. In addition to the ancestral spirits there were nonhuman deities, but their number and importance varied greatly in different parts of the area. Outside a few of the great kingdoms, god cults were less important than the ancestor cults.

There was a lively belief in magic of all sorts, and the medicine men, its practitioners, held an honored position. Professional priests were in charge of the shrines of various gods and directed their worship. Supervision of ancestor worship was normally a function of the head of the kin group. There were also professional diviners who practiced no other type of magic; medicine men's activities were directed mainly toward the healing of disease.

The cattle brought to Africa by Neolithic settlers could flourish in regions where the crops which they had brought could be grown with difficulty, if at all. The result was the development of an African dairying culture similar to the Eurasian one. Among the African dairying societies cattle were the emotional and cultural center of native life. All work with them was pre-empted by men and the cultures were strongly patriarchal and patrilineal. The bride price was always paid in cattle and a man's wealth was reckoned in terms of the size of his herd, irrespective of quality, an attitude which in modern times has resulted in inferior stock and bad overgrazing.

Although most of the historic dairying societies conducted mass hunts to destroy lions and other predators, they rarely hunted for meat. Since game was abundant everywhere in the plateau, this neglect of a significant natural resource seems curious. In several cases the dairying tribes shared their territory with hunting tribes of inferior social status, from whom they obtained the skins of antelopes and other wild animals which they used for clothing. Technology was rather poorly developed in all the dairying cultures. Iron was in universal use for tools, weapons, and even ornaments. The metal seems to have been most plentiful and most skillfully worked in the northern part of the plateau. Smiths everywhere formed a distinct caste of low social status. This may indicate that the iron-working technique was introduced by foreign craftsmen. Mats were woven but the true loom was unknown.

Most of the plateau from Kenya south was occupied by Bantu-speaking tribes who were comparatively recent arrivals in the region. Although cattle dominated their economy at the time they were first encountered by Europeans, they depended much more heavily on agriculture than did the Sudanic and East African dairying tribes. This tendency may have been increased by the fact that they were already in possession of American crops at the time when Europeans first visited this region. There can be little doubt that before their entrance into the plateau the culture of these Bantu invaders was much like that of the West African agricultural villagers. They seem to have brought with them more advanced patterns for political organization, and during the eighteenth and early nineteenth centuries a number of ephemeral empires were developed in this region, each one centering about some great leader and military organizer. None of these empires developed the professional administrators who gave the agricultural kingdoms their continuity. The most famous of these empires was that of the Zulu, created by Tschaka.

In far South Africa a highly aberrant version of the dairying culture was carried on by the Hottentots, a group closely related to the Bushmen in both physical type and language. Their principal domestic animals were cattle and fat-tailed sheep, both of which were milked. Milking was done by women, and cattle were used as pack animals, practices which other African dairying peoples regarded as little short of sacriligious. Instead of occupying more or less permanent kraal, the Hottentots lived in temporary camps and moved frequently. There was a heavy dependence on hunting, carried on by men.

In Africa the line between farming cultures and dairying cultures was closely related to rainfall. From the borders of the Sahara, rainfall gradually increased southward through the western and central Sudan until one reached the humid tropics of the coastal lowlands and the Congo basin. The transition was gradual enough so that farming and dairying cultures were able to co-exist over a fairly wide strip of territory running east and west. Although some tribes practiced both herding and agriculture, the dominant pattern was a symbiotic relationship, dairymen and farmers operating side by side and exchanging their products. However, political dominance of the dairying people over the farmers was the usual pattern. Along the western edge of the great African plateau, on the other hand, the climatic transition was abrupt, and the frontier between the dairying and farming economies closely followed the line of forty-inch rainfall. Where the precipitation was more than this, the presence of the tsetse fly, which carried a disease deadly to cattle, made dairying unprofitable.

The farming economy provided a basis for the development of great and relatively permanent kingdoms which, by all tests except that of literacy, fully merit the title of civilizations. These kingdoms, which will be discussed in the next section, were most numerous and most highly developed in regions immediately south of the Sudan. Although the imperial patterns also penetrated into the Congo, most of the states set up there lacked the elaborate organization of the more northerly ones and certainly represented a less advanced stage of development. Still further south, political centralization disappeared, leaving autonomous communities or small groups of villages recognizing only local chiefs. The patterns of peasant life were so similar throughout the whole area in which the main economic dependence was on agriculture that one is forced to conclude that there was an older cultural substratum, upon which centralizing political institutions had been superimposed in various regions without greatly altering the daily life of the common people.

In the regions of heaviest rainfall the only domestic animals were goats, chickens, and dogs, with rare and sporadic pig culture. Toward the margins of the farming area a few cattle were kept, but there was a strong tendency toward specialization in this as in other economic activities. Cattle-keeping tribes interlocked with farming tribes, and the two exchanged their products. The principal crops of the heavy rainfall area were banana, yam, and taro, the last usually referred to in the literature as *bull yam*. Banana and taro were of Southeast Asian origin and must have been introduced into Africa from across the Indian Ocean. At least one of the yam species grown was also Southeast Asian. The main agents in the introduction of these crops were presumably the same Malayo-Polynesian voyagers who settled Madagascar. Since, except for yams, none of the economically insignificant crops raised in the humid African tropics were of African origin, it is probable that these regions were left to primitive hunting and collecting tribes until a comparatively late date. In the regions of less heavy rainfall, maize, manioc, various millets, sorghum, peanuts, and ground nuts were raised, but it should be noted that here also most of the historic staple crops were not of African origin. It seems safe to assume that anything like intensive agriculture, making possible dense and nonmigratory populations, was a relatively late development in Negro Africa. Since strong centralized states cannot exist without such populations, the Negro civilizations must also be of relatively recent origin.

All the societies who shared the <u>farming</u> economy had <u>well-developed law codes and formal systems</u> of legal procedure. Laws were precisely stated and legal precedence carried heavy weight. Witnesses were called to testify under oath, professional pleaders were employed by both sides, and the whole procedure was strikingly like the European one. Also, as in medieval Europe, trial by ordeal was resorted to in those cases where the evidence was so conflicting that the judge could not arrive at a decision, or in trials for malevolent magic where the actual practice was usually impossible to prove. Poison ordeals were common and far from uniformly fatal to the accused.

<u>Religion</u> in general was much more important among the farming than among the dairying societies. The ancestors were regarded as ever-present, and not only aided their descendants but also disciplined them for any moral slips. The male ancestors in particular were regarded with much more fear than affection, and it may be noted that in many cases conversion to Christianity, with the consequent relegation to limbo of these invisible guardians of the status quo, has resulted in a distinct breakdown in native mores. In addition to the ancestors, there were often regular pantheons of deities, usually

organized on the model of the human kin groups. These deities were, for the most part, associated with forces of nature, but the greater ones were often provided with supernatural messengers and servants who operated as intermediaries in the deity's dealings with humans. The good will of these was often sought more earnestly than that of their divine superiors. As might be anticipated, the god cults reached their highest development in the great kingdoms. For the average villager the gods were little more than literary deities, Beings who were the subject of fascinating myths, but with whom one had little dealing.

Mention should be made of the men's secret societies, which were widespread among the farming tribes. Curiously enough, they seem never to have been adopted by the dairying peoples. The origin of these societies is obscure. It has been suggested that they were developed in imitation of the Marabout orders of the North African Muslim. They may also have been developed out of the puberty initiations universally present. In any case, they were one of the most striking features of the African agricultural cultures. The societies were in part cult groups, but were also organizations for mutual aid, for social control, and, not infrequently, for blackmail. Each society had its masks and characteristic costumes and gave occasional public performances at which these were displayed. Women, children, and any men who were not members were supposed to believe that the masked dancers were super-natural Beings, and anyone who discovered their real identity was killed. The societies had regular recognition signs and passwords, and members were pledged to mutual aid much as in Freemasonry.

The societies thus provided a unifying factor in regions where large political units were lacking, and enabled their members to travel outside their home territory with reasonable safety. Where political control was strong, they were often quite understandably regarded with disfavor by authorities, and in Dahomey they were forbidden on pain of death. Their activities varied with the region, but one of their main functions seems to have been the enforcement of local mores. "Uppity" wives and other nonconformists were likely to be severely beaten or even killed by masked members. The resemblance between the Ku Klux Klan and these west African societies is striking, and may well be more than coincidental. In addition to these socially approved secret organizations, there were others whose acitvities were unqualifiedly antisocial. The witch-societies, previously mentioned, may not have existed in fact, but there was a Leopard Society, whose members regularly practiced murder and cannibalism, apparently as accompaniments to black magic.

AFRICAN CIVILIZATIONS

F E W realize how rich and complex the cultures of many African societies were at the time of the first European contact. In the regions from which most of the American Negroes' ancestors were drawn, there were a series of strong and enduring kingdoms which deserved the name of civilizations on every count except that of literacy. In their arts and crafts these societies were little, if at all, inferior to medieval Europeans, while, in the thoroughness of their political organization and the skill with which social institutions were utilized to lend stability to the political structure, they far exceeded anything in Europe prior to the sixteenth century. It is not too much to say that in their home territory the African Negroes have shown a genius for state-building unsurpassed by any other people, except possibly the Incas of Peru.

Every civilization has drawn into itself elements from many sources, and those of Negro Africa are no exception. Contacts between them and the civilizations of Egypt and the Mediterranean littoral have existed since ancient times. Egypt is known to have traded and fought with the Negro tribes of the Upper Nile since at least 3000 B.C. During the eighteenth dynasty (1580–1320 B.C.) Nubia was conquered and occupied by the Egyptians and a viceroy established there. The Nubians seem to have been overawed by Egyptian civilization and accepted it enthusiastically.

There was abundant opportunity for Egyptian, Near Eastern, Greek, and Roman influences to reach Negro Africa by way of the eastern Sudan. The Hamitic tribes who settled the Nile Valley also extended their occupation over most of the Sahara at a time when the climate there was more benevolent than it is at present. Everything indicates that the Caucasic Hamites began infiltrating the Negro peoples to the south in Neolithic times if not before. The Berbers, who were the historic descendants of the Saharan Hamites, continued this process. Their conversion to Islam, which gave this southward penetration the sanctions of a crusade, merely accelerated what was already a long-established pattern. By the ninth century A.D., Berbers, with some slight Arab admixture, were already establishing a chain of kingdoms throughout the western Sudan. The most important of these were Songhai and Ghana, in the region of the Niger. In the fourteenth century the Mandingo kingdom of Melle conquered the entire western Sudan.

Berbers and Negroes mingled their blood freely, and even the ruling dynasties of these Sudanese kingdoms were predominantly Negro. However, they were self-consciously Islamic in culture, and their political organization followed regular Islamic lines. It has generally been assumed that the pagan Negro kingdoms which arose still farther south derived from those of the Sudan. However, the structure of the pagan kingdoms differed so much from the Islamic patterns that only some sort of stimulus diffusion seems possible. The pagans far exceeded the Islamic peoples in the complexity of their political organization and in the skill with which they utilized existing institutions to strengthen royal power.

The two greatest of the pagan kingdoms were Uganda and Dahomey. The former lay at the eastern end of the line of kingdoms and received minimal Islamic influence. Dahomey, toward the western end of the line, was a much more recent creation and was in the region which received the first impact of modern European penetration. Although it is impossible to say how far this contact modified the native institutions, it unquestionably changed the native economy, shifting the emphasis from ordinary agricultural production to wars for profit. Because of space limitations only the kingdom of Uganda (the civilization of the Baganda peoples) will be described here.

The kingdom of Uganda lies northwest of Lake Victoria. It includes a considerable stretch of shore line protected by outlying islands, so that coastwise traffic was easy. Although the Baganda never developed sails or any craft more elaborate than large plank canoes, the high level of their technological development was reflected in the excellence of these. Canoes were used in war expeditions against neighboring tribes, and the admiral of the canoe fleet was an important officer. More prosaically, fishing was a main source of protein food. Fish were dried and distributed throughout the whole kingdom in trade.

According to the native tradition, the organization of the Baganda kingdom was begun by Hamitic dairying people who invaded the region about five hundred years ago and founded the dynasty which still rules. By the time of European contact these invaders had been completely absorbed both physically and culturally. Due to constant intermarriage, royalty and commoners were of the same Negroid type. The main economic dependence of all classes of the population was on agriculture. Some cattle were kept but they had become essentially luxury objects. The commonest domestic animal was the goat, and a commoner who was so fortunate as to own cattle normally kept them with the herd of his chief. Herding was done by a hereditary group, the Hima, who did not occupy a particularly high social position.

While a variety of crops were raised, the main sources of food were bananas and plantains. These were rarely eaten raw, being by preference steamed and mashed to a pulp. Banana mash was the bulk staple of the native diet, comparable to rice in the Orient, and although other foods were eaten with it, they were regarded as incidental and desirable mainly because of the flavor and variety they gave the meal. It may be noted that milk of either cattle or goats was very little used. In addition to various food crops, a species of fig was planted to provide bark for the bark cloth of which the native costume was originally made.

Baganda agriculture had significant effects on their patterns of production, settlement, and social organization. The banana plants, once established, would continue to send up new shoots and produce fruit for twenty-five or thirty years. This made possible relatively permanent settlements. Moreover, the yield was so heavy that a dense population could be maintained, even though women did all the agriculture. It is said that one woman could care for enough banana trees to feed four men. The result was a society in which there was a very considerable surplus of time and energy, with possibilities for the development of correspondingly excellent manufacturies and complicated rituals.

An unusual feature of the Baganda kingdom, and one which no doubt contributed to the successful functioning of its centralized government, was an extraordinarily good network of roads. These were frequently as much as twelve feet wide, hard surfaced, and with causeways running across swampy ground. The chief of each district had as one of his duties the maintenance of a road between the king's establishment and his compound, while each of the nobles in a district had to maintain a road between his compound and that of the paramount chief. The road system made possible rapid troop movements and an extensive exchange of manufactured goods. There were numerous markets to which both professional craftsmen and local peasantry brought their products. Markets within easy walking distance of each other were usually held on different days, forming a cycle, so that itinerant merchants, at the close of one market, could pack up their wares and move on to the next. Each market was in charge of an official who was responsible for maintaining order and punishing unfair dealing. The government imposed a ten per cent sales tax.

The social and political organization of the Baganda

bore out their traditions of the origins of the state. There were only three hereditary classes: slaves, commoners, and members of the royal family. Since polygyny was the rule and the kings were expected to exceed their subjects in the number of wives, as in all other symbols of prestige, the royal group was fairly numerous. However, as a preventative of civil war, it was customary to kill most of a reigning king's brothers when he came to the throne, and to kill any of his daughters who married or bore a child. As a result the royal group was largely reconstituted in each generation.

Below the members of the royal family, who were debarred from holding administrative offices, there were numerous officials who functioned as administrators. This group bore a superficial resemblance to the European feudal nobility. However, all of them were appointed by the king and owed allegiance directly to him. Since every appointment automatically terminated at the king's death and any free man was eligible for office, these administrators never developed into a distinct hereditary class.

Slaves were, for the most part, prisoners of war or their descendants, although there were also Baganda slaves, children who had been pledged as security for debt and whose labor provided the creditor with interest on his loan. Slaves were in general well treated. Women became concubines and were freed as soon as they bore a child to their masters. The main disadvantage of slavery for men was their immediate eligibility for the numerous human sacrifices required by Baganda ritual.

Commoners were originally grouped in thirty-six patrilineal exogamous clans, but by the time of the first European contact six of these had almost lost their identity through fusion with other clans. Each clan had its chief, selected by a council of the clan elders. Upon his accession, the clan chief took the name of the clan founder and was regarded as in some degree his reincarnation. Each clan had two totems, usually animals, and took its name from the more important of these. Clan members were forbidden to kill or utilize their totems, but had no objection to members of other clans doing so. A clan divided into a series of subclans. The central feature of a subclan's territory was a graveyard for its members. After it had been in use for three generations this graveyard, with the plantations about it, became the inalienable property of the subclan, not subject to royal seizure. Each subclan had its chief and usually a temple in which its founder or some clan deity was worshipped.

The organization of clans and localized subclans was certainly older than the Baganda state. The Hamitic invaders superimposed the administrative framework of the state upon it and were careful to keep the two severely separated. Clan and subclan chiefs were in general debarred from participation in the national government, and officials were rarely appointed to rule over their own clansmen. At the same time, through the ascription to the various clans of numerous more or less honorary offices, the clan loyalty was used to bind the subjects to the central government. To cite only a few examples of these, the post of custodian of the royal tombs was hereditary in the Monkey Clan, the king's guard was drawn from the Rat Clan, the men who carried the king on their shoulders whenever he went outside the royal compound were recruited from the Buffalo Clan, the royal gatekeepers came from the Mushroom Clan, and the royal drummers from the Hippopotamus Clan. A wife from the Otter Clan made the royal bed. Every clan sent wives, and from time to time levies of boys and girls were drawn from the various clans for service in the royal compounds and the households of the highest officers.

The whole structure of the state centered on the king, whose functions were as much religious as political. Immediately below him were two officials, the *Katikiro,* or prime minister, and the *Kimbugwe,* keeper of the king's umbilical cord. The former took charge of the administration of the kingdom, while the other had charge of the national shrines. Their offices thus corresponded to the two major aspects of the royal office. The entire kingdom was divided into ten districts, over each of which ruled a great official *Basaza,* or earl. Within his district the principal duties of the *Basaza* were to administer justice, maintain order, and supervise public works. He also had to provide a contingent of troops in time of war, keep certain buildings in the royal compound in repair, and provision the king's household for one month in every ten. The earl of each district had special duties. The *Basaza* of Kayadondo, the district in which the royal establishment was situated, substituted for the king on the various occasions when the monarch was in seclusion. Because of the sacred nature of the royal office, these were fairly frequent. The *Basaza* of Busugu occupied a position of great importance, since he had charge of all the royal offspring, who were forced to reside in his district, and played a major role in the selection of a new king. The *Basaza* of the district of Busiro was custodian of the royal tombs, and his post was the only one which was hereditary in a particular clan. All other *Basaza* appointments were terminated with the death of the king, although a *Basaza* might be reappointed and, in any case, would usually be succeeded by another member of the same clan. Every *Basaza* kept one establishment in the capital and another in the district which he ruled. Each establishment was supervised by a steward who acted for the earl in his absence.

Below the *Basaza* there were six grades of minor nobles ruling over subdistricts. These nobles were appointed by the king with the advice of the earl but were responsible to the king alone. Like the *Basaza,* they maintained establishments in the capital, and all officials were expected to spend much of their time there. The whole order of nobility together formed the great council of the kingdom, which was in almost constant session.

One of the main duties of all officials other than palace functionaries was the administration of justice. Personal revenge was rigidly forbidden except during the lawlessness of an interregnum. There was an elaborate law code which was amended from time to time by royal decree. Nobles of each grade acted as magistrates in their own districts, but appeal was possible from lower to higher courts until the case reached the king himself. In litigation both the plaintiff and the defendant were required to post a bond in the same amount, and this was forfeited by the loser, a useful mechanism to discourage unnecessary litigation. Ordeals were resorted to when the evidence was inconclusive, and torture was used to extort confessions. Suspects might be kept in the stocks while waiting trial, but there were no facilities for prison sentences and the commonest punishment for minor crimes was mutilation, ranging from ear or nose clipping to castration or amputation of limbs. Those guilty of capital crimes were often reserved for human sacrifices.

Taxes were collected irregularly and levied whenever the royal treasury became depleted, but the methods of collection were well organized. Six tax collectors were appointed for each district, one each by the king, the queen-sister, queen-mother, the prime minister, the keeper of the national fetishes, and the earl of the district. The collectors visited each noble and fixed the tax to be paid by his territory on the basis of the number of compounds it contained. Taxes were paid in kind, and two months were allowed between the levying of the tax and its collection to give the peasants time to get together the necessary goods. The king received half of the total. The rest was divided between the queen-mother, the queen-sister, and the two great ministers, while each *Basaza* and baron received a share of the tax collected from his district. Peasants were drafted as soldiers and also for labor on public works. There was a curious arrangement by which a man who had been drafted for labor had to pay a substantial sum to the overseer before he began work, although he received no compensation for his work.

Royalty was sharply differentiated from commoners and administrators. The central figures were the king, the queen-mother, and queen-sister. All of these, but the king in particular, partook of a personal divinity reminiscent of ancient Egypt. He was hedged about by elaborate ritual, and everyone who approached had to prostrate himself. Although the king never submitted to marriage, he had innumerable wives who had been presented to him as gifts or bribes, whom he had inherited from his father's harem, or who had simply caught his eye. Among these,

the wife who had been acquired for him by his royal
father was preeminent. All wives lived in the royal compound and were subject to strict chaperonage to insure
the legitimacy of any children born to them. All kept their
mothers' totems in recognition of their kinship with her
clan. In addition they respected the lion and leopard totems.

Each prince, as soon as he was weaned, was turned
over to the earl of Busugu, who appointed a guardian for
him and assigned him a small estate. The eldest son, who
was debarred from inheriting the kingship, shared with
the earl the supervision of his royal brothers, while the
eldest daughter of the king was similarly responsible for
her sisters. Few of the royal sons survived the death of
the father for any great length of time. When the heir had
been selected, he and his mother gathered up all brothers
who might have any claim to popular support and sent
them to a particular place where they were put in a stockade under strict guard and allowed to perish of thirst and
hunger. The royal daughters were treated with great respect. They were forbidden to marry or to have offspring
but were not required to be chaste. Some of them became priestesses, while others, as free women supported
by small estates, lived in promiscuity.

At the death of the king there was a hurried confer-
ence of the great ministers, the earl-guardians, and the
king's eldest son. When they had decided who the next
king was to be, the royal death was announced by extin-
guishing the sacred fire which burned before the entrance
of the king's house, strangling its keeper, and sounding a
special drum used at no other time. The drum telegraph
carried the news to all parts of the kingdom, and the
country immediately fell into anarchy. Earls and barons
fought with each other, and the strong looted their
weaker neighbors. All the princes were summoned to the
capitol, and the earl-guardians announced who would be
the next king. After this, the prime minister challenged
any disappointed candidates and their supporters to a test
of arms. The mother of the new king assumed the office
of queen-mother, and one of his sisters or half-sisters was

selected to be the queen-sister. Some of the most important officials were also appointed at this time. The king went through a complicated ceremony known as "eating up the country" in order to legalize his claim to the throne, but the coronation was postponed for six months, during which time the new king was in mourning for his father.

The earl-guardian of the royal tombs took the dead king to his district, where the body was mummified. When mummification was completed, the body was carried to the building which served as its tomb. Subjects brought offerings of bark cloth, which were piled inside until the house was filled to the roof, after which the door was sealed. Four of the king's personal attendants, four of his wives, and hundreds of slaves and captives were clubbed to death and their bodies left lying around the building. Six months later the house was opened and the head of the mummy removed and cleaned. One man drank beer and milk from the skull and thereafter became the medium through whom the ghost of the dead king spoke to the people. The skull was replaced in the tomb, but the jawbone, together with the umbilical cord, was deposited in a temple in the dead king's compound. Each king's establishment was kept up in perpetuity. The dead monarch's ministers, palace officials, and numerous wives continued to serve his spirit, and, as each official died, a new man was appointed as substitute. The reigning king was expected to visit his father's temple once during his reign. At the conclusion of this visit he gave a signal, and hundreds of the onlookers who attended every royal progress were seized and sacrificed to his father's ghost.

The coronation came at the end of the king's mourning period. He and the queen-sister took the oath of office and were invested with the royal robes. Two men captured on the highway were blindfolded and brought before the king. One of these he wounded with an arrow, and this unfortunate was taken by a raiding party to the borders of a neighboring kingdom with which the Baganda were habitually at war, maimed, and left to die. The second man was taken to a place of sacrifice, where eight other men were slaughtered one after the other and their intestines draped around his neck. Thereafter he received a special title and was placed in charge of the king's wives. Lastly, the earls built new compounds for the king and for the queen-mother and queen-sister. Each of these ladies had her own court, ministers, and court officials paralleling those of the king in title and function.

Baganda supernaturalism was strongly tinged with magic. Here, as everywhere in Africa, there were medicine men whose activities included the making of fetishes, working of magic, and healing of disease. Medicine men were sharply differentiated from priests, who were attached to the service of particular deities, but there was some duplication of function between the two groups. Thus divination, which was one of the medicine men's important activities, was also carried on by the priests. While the medicine men divined by observing the fall of cowrie shells, studying the entrails of fowl, and other objective techniques, the temples maintained oracles.

Baganda religion centered about the worship of the dead. Ordinary souls were believed to become reincarnated a few years after death in children of the same clan. The child was given the dead person's name, and worship of the soul ceased. During the interval between death and reincarnation, sacrifices had to be made to the ghost. Although generally friendly to relatives, ghosts were quick to revenge neglect and to punish improper behavior, and their anger was frequently considered a cause of disease.

Even the greatest gods of the Baganda were really ghosts, since all of them were believed to have once lived on earth as men. Each clan worshipped as its principal deity the spirit of its first ancestor. This ancestor was also incarnated in the clan chief, who assumed the ancestor's name when he took office. As a spirit, the ancestor was provided with a temple, priests, and all the appurtenances of divinity. The logical inconsistency involved in such multiple beliefs troubled the Baganda no more than it did the ancient Egyptians. All dead kings were regarded as national deities and were frequently consulted by the reigning monarch. The social and political organization of all the Negro kingdoms had numerous features in common. It would seem that their basic institutions all represented various elaborations of much the same themes. In all of them the peasantry was organized into more or less extended kin groups, with chiefs who functioned both in adjusting disputes between members and as priests of an ancestor cult. This kin organization was kept rigidly separate from the bureaucratic organization upon which the functioning of the state depended. Even when posts in this bureaucracy were hereditary, the kin group leaders were debarred from them. All the Negro kingdoms were highly autocratic, with power of life or death vested in the king. He also represented the court of last appeal in legal cases, and one of his important functions was dispensing justice. While benevolence in a king was appreciated, he was likely to be regarded as a weakling if he never utilized his powers arbitrarily. The person of the king was always sacred, and his physical condition was thought to affect the well-being of the state. In conjunction with this there were often formal provisions for the killing of infirm or senile rulers.

The royal ancestors were everywhere the subject of a national cult and functioned as guardians of the kingdom. The royal establishment was always elaborate and absorbed much of the national revenue. It included guards, an elaborate cadre of court officials, and hundreds of wives. Although rarely rigidly secluded, the king's wives were usually guarded to prevent adultery. None of the Negro kingdoms had legislative bodies or any other device for popular representation in government. Although the king usually had a council, the members were appointed by him and their duties were purely advisory. Like the kin group leaders, the king's own kindred were normally excluded from office. Women of the royal group everywhere enjoyed a high degree of freedom in sexual behavior, yet they were either prohibited from bearing children or their children were excluded from the succession.

It seems unlikely that, in the resurgence of African

culture which may be expected to take place within the next century, these long-established patterns will be ignored. In particular, it is highly improbable that any attempt to impose the reality as well as the outward forms of democratic government upon the African civilization will be successful.

8 INDIA

PREHISTORIC INDIA

EUROPE owes its continental status to Greek parochialism; India has been deprived of such status by the same sort of limited perspective. The great peninsula is as large as the continent of Europe exclusive of Russia, and its inhabitants comprise one-fifth of the world's population. Its climates present every gradation from glacial peaks to lush tropical jungles, and to deserts as forbidding as the Sahara. Throughout the historic period there has been no other region of equal size occupied by as great a variety of races, languages, and cultures, and this situation continues even today. Tribes of genuinely primitive hunters and food-gatherers are to be found within two or three hundred miles of great modern cities, and the largest steel mills in the world match their assembly lines against village artisans carrying on hereditary occupations by techniques which were old when Alexander of Macedon made his raid into the Punjab. No adequate description of such a country can be given in a single volume, let alone within the scope of a single chapter. The present discussion will, of necessity, be confined to those aspects of Indian life which serve to indicate the place of Indian civilization in the world picture and the role which it has played as both a receiver and donor of culture elements.

India is geographically more isolated than any other part of Eurasia. On the north it is cut off from the rest of the continent by the enormous barrier of the Himalayas, a sort of Maginot line against invasion. The western end of this rampart rests upon the deserts and mountains of Baluchistan, while its eastern end is buttressed by the equally formidable jungles and swamps of Assam. Like every static defense, this Himalayan bulwark was breached repeatedly, but behind it India presented a more formidable defense in depth. A Mongol general who had raided into the Indus Valley wrote back, "This is an evil land. The water is bad and the sun kills men." The successive waves of northern invaders found themselves in a crowded and a long-lived-in land where, no matter what their skill in arms or the rapidity of their initial conquest, they were confronted thereafter with an unending war against climate and disease. In the slow, continuous struggle for survival which followed every new conquest and occupation, the older population always came off best. The invaders could survive only by mingling their blood with that of the conquered and accepting much of the Indian way of life. Their descendants became an integral part of India, finding places in the elaborate yet flexible structure of Indian society and religion. In India the mosaic pattern, already mentioned in connection with the Near East, reached its climax. There the problem of integration was solved by creating a sort of jig-saw puzzle in which innumerable subsocieties of diverse origin were fitted together to form a coherent picture, a working whole in which each unit has its place, protected by specialized activities and religious sanctions. Thanks to this system, Indian civilization has been able to maintain itself for at least three thousand years as a distinct, easily recognizable cultural entity. It has borrowed extensively, like all civilizations, but it has borrowed selectively and shaped its borrowings to its own patterns.

From the point of view of the social anthropologist India has no race problems. Physical type is only incidentally an indication of social status. Although *Varna,* meaning color, is the Sanskrit term for the four great divisions in the system by which castes are classified, and the classical explanation for caste is that it came into existence to protect the dominant Aryan group from miscegenation, today the black South Indian Brahman is no less aristocratic for that reason, nor is the white-skinned, grey-eyed untouchable of some northern Indian regions any more elevated because of his pale complexion. Fairness, however, is a criterion of beauty much as it is among American Negroes.

For the study of race as a physical phenomenon India presents a fascinating series of problems. Invaders who entered India in complete ignorance of the caste system and took to themselves concubines from the local population were, within a few generations, converted to caste practices and began carrying on a quite unconscious experiment in the fixation of hybrid characteristics. Gangs of bandit adventurers, who gained control of territories in times of confusion, soon claimed caste status for themselves, in bland indifference to their heterogeneous origin. Lastly, practically every religious reformer who has arisen in India has begun by denying caste and welcoming converts from all regions and levels of society, only to have his sect transformed into a caste within a few generations. What one actually finds at present, if one studies Indian castes as the functional local groups on which the system is based, is that the members of any caste, even one only a few centuries old, tend to show a sort of family resemblance.

Our knowledge of Indian prehistory is still extremely sketchy and based largely on surface finds rather than systematic excavations. However, these indicate that India, since the most ancient times, has been the meeting ground for two fundamentally distinct culture complexes. In the old Paleolithic, northwestern India was the seat of a hand-axe culture belonging to the general African-Western Eurasian co-tradition. Eastern and southern India, on the other hand, had chopper- and flake-using cultures of the Southeast Asian co-tradition. The border between these two cannot be accurately traced at present. It is highly probable that it fluctuated with climatic changes during the many thousand years that the two co-traditions shared the peninsula. One may anticipate that the distribution of each will be found linked to particular ecological conditions, the hand-axe cultures occupying

regions where the natural environment was like that of
Southwest Asia, the chopper- and flak-using cultures regions where the ecology was of Southeast Asian or Indonesian type.

By 3300 B.C. at the latest, the Indus Valley was occupied by a great civilization which had been developed out
of the Southwest Asian Neolithic base. It followed the
Southwest Asian tradition in passing through successive
stages of copper and bronze utilization. It had come to an
end before the introduction of iron. The staple foods were
wheat and barley. No rice has been found so far. Numerous representations of cattle, including some showing
their use as draft animals, suggest that the economic base
of the culture was a mixture of farming and dairying. The
wheel and loom seem to have been known from the first.
It is impossible to say whether the plow was used, since
no examples or representations of it have come to light.
This is in sharp contrast with the numerous miniature
carts, modeled in clay or cast in bronze, which seem to
have been favorite toys of the Indus Valley children.
Grain was apparently hulled in mortars, and one of the
sites shows brick-floored circles polished by generations
of bare feet, in the center of which the wooden mortars
were set.

Cotton probably was cultivated, since cotton cloth
has been found. Flint, copper, and then bronze were cast
in a variety of forms. Tools included adzes, axes, and saws
with offset teeth. One of the most interesting finds is a
piece of a bronze ruler with divisions accurately marked,
showing that the Indus Valley people were already conscious of small exact measurements. There were also
bronze weights arranged in a complicated scale. Pottery
was abundant, and even that from the lowest level so far
excavated was wheel-made and well-fired. Much of the
pottery was coarse cooking-ware, but the better jars were
painted black on a red ground and burnished to a lacquer-
like finish. The designs were mainly floral and showed
little vigor or originality. There were innumerable little
clay figures which are presumed to have been toys. So
many of these have come from one site that it must have

been a center in which they were manufactured for export.

The cities of the Indus civilization were carefully laid out on a gridiron plan, with a main thoroughfare or thoroughfares connected by narrow ways. There can be no question that they were deliberately planned and then constructed, a practice which has continued all through Indian history. A striking feature of all the sites so far excavated is the absence of anything which could be construed as a temple or palace. At Mohenjo Daro there are the remains of an extensive roofed area with numerous pillars but no interior walls, probably a bazaar, a large building with numerous rooms which may have been an administrative center, and a large and extraordinarily well-built swimming pool surrounded by cubicles which look like dressing rooms. It seems likely that the last was used for some sort of ceremonial purification comparable to that practiced by modern Hindus. Mohenjo Daro was unfortified and there was a striking lack of weapons among the finds. This led early writers to picture an idyllically peaceful society. Subsequent excavations have shown that some of the cities were walled, while at least one had a heavily fortified acropolis. Even at Mohenjo Daro there were signs that the city had been attacked and its inhabitants slaughtered.

The Aryans have been the most advertised of all the groups which have invaded India, and numerous beliefs regarding them have become practically religious dogmas. According to the classical formulation, they entered India about 1500 B.C., killed or reduced to slavery the aboriginal population, established the institution of caste in order to maintain the purity of their blood, and then turned from warfare to mysticism and developed the pantheistic and spiritual evolutionary concepts upon which all later systems of Indian philosophy were based. They became the ancestors of the three highest groups in the caste classification and gave their language to most of India.

The Aryan invasion of India was, after all, only one of a series of movements which carried Indo-European-speaking people from the eastern steppes into the more civilized regions. The invaders everywhere created and preserved a considerable literature, verbally transmitted, and the accounts which all these literatures give of their life have so many features in common that their original culture can be reconstructed with considerable accuracy. The picture it gives is of seminomadic tribes of cattle-lifting, chariot-racing raiders, equally addicted to gambling and hard liquor, and interested in the supernatural only in time of need.

The material on which reconstruction of Aryan life must be based is the direct antithesis of that available for that of the Indus Valley civilization. The latter has left a wealth of remains and no written records. The Aryans in India have left practically no remains, but a wealth of literature. It is a case of circumstantial evidence versus testimony. A few stone posts which may have been used in the sacrificial rites described in the *Vedas* have been found, but no Aryan occupation site or graveyard has ever been identified. The literature on which reconstructions of early Aryan life are based is included in four collections known as the *Vedas*. The *Rig Veda*, which, on the evidence of its language, must be the oldest, consists of hymns partly sung, partly recited at sacrifices. The *Atharva Veda* is the most primitive of all in content if not in its language. It is a book of magic consisting mainly of spells, incantations, and medical prescriptions. The *Sama Veda* is a collection of the songs used at sacrifices. It includes verses from many of the *Rig Veda* compositions, together with others of later origin. The *Yajug Veda* consists of *Mantras*, i.e., prayers and mystic formulae.

As the Aryan invaders settled down they could scarcely have failed to take on many elements of blood and culture from the older population. They seem to have been unusually reluctant to admit this. One of the most puzzling features of the Vedas is the references to the aboriginal population, the Dasyus, as black-skinned and flat-nosed. While these adjectives might be applied to some of the proto-Australoid people of southern India, they certainly were not applicable to the predominantly Mediterranean population of northwestern India, the people with whom the Aryans must have had their first and presumably hostile contact. The Dasyus are also described as savages in some hymns, while in others the gods are appealed to for aid in overthrowing their cities and stone-walled forts.

There can be no doubt that the Indus culture contributed very heavily to the development of later Indian civilization. In fact, one can recognize many more resemblances between it and the historic civilizations of India than between the latter and the seminomadic cattle-keeping culture of the steppe region from which the invading Aryans came. One is tempted to believe that during the interval between the arrival of the Aryans and the completion of the Vedas a fusion took place between the invaders and the survivors of the Indus civilization. In the growth of a hybrid folklore it would be quite possible for memories of the struggle which the ancestors of the Indus Valley people had had with proto-Australoid aborigines in northwestern India to become confused with the battles between the Aryans and the weakened and culturally decadent survivors of the older civilization.

The main difference between the later Vedic and the historic periods was in connection with social structure and religion. The institution of caste had not yet come into existence. There was a division of the population into warriors, farmers and craftsmen, and priests. An arrangement similar even to cognate terms for the various groups was also present among the earliest Persians, to whom the early Indian Aryans were closely related. It is significant that in neither system was there a category comparable to the later Untouchables. Even priests were not yet a clearly differentiated group. Every head of a family functioned as a priest in the frequent sacrifices which the Vedic religion required. The Brahmans of the period were a small group of experts who served as chaplains to aristocratic warrior families, and whose services were sought on occasions when difficult rites had to be performed correctly. They were still dependent on the warrior aristocracy and clearly subservient to them.

Ascetics were already present by the end of the Vedic period. They were individuals who had withdrawn from ordinary social contacts and activities and had retired to a hermitage in the forest. There they gave instruction to those who sought to penetrate into the nature of the universe and of man. Even at this date the emphasis was on man. The later Hindu concept of the material world as illusion was already present at least in embryo form. Ascetics were supported by voluntary contributions from the local villagers, who were glad to provide the food and minimal comforts required in the Indian climate in return for the magical benefits conferred upon the community by the ascetic's presence. Even the touch of his hand when receiving a gift conferred a part of his spiritual power on the donor.

How much later Hindu religion owed to the Aryans is still an open question, but their contribution was certainly less than that ascribed to them by Brahmanic writers. Of all the Vedic gods, only Vishnu survived to become an active deity of developed Hinduism, and even his attributes had been changed beyond recognition. The doctrine of reincarnation, basic in later Hinduism, seems not to have been held by the early Aryans. The patterns of asceticism, and of a hereditary priestly group dominating society by its learning and skill in dealing with the supernatural, were both highly incongruous with ancient Aryan values as these appear in related cultures outside India. If one turns directly to the original evidence, ignoring the wealth of rationalizations and interpretations developed by later writers, one is forced to conclude that the Aryan invasion of India followed very much the course of most subsequent invasions. In these the early political and military dominance of the invaders was followed by their absorption, and a resurgence of the older culture. In the long run the Aryan invasion may prove to have been little more than an episode in the long evolution of a distinctive Indian civilization.

The main argument which can be advanced against this view is the acceptance of Aryan languages throughout most of India. However, this problem is not exclusively an Indian one. In nearly all the regions invaded by Indo-European-speaking peoples they succeeded in establishing their languages, even though their culture and even physical type soon disappeared. In fact the only region in which this did not occur seems to have been in the general Mesopotamian area, where the Indo-European languages came into competition with equally vigorous and equally foreign Semitic tongues. Why certain languages survive in acculturation situations and others do not is one of the most interesting problems of culture dynamics, and one for which we have as yet no solution.

EARLY HISTORIC INDIA

A N Y discussion of Indian history is complicated by the singular lack of interest in history which the Indians themselves have displayed. A *Weltanschauung* which regarded the universe as an illusion and events as occurring in repetitive cycles was understandably uninterested in exact details of time and place. The Brahmans, who enjoyed a monopoly on education, fixed their attention on philosophy and religion rather than on the passing show. Moreover, since they always claimed to find ancient sanction for their current practices, they were less than interested in tracing cultural developments. As a result, Indian cultural history must be reconstructed mainly from the incidental background materials in romantic and religious literature, from archaeological monuments, and from the accounts of foreign visitors.

Even Indian political history is vague at many points. It does not begin to meet Western standards of precision until after the first Muslim invasion. To one who is not a specialist in the field, the names of the innumerable Indian dynasties and kings who have functioned during the last twenty-five hundred years are largely meaningless, and their rise and fall matters of indifference. For that reason the only political events mentioned will be those which seem to have had lasting cultural significance.

On the basis of the source materials available for the earliest historic period, it is possible to divide the whole of India into three regions. Northwestern India was brought into contact with Western civilization by the sixth century B.C., when Darius the First annexed the Punjab and Sind to the Achaemenian Persian Empire. This was followed by the conquest, actually little more than a raid, of Alexander the Great and the establishment of successive dynasties of invaders from the northwestern mountains and steppes, all of whom rapidly assumed the more obvious elements of Hellenistic culture. European descriptions of the region began with an account by Skylax, a Greek, whom Darius sent to explore the Indus in approximately 500 B.C.

For northeastern India we have no early foreign sources and almost no local historic writings. However, early Buddhist literature contains abundant references to this region as far back as the fifth century B.C. In southern India the record begins somewhat later, the oldest writings dating only slightly before the beginning of the Christian era. This region was in frequent contact with other ancient civilizations and there are numerous references to it in Greek literature from the first century and thereafter.

By the dawn of their respective histories the three Indian regions had numerous cultural features in common, but also well-marked local differences. Northern and southern India were sharply divided by language. The Indo-European-speaking peoples of the North had inherited more of the Aryan tradition. The Dravidian-speaking peoples of the South had retained numerous practices which were certainly non-Aryan.

By the fifth century B.C. northern India had developed many of the cultural characteristics which have survived there to the present time. The life of the ordinary villagers seems to have changed little between that period and the revolution which is now being initiated with the arrival of radios and easy transportation. The modern time-traveler who returned to this horizon would be impressed by the extent of the forests and the universal use of wood for construction. Even such great cities as the Mauryan capital of Pataliputra, with its palace and temples, was built entirely of wood and protected by a stockade and a moat. In much of the same region today the peasants are hard put to it to find sufficient timber for rafters and do their cooking with cakes of dried cow dung. He would also have been impressed by the comparative scantiness of the clothing worn in the eastern part of the region. The ordinary costume of men was limited to a loincloth made from a single narrow strip of cotton, while women wore only a short kilt. The rich compensated for the inexpensive character of such dress by the fineness of the fabrics used and by jewelry so abundant that women must have found it a genuine burden.

The same differences in economic status which impress the modern traveler in India today seem to have been present even in this period. Although the villager's economic status was probably better than it is today, he paid one-sixth of his harvest in direct tax and was further exploited by a state salt monopoly, a sales tax, and various other exactions. However, it seems that even at this date differences in income were reflected more in display than in standards of living. The pillars of Chandragupta's palace were sheathed in gold, but he slept on a mat and ate much the same simple, if highly spiced, food as the average peasant. When, in his old age, he retired to a forest hermitage, he had to surrender few creature comforts.

The four great caste divisions: Brahman, Kshatriya, Vaisya, and Sudra, were already in existence in northern India, but there are no indications of the innumerable subdivisions of these which characterize the modern caste system or of the elaborate ceremonial regulations which govern the interrelations of individuals of different castes today. In northeastern India the struggle for power between Brahmans and Kshatriyas had not yet been resolved at this period. The Brahmans had not resigned themselves to the role of advisors to kings or realized the numerous advantages of power without responsibility, nor had the Kshatriya given over all claims to learning or to direct access to the supernatural. It is interesting to note that the activities of the Kshatriya were much more in keeping with the character of the earlier Aryan invaders than were those of the Brahmans.

By the beginning of the historic period, religious beliefs and practices in northern India had taken on a number of distinctive characteristics. Outstanding among these was the belief in reincarnation and the concept of *Karma.* Although the Greek Pythagoras had taught reincarnation, and there are references to it in Celtic mythology, the belief does not seem to have been present in the older Vedas, nor did it form a part of the general Indo-European cultural heritage. We know that a belief in reincarnation, with various elaborations, has arisen independently in many parts of the world, and its Indian form may very well have been developed by pre-Aryan philosophers seeking to find a logical solution to the problems created by man's determined denial of the possibility of his own extinction.

Whatever its origin, the Indian version of the soul's destiny was far more logically consistent and intellectually satisfying than that developed within any other cultural tradition. While the doctrines of various Indian sects differed as to the beginning and the end of the soul's journey, they all were in essential agreement on the middle portion, that which had to do with the individual's immediate past and future. The soul began as an unformed, amorphous aggregate of spiritual forces, which infused the body of some low form of life. Upon the death of its host it passed to another body, bringing with it the experience which it had acquired in the previous incarnation. Through life after life this accumulating experience molded and consolidated the soul. In addition to experience, each soul accumulated a running account of what might be termed spiritual credits and debits, the result of good and evil deeds performed in its incarnations. These together constituted the individual's *Karma,* which determined the particular position in society into which he would be reborn and the good or bad fortune which he would experience.

The most direct road to spiritual advancement was to become an ascetic. The principal object of Indian asceticism has been to achieve identification with the infinite and to experience states of ecstacy in which the soul apprehended the universe. The ascetic progressed to his goal by progressive steps. The first of these was the breaking of all worldly ties and retiring to a forest retreat where he could devote himself to meditation and to exercises designed to give him complete control over his body. The next step was the conquest of the mind, achieved when the individual was able to arrest the thought processes and free his soul for deeper experience. Whatever the skeptical Westerner's reaction to these concepts, he must recognize the value of Indian asceticism as a social mechanism. Ascetic life was open to members of all three of the upper castes and functioned much as did the Western religious orders in the Middle Ages, appealing both to mystics and to those unable to face the stresses of secular existence. Not only the seeker after spirituality, but the prince who tired of his role, the husband who found his wife insufferable, or even the merchant relentlessly pursued by his creditors could join the ranks of holy men.

From the very beginning of the historic period there was a sharp distinction between the Brahmans and the ascetics. Brahmans could become ascetics, but most of them did not. The Brahmans were skilled workers with the supernatural, professional priests who knew the long and complicated rituals prescribed by the Hindu religion. Outside their religious duties they led normal lives, except for the limitations imposed by the regulations of their caste. Many of them were eager for wealth and social control, and it is clear that during the early historic period they were constantly building up their power in northern India and seeking to convert aboriginal tribes to Hinduism.

The increasing pretensions of the Brahmans, and the development of more and more elaborate and expensive rites which only they could perform, was met in the sixth century B.C. by a religious revolution instituted by two great leaders, Gautama Buddha and Vardhamana Maha-vira, founder of the Jains. Both of these men were born as members of the Kshatriya caste, both became ascetics, and both accepted the doctrines of reincarnation and *Karma* without question. However, in both cases their teachings were antithetical to Brahmanic ritualism. The Jains still survive as a minor sect, characterized by a highly devel-oped ritualism and an extreme reluctance to take life in any form. The Jain priest going about his duties swept the path before him with a broom to remove any insects which might be trodden upon, and would not drink water in the dark lest he swallow and destroy some minute form of life. The most important tenet of the faith was its insist-ence upon *Ahimsa*, "harmlessness," a pattern of consistent nonresistance. The late Mahatma Gandhi, although not a Jain himself, had been strongly influenced by Jain doc-trines. Although Jain missionaries made many converts in southern India, the religion had never spread outside the peninsula. The doctrines of Buddha, on the other hand, have been a force in world affairs for two thousand years.

BUDDHISM

B U D D H I S M has been India's most impor-tant contribution to civilization. Although now practically extinct in its homeland, it has become a world religion, with innumerable sects and with followers half again as numerous as all Christians combined. Buddhism is impor-tant not only as a religion but as an expression of basic In-dian philosophy. Siddhartha, also known as Gautama, as Sakyamuni, and as the Buddha, was a historic personage who was born in 563 B.C. and died in 483 or 486 B.C. Euro-peans find these multiple names puzzling. Siddhartha was his childhood name, Gautama his clan name, Sakyamuni his title as an ascetic, and "The Buddha" his divine ap-pellation. He lived to instruct numerous disciples and to supervise the organization of the religion which he founded. The records of his sayings and of the various events in his life, although transmitted for at least a century by word of mouth, are probably accurate. However, as with the founders of all great religions, the myth which has sprung up about him has become more important than the facts.

There is an ancient Hindu doctrine that a god will incarnate when some great evil threatens the world and thus save it. Thus Vishnu, as preserver, has had numerous *avatars*. According to orthodox Buddhism, Sakyamuni was only one of a series of Buddhas who have come at various times in the past and who will come in the future. He had already experienced innumerable incarnations, stories of which are preserved in the *Jatakas,* a charming collection of folklore. Having achieved the highest point of spiritual development, that of a Bodhisattva, he rested with the gods in the highest heaven. Moved by compassion for mankind, he took upon himself the burden of a last reincarnation. He called all the gods together and instructed them in Buddhist law. He also presented to them his successor, the Bodhisattva Maitreya, the time for whose appearance on earth the Buddhist world believes is approaching. Gautama then looked about for a suitable mother from whom to be reborn. He chose Maya, the wife of the ruler of the Sakyas in Nepal, on the border of northeastern India. When he announced his decision, all nature made demonstrations of joy. A cloud of singing birds settled on the palace and all the trees bloomed out of season. Maya retired to the women's quarters, where the Bodhisattva appeared to her in the form of a pearly white elephant with six red tusks, certainly a more picturesque visitant than the Christian Angel of the Annunciation. When her time arrived, Maya went to the park of Lumbini outside the gates of the city, and Buddha was born from her right side as she stood erect. The gods Indra and Brahma received the newborn child in their arms, and the two kings of the Nagas, the serpent deities of aboriginal India, sent streams of hot and cold water for bathing the child. The moment that he was born, Siddhartha took seven steps toward each of the four cardinal points, thus taking possession of the world.

Mother and child were borne to the palace in a chariot drawn by angels. The mother died of happiness seven days after the birth and was immediately reborn in heaven among the gods. Siddhartha was reared by his mother's sister, Mahaprajapati. The child, according to the legend, was born with various auspicious marks, such as webbed fingers; a bump on his head; large, elongated ears; and the marks of the wheel of the law on the soles of his feet. A great sage who saw him prophesied that he would either become King of the World or the Savior of Mankind. When the child was first taken to the temple, the statues of the gods prostrated themselves before him. He disputed with the wise men, his teachers, and astonished them by his wisdom. When, in his early teens, he sat in meditation for the first time in the shadow of a tree, the shadow of the sun remained stationary so that he would be sheltered and his meditation undisturbed.

When he came of age his royal father chose a wife for him, but his future father-in-law doubted whether the beautiful, dreamy young man had the necessary strength to make an able husband and ruler. He therefore resorted to the competition of suitors, a theme which occurs in legends the world over. He offered his daughter to the one who could draw the strongest bow and shoot an arrow farthest. Siddhartha, of course, far outshot any of his competitors. He then married Yosodhara and a series of secondary wives who were sent with her. However, the delights of the harem failed to satisfy him, and he meditated upon the sorrows and evils of the universe.

His meeting with an old man, a sick man, and a corpse, and his charioteer's assurance that these things were the unavoidable fate of man, focused his discontent. He begged his father to allow him to become an ascetic. His father refused and tried to divert his mind with new pleasures. A son was born to him, and the event was celebrated with a great festival, but Siddhartha himself greeted the news with: "This is one more tie to break." On the very night of the festival he fled the palace, accompanied by his charioteer, Chandhaka. The deities bore up his horses' hooves in their hands so that the guards would not hear his passing. At the edge of the forest Siddhartha said good-bye to horse and charioteer. He cut off his long hair and exchanged clothes with the first peasant he met, who was, needless to say, a god in disguise. He visited various groups of holy men and finally became the disciple of Arada Kalama. After undergoing the usual instruction in meditation and ascetic practices, he became a holy man. He finally settled in southern Bihar, chosen because of its natural beauty, and gathered about him a group of five disciples. He practiced great austerities and his fame spread far and wide.

At length Siddhartha's austerities became so great that the gods feared for his life and sent his mother from heaven to beg him to desist. In less romantic terms, he came to the conclusion that austerity could not give him what he sought. He ate, bathed, and announced his decision to give up fasting and yoga practices. His five disciples promptly left him. He wandered for a time, then, at Bodh-Gaya, seated himself beneath a pipal tree and entered into the sublime meditation which was to reveal to him the path of salvation.

From this time on, Buddha's career, as recorded in the legends, was a continuous series of miracles. In sober fact, he seems to have lived for forty years after the enlightenment and to have dealt wisely and realistically with the innumerable problems which arose during the founding of the new religion. Although at the beginning of his mission he met with some skepticism and even open hostility on the part of a few individuals, he was never persecuted. He even underwent successfully the acid test for any prophet, returning to his home and converting the members of his own family. He enjoined poverty, chastity, and benevolence in his followers, and gave them a distinctive costume, the yellow robe and tonsure. He organized them into monastic groups, whose government was modeled upon that of the small republics still extant in northern India at the time. During the dry season the

monks and nuns, for women had been admitted to the religious community with some reluctance, went forth to
preach the gospel. In the rainy season they returned to
the monastery and spent the time in meditation and discussion.

During the forty years after his enlightenment Buddha lectured to his followers and gradually clarified his
doctrine. He denied the value of caste distinctions, not as
difficult at this time and place as it became later. He also
denied the efficacy of ritual and sacrifice, a body blow at
the Brahman supremacy. He did not deny the existence
of the gods, but he claimed that they were unable to aid
men in their striving toward the final goal; they too were
tied to the wheel of life. Even more significant, he condemned the belief in the transmigration of souls, although
this was so deeply rooted in Indian thought that it became
one of the basic tenets of the emergent religion. He even
questioned the existence of the soul as a distinct entity,
holding that it was merely the Karmic accumulation of
good and evil deeds held together by desire. When one of
his disciples questioned him regarding the beginnings of
the world, he answered that the question was unprofitable,
thus forever saving Buddhism from the conflict between
a primitive cosmology and an evolving knowledge of the
nature of the universe which has so plagued Christianity.

All this negativism was intended to strip away super-
stitition and to leave the individual free to follow the eight-
fold path. This involved, first, right views, which seems to
have meant largely the insistence upon truth as this could
be arrived at by logic. Second was right aspirations, which
were to take the place of the base personal cravings which
he condemned. They included such things as an abstract
love for the service to others, love of justice, and the like.
Third, fourth, and fifth were right speech, right conduct,
and right livelihood. Sixth was right effort, which meant
the intelligent planning of action toward the ends indicated in the rest of the doctrine. Seventh, right mindful-
ness, seems to have meant the elimination of individual
pride of accomplishment in the face of the realization of
individual imperfection. Eighth, and least clear, was right

rapture, which seems to have meant the joy to be derived from meditation and contemplation as distinct from ecstasies of the Dionysian type.

The incoherent animistic beliefs of the farther Asian peoples could oppose no resistance to the closely reasoned, logical systems which the Indian missionaries brought, while the religious paraphernalia of images and pictures, and the beautiful and dignified rites which accompanied them, had an overwhelming appeal. Even in China, where Buddhism was faced with a group of well-defined philosophic systems, the metaphysical doctrines and comprehensive appeal of Buddhism won the support of a large segment of the population during the disordered period from the second through the sixth century A.D. Later, when Buddhism was dying in India, new sects were being created in China under the inspiration of Sanskrit texts brought back from India by zealous pilgrims. The new doctrine then spread from China to Japan, where even today Buddhism is a living philosophy.

Buddhism was the first religion to send out missionaries. In Buddha's own lifetime he sent forth hundreds of disciples to carry the good news to all parts of India. The Indian patterns of asceticism and withdrawal from the world, already well established by Buddha's time, added an important ingredient to this missionary complex. The begging priest could move among hostile peoples and disordered nations with impunity, since he was too poor to be worth robbing and also carried with him the mystery of supernatural dedication. One does not lightly injure a man from whose death or robbery nothing is to be gained, especially when, at the same time, there is an excellent chance of offending the higher powers by such an act. It was not until more than a thousand years after Buddha's death, when his monks found themselves confronted by Muslim fanaticism, that they lost this immunity. Prior to that time they were able to wander east and west over the immemorial caravan routes and seaways, bearing with them everywhere the tidings of the law and welcomed alike by villagers and kings.

PRE-COLONIAL INDIA

T H E development of modern Indian culture
has involved a synthesis of elements from many sources.
The fusion of Aryan culture with what were probably
numerous aboriginal cultures went on for millennia, the
Aryan elements being diffused progressively eastward and
southward. Beginning with the Persian and Greek invasion, northwestern India was the scene of numerous
evanescent conquests, in all of which the cycle of events
seems to have been much the same. The early and rapid
victories of the invaders were followed by gradual absorption and the final overthrow of alien rule by neighboring
native states. The Muslim invaders were to introduce a
new pattern.

In 712 the Arabs conquered Sind in the lower Indus
Valley, and the province became the first independent
Muslim state in India. From the eighth to the eleventh
century, western India was in close contact with the Arab
world through trade, cultural relations, and missionaries
who brought the religion of Islam to a tolerant India. It
was not until about 1000, when a Turk from Afghanistan,
Mahmud of Ghazni, cruelly pillaged northern India and
annexed the Punjab, that Islam became equated with political power, brutality, and religious fanaticism. After
Mahmud's death there were no invasions until the end of
the twelfth century, when another Afghan conquered
Delhi, this time establishing a Sultanate which, during the
next 150 years, gradually spread its dominion southward
on the heels of refugees from Muslim tyranny. During
that time the conquerors, an Indo-Aryan people closely
allied to the Indians, underwent some Indianization
through cultural synthesis. Toward the close of the fourteenth century Delhi was mercilessly sacked by Timur,
who left all of northern India greatly weakened. In 1526
Babar, a cultivated Turco-Mongol descendant of the Ti-
murids, took Delhi and founded the Mogul Empire in India.

The Moguls were not barbarous invaders but representatives of the ancient civilization of the Near East, reinvigorated by Muslim fanaticism. They were not impressed by Indian culture in the north, which was in a state of decay, and they missed the luxuries of their homeland in Central Asia. (It was Babar, for example, who laid out the plan for the city of Agra; his grandson, Shah Jehan, who built the glorious Taj Mahal.) Nor did they value the abstract philosophy in which the Indians were supreme. Continuous relations with the West and prescribed pilgrimages to Mecca kept these invaders in close touch not only with the Muslim center but also with the Safavid Renaissance in Iran.

Between the *weltanschauung* of Hinduism and Islam there lay an unbridgeable gulf. It would have been difficult to find two civilizations more antithetical. The Muslim invaders were uncompromising monotheists, with a burning faith in the immanence of a highly personalized anthropomorphic deity; the Hindus were polytheists willing to recognize the existence of innumerable deities, since they regarded all of these, in the last analysis, as merely manifestations of an impersonal world soul (Brahman). The Muslims had a violent aversion to all forms of image worship; the Hindus had been accustomed for millennia to approach their deities through visible material representations. The Muslims insisted upon the brotherhood of all true believers and in practice allowed a high degree of individual social mobility. The familiar *Arabian Nights* motif of the mendicant raised to wealth and high political office overnight was only the romantic expression of a cultural ideal. The entire Hindu social system was based on social inequality and fixity of inherited status. Most of all, Muslim values were dynamic. "Islam" meant "submission to the will of God," but in practice consisted in the dignified acceptance of a *fait accompli* when no alternative appeared possible. The Hindus, on the other hand, glorified passive resignation and other-worldliness. The Hindus' loss of political power after the Muslim invasion no doubt reinforced tendencies toward passivity and denial of the reality of the external world. They cloaked themselves in a

protective mantle of exclusiveness. The caste system crystallized and the seclusion of women (*purdah*) developed
rapidly, as did untouchability. But exclusiveness, passivity,
and other-worldliness were already present when the Muslims arrived. Since, as we have seen, they were foreign to
the early Vedic religion, they may well have been of
Dravidian origin, becoming more deeply impressed upon
the Indian population during the long period when Buddhism was ascendant.

It is quite impossible to trace the successive steps by
which Indian society and religion arrived at the forms
which they manifested at the time of the first European
contact. As has been previously noted, the Indians have
been singularly uninterested in history and the applied
sciences, and the Brahmans have maintained the pattern
of claiming both remote antiquity and Vedic origin for
any and all forms which they favored. By the Colonial
period Indian religion and society had been integrated
into an indissoluble whole. Daily life and social intercourse
were ritualized to a greater extent than in any of the other
world civilizations, and every detail was reinforced by
supernatural sanctions. Even the caste system was justified
by elaborate theories of spiritual development. As the result of the work of many sages over centuries, Hindu religion and philosophy had been brought into a working
whole.

In contrast with the universal gods of the Vedic
Aryans, the Dravidians seem to have had innumerable
local deities. Thanks to the pantheistic concepts of the
Brahmans and their doctrine of reincarnation, it was possible for them to equate the local gods and heroes with
beings of their central pantheon, thus converting both the
deities and their worshippers. The conflicting attributes of
these adopted deities and the contradictions in the legends
associated with them could always be explained by the
concept that the gods, like men, were reborn repeatedly
and that the conflicting tales referred to different *avatars*
(reincarnations). Many of the deities which had been
locally popular in the Dravidian south had considerable
popular appeal, and their worship spread over most of

Hindu India. Buddhism and Jainism were both heresies of an orthodox Brahmanism. Buddhism, particularly in its early stages, was, as we have seen, fundamentally philosophic and monastic and probably was continually in conflict with popular belief in local deities, although many of them were incorporated into the Buddhist pantheon. When Buddhism suffered for want of royal patronage these aboriginal deities reappeared in a resurgent Hinduism which, around the sixth century, began to weaken the Buddhist hold on India.

The two main deities of this later Hinduism were Siva and Vishnu. The chief gods of ancient times, Indra and Brahma, fell into virtual obscurity. Vishnu, orginally a form of Surya (the sun) now became the god sustaining the universe. His numerous avatars show how various divinities were consolidated in the person of one god. Even the Buddha was explained as an avatar of Vishnu. Siva seems to have been a pre-Vedic divinity; his home, Mount Kailasa, was in the Himalayas, and the forms of most Hindu temples reflect the outlines of his mountain abode.

Although in common practice Hinduism is polytheistic, it may be said to be monotheistic in that all divinities are regarded as aspects of one universal power. Hindu philosophy posits three great beings or manifestations of the basic world force: Brahma, the creator, Vishnu, the preserver, and Siva, the destroyer. This is consistent with the Indo-European pattern, in which 3 is the most sacred of all numbers and the male principle is uniformly given precedence over the female. But according to the Saivas all three are manifested in Siva himself, and according to many, Siva and Vishnu are only aspects of the One. This philosophic attitude led to complete tolerance among the various sects, so that almost entirely different practices and ways of thought were acceptable within the one religion. The worship of vital forces was uppermost in Saivism, while other sects paid devotion to the *Sakti* (female principle). During the seventh and eighth centuries the doctrine of *Bhakti* (devotion to a personal god) came into prominence, and soon thereafter the great philosopher-missionary Shankar organized the first Brahmic monastic orders and, in his remarkable travels all over India, preached for the unification of beliefs. The thousands of Hindu temples constructed during and after the time of Shankar reflect the fervor of that Hindu Renaissance.

The source of much of Hindu doctrine is the *Bhagavadgita* (*Gita*), an enchanting dramatic poem in dialogue which is primarily ethical in its teachings. It condemns inaction and posits three main paths to salvation (*moksha*): action (*karma*), knowledge (*jnana*), and devotion (*bhakti*). The *Gita,* which was written some time during the first two centuries B.C., is a section of the *Mahabarata.* This work is a repository of Indian mythology, legendary history, and early philosophic speculation. The other epic, the *Ramayana,* has been a source of great inspiration to the Hindus, especially through its vernacular rendering in medieval times. For centuries their tales of gods and goddesses, heroes and heroines, have been woven into the fabric of the people's lives. From them various sects chose their deities, both major and minor.

The Hindu peasant left philosophic speculations to the Brahmans, and followed the prescribed rites in order to get practical benefits. In addition to the particular god of his sect, he worshipped local spirits, legendary heroes who were in some way connected with his caste or region, and even in some cases prayed to his own ancestral spirits. He would attempt at least once in his life to make a pilgrimage to one of the great temples dedicated to his patron deity. The festivals of different gods were held at different times and places. Such gatherings brought together great numbers of worshippers and provided a welcome break in the monotony of village life. A fair was usually combined with the religious celebration. Between pilgrimages he might worship his particular god at a private shrine, but he would not neglect the village shrine dedicated to some local deity. This was presided over by a resident priest, not always a Brahman, who would be called on to assist whenever elaborate rites were needed. In addition, he would address any god who might be of assistance to him in current need. Thus the merchant would pray to Ganesh, the elephant-headed god, for help in business, while at the time of a smallpox epidemic offerings would be made to Durga, the goddess of smallpox, one of the less lovable consorts of Siva. The average Hindu, whether peasant or Brahman, did not question the existence of innumerable deities and was as tolerant of other sects as the followers of one Christian saint are toward those of other saints.

The economic basis of pre-Colonial village life lay in a delicate balance between agriculture and industry. Cities were primarily administrative and religious centers, and were usually small, except for those on the coast or on rivers where water transport simplified problems of supply. A striking feature was the building of fortified cities and the development of city planning as an art common to both Hindu and Muslim. A ruler, wishing to escape from the influences of his predecessor's reign, would pick a new site, construct a planned city, and then move a population into it by a combination of force and persuasion. The duration of such cities depended to some extent on the skill with which the site had been chosen. In most cases the movements were only over a short distance, and in many localities there are clusterings of old and new cities within a small area.

The bulk of the Indian population occupied rural villages with an average of four hundred inhabitants. Groups of villages were often united in a county council, which acted as the final tribunal in civil affairs. Many of these communities were isolated, with little outside contact. Land holdings followed the immemorial pattern of the Near East, with cultivated fields immediately above the village and pasture beyond. Joint property ownership and survivorship inheritance, which also followed Near Eastern patterns, prevented excessive fragmentation of holdings. The joint family also provided for the needs of each worker and nonworker among its members. The village grain share system (*Jajmani*) continued to provide a fixed annual share of the harvest to the village carpenter, smith, potter, priest, barber, etc., in return for services performed throughout the year. Economic patterns remained stabilized and there were few mechanical improvements in workmanship. Techniques of craftsmanship were transmitted within hereditary groups (castes) and guarded as trade secrets. The lack of material advance may have resulted from these occupational monopolies, which limited competition and discouraged invention.

Indian culture was characterized by an extreme development of ascribed status and role, which made it the most static and most perfectly integrated culture so far developed. The foundation of the society was threefold: village self-government, the caste system, and the joint family. The caste system was reinforced by a series of supernatural sanctions and rationalizations derived from a highly complex and formal religious and philosophical system. A caste is a closely organized body equipped with a common tradition and a strong esprit de corps. It has a chief and a council. Its members meet on occasion in assembly of more or less plenary authority. They join in the celebrations of certain festivals and they have jurisdiction over their members, with power to impose penalties, the most severe of which is expulsion from the caste.

No matter how diverse the actual origins were, all castes are, in theory, arranged in a graded series of social prominence, based on their supposed derivation from Brahma's body. Each of the four main castes is divided into hundreds of subcastes, each of which has one above and one below it in the social order. Since the Indian populations have been relatively static, this arrangement could be maintained. While it is impossible for an individual to rise in the caste hierarchy, it is possible for an entire caste to rise as a whole. This is done by keeping the formal regulations with respect to prayers, ceremonial cleanliness, and so forth, with special strictness. A Sudra cannot become a Kshatriya, and no caste can become Brahman, but it is possible to elevate a subcaste a notch or two by this method.

The caste system is excellently adapted to keeping a highly complex but static culture functioning successfully. Caste has become a basic pattern of Indian life and most new social elements are interpreted and adjusted in its terms. Even the native Christians and Muslims, although they did not accept the Hindu hierarchy, divided into sub-castes. On the other hand, many Untouchables espoused Islam, and later Christianity, in order to escape from their miserable status.

British colonial rule in India, among other things, dealt a body blow to the autonomy and self-containment of the village and further fractured the caste system. Today in independent India other significant forms of social relationships are in the process of drastic reform. Through the enactment of new laws, changes are now taking place in caste relationships, land ownership, and in the structure of the joint family. These events, the consequences of which are still being worked out, will not be discussed in the present volume.

9 CHINA

C H I N A has had a culturally unified population for a longer continuous period than any other civilization of the world, although it is by no means the oldest. China's civilization took shape much later than those of the Indus Valley, the Near East, or Egypt. China's culture, however, became integrated early and, unlike the other great early cultures, has never collapsed, but has continued its development with varying degrees of effectiveness ever since. Contacts with other cultures have been numerous. The Chinese have been conquered and ruled by several foreign dynasties, but have always managed to impose their own culture on their barbarian conquerors and eventually to absorb them and re-establish their own line. They were the first civilization to evolve a really workable and stable government which could handle a large population made up of both city and rural areas, and they have never been truly overthrown.

According to the Chinese historian, Mencius, Chinese history moves in 500-year repetitive cycles. The pattern has always been: domination by a foreign conqueror; absorption of the conqueror; a period of confusion; and finally, when the Chinese are once more reorganized under a Chinese dynasty, a period of aggressive world policy and conquest. If history repeats itself, China should be able to dispose of the Russians and become a world power in its own right within another couple of hundred years. The idea that the Chinese are a simple, friendly, nonwarlike people is far from the truth. China has been a world power during several periods of her history and has spread her conquests to an amazing distance.

The earliest Chinese date which can be assigned with any probability is 2250 B.C., based on an astronomical reference in the *Book of History*. However, development was rapid, and, by the beginning of the Shang Dynasty, approximately 1750 B.C., China had drawn abreast of the Western civilizations. Since that time it has maintained an enviably high level of culture, and a continuity of tradition unequaled elsewhere.

Several factors contributed to this. Chinese crops and cultivation methods were probably the best in the world prior to the introduction of modern scientific agriculture. They made possible the support of a population as dense as that of Egypt or Mesopotamia over a vastly larger area. The Chinese, from very early times, concerned themselves with the practice and theory of government, and well before the beginning of the Christian era had developed techniques for recruiting superior minds into the government service. Wicked men, and equally wicked women, have ruled in China, but few fools have held power, and these only briefly. Thanks to techniques of training and selection, the Chinese administrative system during the last two thousand years has been able to combine the advantages of the British government service with a broad utilization of human resources like that created by the American democratic system. Lastly, the development at an exceedingly early time of a system of writing, which was divorced from spoken language, made it possible to incorporate into a single state and cultural tradition groups speaking many different dialects. It also made available to the administrator the experience of past rulers in a way impossible in the West, because of the frequent language changes which have taken place in the history of every European state.

In sharp contrast with the Indians, the Chinese have always been historically minded, and the amount of Chinese literature dealing with the past is enormous. Unfortunately, their desire to use past events to point a moral and their fondness for systematic organization have resulted in the frequent rewriting of the earlier records. Thus, the *Bamboo Books,* which give earlier accounts of the same period covered by other classics, present a much less idyllic society. However, much of the cultural information presented incidentally in all of these writings undoubtedly has a sound factual basis.

The earliest Neolithic phase in northern China was clearly a part of the Circumpolar co-tradition. The sites contain circular pits usually referred to as pit-houses. These are so small that they are more likely to have been underground granaries or storage rooms. If lived in at all, they probably served as cold weather dormitories. The earliest crop seems to have been a large, strong-stalked millet, *kaoliang,* like that still grown in the region. Some of the accidental impressions on pottery have been interpreted as made by rice, but, if so, the presence of this cereal in northern China by at least 2500 B.C. presents a puzzling problem. With the millet and rice (?) culture the people also kept dogs and pigs, both used for food. Before the close of this early Neolithic phase sheep and cattle also appear, but the infrequent horse bones found in sites probably indicate that the animal was hunted rather than domesticated.

There are no inscriptions from any period earlier than Shang. The *Book of Changes,* which deals with origins of things Chinese, states that before the invention of written characters records were kept and messages sent by means of knotted cords. The Peruvian use of these appliances (*quipus*) proves how effective they can be. The *Book of Changes* itself was revised and re-edited several times, so the statements contained in it must be taken with all the usual reservations. As a further complication, the scholar-philosophers, through whose hands it passed, thought in terms of a logically organized universe whose order was perceived by the semidivine rulers of the earliest times. Only when these rulers had established the observances necessary to strengthen and maintain the cosmic order did they turn their gifts to the invention of utilitarian appliances.

The historic period begins with the Shang Dynasty (1766-1122 B.C.). Although frequently mentioned in the classical literature, this dynasty was considered mythical until a few years ago, when bones scratched with very archaic characters came to light in the region about the great bend of the Hwang Ho. Since then royal tombs of the dynasty have been systematically excavated, and most of the Shang emperors listed in the *Book of History* have been identified in contemporary inscriptions. The combination of excavated objects, contemporary inscriptions, and traditional literature makes it possible to get a better picture of the conditions during this dynasty than we have for many later periods. The Chou dynasty, which succeeded the Shang, has left a wealth of literary records, but no Chou site has been excavated by satisfactory modern scientific methods. Chinese antiquarians' interests have provided a market for ancient bronzes and stone carvings, and tomb robbing has been a common if disreputable occupation since at least the beginning of the Christian era. It has brought to light many wonderful works of art, but not much can be told from objects out of context. The excavation of the Shang royal tombs at An-yang still remains an isolated example of scientific work. The finds which have proved most valuable for throwing light on the daily life of the upper classes are the Shang oracle bones. The rulers of the Shang period were deeply interested in divination and practiced it according to several methods. The favorite system was scapulimancy (divination using the bone of the shoulder blade). The Shang diviners scratched questions on the bones, heated them, and interpreted the answers from the cracks which appeared. The inquiries dealt mainly with affairs of the royal palace, proper times for performing rituals, weather and crop prospects, and the probable outcome of raids.

The Shang aristocracy seems to have led a luxurious existence. Evidence of this is to be found in the royal tombs of the dynasty, which were regarded as dwellings for the dead and fitted with furnishings appropriate to a palace. In the tomb were placed weapons and armor of bronze, stone and jade carvings, and bronze ceremonial vessels which reveal a vigor and sophistication of design and a technical skill in casting which has never been surpassed.

The structure of the Shang Empire seems to have been intermediate between that of a conquest state and a federation. The various districts which composed it were politically self-contained, and there was no suggestion of anything like an imperial council or general assembly of nobles. Each district was ruled by its own hereditary noble family, who had submitted to the emperor and shared the benefits of the rites which he performed. The strength of the central power depended largely on the personality of the emperor. When the emperor was weak, the nobles made war upon each other. At all times the empire was at war with one or another of its non-Chinese neighbors. There are repeated references in the oracle bones to a tribe designated as "shepherds," who lived to the west of the Shang territory. These were regularly raided for slaves and particularly for sacrificial victims. In the lists of sacrifices one finds "shepherds" noted on a par with other domestic animals offered.

Shang culture had an unusually strong religious and magical orientation, although at the same time it was quite devoid of mysticism. Each village performed its own ceremonies related to its annual round of activities and also worshipped its own ancestors. The district nobles performed other rites for the benefit of the district. Apparently each district had a somewhat different series of secondary deities, as well as spirits of the local mountains and streams. Lastly, the emperor performed rites in honor of the highest group of deities, especially the celestial beings, thus benefiting the entire state. The rites performed by the nobles and by the emperor were rigidly formalized. There were strict regulations as to the type of sacrificial vessels to be used on each occasion and the appropriate offerings. There can be little doubt that the procedure followed in the rites was equally conventionalized.

The origins of the Shang are obscure. Apparently their ancestors came into China from the northwest by the route which conquerors have followed throughout Chinese history. Moreover, the beginning of the dynasty, approximately 1500 B.C., corresponds rather closely to the invasion of India by the Aryans and of the Near East by various steppe peoples who were also horse breeders and chariot users. The generally accepted theory is that the Shang were responsible for the introduction into China of a whole series of culture elements of Western origin, notably the cultivation of wheat and barley, the use of horses, chariot fighting, bronze casting, and writing. Wheat and barley do appear first at this period and are unquestionably of Western origin, but horses as well as cattle and sheep were already known to the Lung Shan peoples. There is no indication that the establishment of the Shang dynasty led to any great increase in animal husbandry. Moreover, they did not use milk, an incomprehensible feature if the Shang culture was derived from either of the co-traditions of the steppes.

Whatever the Shang origins may have been, the beginnings of this dynasty found northern China a region of independent tribes with varied Neolithic cultures, while its end saw the same region possessing a unified, unmistakably Chinese civilization. In many ways the Shang period foreshadowed the later course of Chinese history. It began with a foreign conquest, followed by the acculturation of the conquerors. It witnessed the elevation of writing to the position which it enjoyed in later Chinese culture and the emergence of respect for learning. It saw the formalization of religious rituals and the triumph of technique over emotions in the relation of man to the supernatural. Above all, it crystallized the pattern of assigning the most important secular and sacred duties to the same individual. The development of a literate aristocracy who were simultaneously priests, warriors, and rulers resulted in a complete and indissoluble fusion of church and state.

Moreover, the result was in no sense a theocracy. Chinese attitudes were eminently practical and made religion a supplement to administration. These patterns survived throughout Chinese history and saved the country from the struggles between priest and ruler which disrupted so many other civilizations. Even the downfall of the Shang dynasty set a pattern for propaganda which was followed by each of its successors. The Chou invaders who overthrew the dynasty depicted the last Shang emperor as a monster of vice and cruelty, and themselves as liberators sent by a benevolent supreme being to punish the Shang Dynasty for its crimes and to restore order to the commonwealth.

EARLY HISTORIC CHINA

W I T H the Chou Dynasty China emerges into the full light of history, and Chinese culture takes on most of its characteristic patterns. Many of these patterns were already in existence in Shang times, but it was during Chou that they became integrated into a coherent whole. The Chou was less a dynasty than a period. Although in the dynastic lists it is usually given as extending from roughly 1000 B.C. to 221 B.C., the temporal control of the Chou emperors came to an end about 770 B.C., when the capital was moved east to the city of Lo-yang. Even before this, the disruptive forces inevitable in any feudal system had begun to weaken the central power. The accomplishment of the Chou dynasty proper was to set up a system of thoroughly integrated social, political, and religious institutions within which culture patterns already present in China or borrowed from the barbarian cultures to the west could be developed and organized. It is difficult to tell how far the founders of the dynasty were personally responsible for reducing the pre-existing patterns to a system. The first Chou emperors were in an unusually good position to do this, once they had already had experience in integrating elements from the Hsia culture with that of the barbarians of the steppes.

The history of the Chou rulers, as recorded in the *Bamboo Books,* reveals a combination of an inflexible will toward power, worship of order, and a profound respect for the proprieties. Until the very end of their vassalage to their Shang emperors they treated these with all the out-

ward symbols of respect, while drawing more and more of
the petty states which composed the empire under their
own control. When King Wen deposed the last of the
Shang emperors and founded the Chou dynasty, he did
so with all the marks of polite regret, and proceeded at
once to put the society and state in order on the basis of
what was, on paper, or more properly bamboo, a rigid system. According to the Chinese historians, always devo-
tees of the Great Man theory, the new system involved
changes even in family organization, and it apparently did
involve a change in the rules of descent among the nobility. However, to change the family structure of any
society is a task of the first magnitude, and it seems probable that what actually happened was that the noble families who had survived from the Shang Dynasty were encouraged to alter a few of their practices in order to bring
their family system into accord with that already existing
among the Chou nobility. Since the main function of the
peasantry was paying taxes, it is highly improbable that
the new dynasty tried to modify their familial habits.

The Chou nobility were organized into joint families
much like those of the Chinese aristocracy in all later periods. The nucleus of these families was a group of males
descended from a common ancestor, sharing a common
residence and functioning as a corporation under the control of the oldest member. The joint families and the larger
name-groups to which such families belonged were strictly
exogamous. Control was strongly patriarchal. Women
born into the joint family were not regarded as actually belonging to it. They were not introduced to its ancestral
spirits, but on marriage were introduced to the ancestral
spirits of the husband and became thenceforth members of his family group. Marriage was theoretically monogamous, but when a noble bride went to her husband's
house she was usually accompanied by a younger sister and
various serving women who automatically became the
husband's concubines. The position of women was high.
Although noble women were secluded, they were not confined in harem fashion. Even at this period women frequently received a literary education, and there are many

indications that husbands frequently consulted their wives even in affairs of state.

In the organization of the Chou empire the basic relations existing between males within the family were taken as a model. The most important of these was that between father and son. This was supposed to be mirrored in the relations of the emperor to the supreme being and to his subjects. This period saw the birth of the imperial title, "Son of Heaven." The emperor stood in the relation of a son to the supreme being, while at the same time he stood in the relation of father to his subjects and was supposed to exercise toward them the twin parental functions of benevolent support and enforcement of good behavior. A second familial relationship strongly insisted upon was that created by the age differences between different generations, and between older and younger brothers. Juniors should always respect and obey their seniors. This was reflected in the attitudes and obligations of different ranks of the nobility toward each other. Lastly, and not of familial origin, was the relationship of mutual assistance and trust implied in friendships which could be used as a basis for loyalty between the feudal lord and his noble followers.

Under the Shang Dynasty there had been a steady growth of cities, and the trend continued in the Chou period. The Chou nobles were city dwellers. Towns were fortified and served as centers for administration and for the concentration and storage of the taxes paid in kind by the peasantry. They also became centers for trade and for the manufacture of articles required by court life. The feudal courts consisted of the feudal lord's family, his aristocratic followers, and his advisors and officials, not all of whom were of noble origin. They became the centers of learning and luxury, and provided a new stimulus for the development of civilization.

The highly centralized political system established by the founders of the Chou dynasty soon proved unworkable. Several causes contributed to its breakdown. The original system placed too much responsibility on the emperor, while the strict rules of succession left his personality to chance and often brought to the office weak or evil rulers. The empire was under continuous pressure from barbarian tribes on both the northwest and south. The Chou nobility became more and more a military nobility, whose only congenial activity was war. They were as willing to increase their estates at the expense of weaker neighbors as they were to protect the empire against foreign aggression. As late as 700 B.C. the Chou armies still followed the old organization of chariot-driving nobles surrounded by light-armed infantry, but the old feudal levies of untrained peasants were replaced more and more by standing armies of professional soldiers. This increased the charges upon the peasantry, who now had to support their lord's military establishments as well as paying the costs of his court. Such courts were now established in many cities, and vied with each other in luxury and ostentatious display. The border lords employed more and more foreign mercenaries, and the depredations of these poorly disciplined barbarian troops added to the earlier troubles of the common people. There were repeated peasant revolts, and one of the causes frequently cited is the destruction of crops and property during the nobles' great hunting parties. This suggests that the Chou nobles held large-scale surrounds and game drives like those of the later Mongols.

Under the stress of constant warfare the nobility increasingly delegated both education and civil administration to an emergent group of professional scholar-bureaucrats. Education, which had previously been a monopoly of the noble class, thus became proletarianized, and schools teaching all of the old noble subjects, with the possible exception of archery and charioteering, were opened in many cities. The office of political advisor to a feudal lord offered a profitable career, and commoners who had studied history and learned political skills sought the patronage of rulers and found it quite consistent with their ideas of honor to leave their native states and take service with whatever noble would pay them most liberally. The philosophers of the sixth and fifth centuries B.C., such as Confucius, Mencius, and others, were drawn from this group of scholar-bureaucrats, and in view of their background it is easy to understand the preoccupations of their philosophic systems with social and political problems.

The constant state of warfare and uncertainty, and the incorporation of more and more barbarians into Chinese society, seems to have weakened belief in the efficacy of the old formal sacrificial rites. Since the performance of these rites was, in theory at least, the main function of the emperor, this also served to weaken the central power. By 700 B.C. the empire had broken down into fourteen contending states, and the role of the Chou emperor had become somewhat like that of the Holy Roman emperor in medieval Europe. It carried great prestige but little actual power or emolument. The emperor's political control was limited to the single state, a relatively small one, of which he was traditional ruler, and his revenues to the taxes paid by its peasantry.

In approximately the fourth century B.C. a new feature appeared. Prior to this time the strength of the Chinese armies had lain in their armored chariots. Cavalry now began to be used by the northwestern states. It seems probable that this period marked the development, presumably in the steppes, of the equipment and tactics necessary for effective mounted warfare. The combination of the tree saddle, stirrups, the composite bow, and drilled horsemen able to charge in line as well as to maneuver, was an innovation in warfare as revolutionary as the development of the tank or airplane in later times. It changed the balance of power along the entire frontier where China met the steppes.

With the coming of the barbarian mercenaries Chinese warfare took on a new and more sanguinary aspect. The civilian population of the fortified cities, which formed the strong point of the feudal defense, was discouraged from determined resistance by systematic massacre inflicted on towns which were captured after stubborn defense. Also, captured soldiers, who in earlier days had usually been set free at the end of a campaign with nothing more serious than some mark of humiliation such as a clipped ear, were now systematically executed in order to weaken the trained manpower at the disposal of the enemy. Meticulous records were kept of the number of heads taken, and it is said that after the capture of the city of Ch'angping 400,000 persons were beheaded. Even allowing for the exaggeration usual to Oriental scribes, the continuing loss of life must have seriously depleted the population and left room for a strong influx of immigrants from the neighboring barbarians. Since the Chinese economy depended heavily upon the presence of a large tax-paying peasant population, it is quite possible that this immigration was encouraged by the feudal rulers. The invaders readily became acculturated, and the influx seems to have had little effect upon the Chinese civilization.

In spite of, or perhaps because of, the ills from which the nation suffered, the time immediately preceding the period of the Warring States was one of extraordinary intellectual activity. The rise of private schools, which functioned side by side with those supported by the state and eventually took over most of their functions, and the admission of commoners to these, provided what was unquestionably the largest group of educated intellectuals which existed anywhere in the ancient world. These intellectuals were all confronted by the very practical problem of finding some way in which to alleviate the sufferings, obviously due to governmental mismanagement, which were making life unbearable. Various philosophers found various answers. Among the resulting systems those founded by K'ung Tzu (Confucius), Lao Tzu, and Mo Tzu were the most important. The first two were able to exert a profound influence on Chinese culture, and the Confucian school in particular, thanks to official support, was directly responsible for the development of numerous governmental patterns. It is difficult for a European scholar who is unable to read Chinese characters to get a clear picture of these philosophies. The telegraphic brevity of Chinese sentences is not correlated with an equal clarity, and one finds numerous differences in the interpretations which Chinese scholars themselves give to the earlier texts.

Confucius was of northern Chinese origin, and the seat of the school which he originated was in the state of Lu, still ruled in his time by dukes of the Chou family. Confucius himself was the greatest scholar of his day, with a deep interest in historical precedents and a belief that the tightly organized state set up by the first Chou emperor had been a golden age. He revised and idealized the records from this period, putting them in the form in which they still survive. His teaching was ethical in intent but was wholly without supernaturalism. It is difficult to translate his concepts into Western terms, but he believed that there was a natural sympathy existing between persons. This found its strongest expression within the family circle, but ideally was extended until it enveloped the whole of mankind. In order to put this sympathy into operation it was necessary to have a correct definition of what he called "names." In the Confucian philosophy this term had a significance reminiscent of the Platonic absolutes. The "names" were regarded as realities existing in the world of ideas.

In practice, Confucius was a precisionist and expended most of his energy in clarifying the various social roles. Like other scholar-administrators of the time, he was peripatetic, going from one court to another in search of a patron who would be willing to put his theories into practice. Eventually Confucius was appointed to a minor governmental post in the state of Lu. It is told of him that in his later days at the court of Lu he accompanied his ruler on a tour and remarked that the order of progress illustrated the state of wordly affairs: pride and vice (i.e., the ruler and his favorite concubine) leading the procession, and wisdom and virtue (i.e., Confucius) following far behind.

The Confucian school underwent further development at the hands of two disciples, Mencius and Hsün Tzu, who agreed on the initial concept of "names," but differed diametrically on the question of whether morality was in conformity with nature and consequently on the efficacy of "sympathy" as the motivating force in good behavior. Mencius believed in the inherent goodness of hu-

man nature. According to him the individual, if not interfered with, would turn toward good as automatically as
water runs downhill. His followers therefore objected
strongly to all sorts of social compulsion. Hsün Tzu, on
the other hand, held that human nature was intrinsically
neither good nor bad. He believed that righteousness was
a habit to be acquired only through the repetition of good
behavior. He might be thus classed as the earliest representative of the Learning Theory school of personality psychology. Consistent with this view, he also questioned the
authority of the remote past and thought of the development of society as a progressive process which could be
best understood and guided by contemporary sages.

After various vicissitudes the Confucian philosophy
was ostensibly accepted in the later Han dynasty as a guide
to the organization of the empire. There is a tradition,
probably apocryphal, that one of the Han emperors, who
found his rule increasingly disturbed by the resurgent
power of the old feudal nobility, called in a Confucian
scholar and asked him how this group could be rendered
harmless. The scholar is said to have replied: "Allow them
to distribute their estates equally among their sons." The
emperor was so much struck by the wisdom of this advice
that he established Confucianism as the official philosophy
of the realm.

Even if this story were true, neither a single episode
nor even official favor can explain the way in which Confucian philosophy has been able to dominate Chinese
thought for nearly two thousand years. The clue probably
lies in that characteristic of Chinese character which
Francis Hsu has termed "situation oriented." According to
this penetrating analysis, the average Chinese is anxious
to understand many situations in which he finds himself
and to adapt his behavior to them. His desire to adjust
successfully is given precedence over any abstract value
system. The Confucian philosophy, with its clear definition
of statuses and roles, clarifies the social situations which
play a predominant part in any individual's life and provides him with ready-made behavior patterns.

The philosophy of Lao Tzu presents a contrast to

that of Confucius at practically every point. Where the Confucian school concentrates on human relations and pays tribute to the supernatural only in its insistence on the proper performance of rites, the school of Lao Tzu ignores human relations and concentrates instead on the understanding of the universe, including aspects of it which we would consider supernatural. Where the Confucian school seeks for an ever clearer definition of concepts, and in this search lays heavy emphasis on scholarship and particularly on the study of history, the school of Lao Tzu turns to meditation and introspection and is content to leave its fundamental concepts vague and to seek the answer to problems in inspiration rather than precedent.

It is an interesting fact that this school, commonly called Taoism, originated in southern China and was obviously an attempt to organize attitudes and beliefs already long established in that region. Taoism obviously developed from the old nature worship and disorganized supernaturalism which preceded the emergence of a politically unified China. Folk elements entered into it so strongly that we do not even know whether or not Lao Tzu was a real individual. There are a large number of Taoist deities, some of them supernatural beings, such as the king of heaven and the goddess of mercy. This goddess, an ancient deity called Hsi Wang Mu, has been equated with one of the Buddhist saints and also, in some localities which have become Christian, with the Virgin Mary. Other Taoist deities are early heroes of legends. The Taoist god of war is a famous general who died in the third century. It is interesting to speculate whether Taoist mysticism and that of India may not go back to some component of the old Southeast Asian co-tradition, since this exerted an influence on both religions.

The fundamental concept in the philosophical system of Lao Tzu was that of a universe in a constant state of change and reorganization within the force field created by two opposing principles, the *Yin* (female) and the *Yang* (male). The Chinese sage did not conceive of these principles as in conflict. They were in balance like the opposite poles of a single magnet. Both forces were completely impersonal and amoral. The idea of the universe as a field of battle between Ormuz and Ahriman or between the Christian God and the Devil, with every individual required to pick his side and take active part, was totally alien to the Taoist philosophy. The Yin and Yang were conceived as being normally in a state of balance which might be temporarily disturbed. The wise man followed the middle way, the Tao, which was revealed to the individual as a result of meditation, especially in the presence of nature uninfluenced by human activity. The typical Chinese landscape, with mountains, a waterfall, great trees, and, somewhere in the foreground, a tiny human figure seated in meditation, was the perfect expression of this Taoist concept. In the presence of nature and its sublime forces man was small indeed, and his wise course was to gain an understanding of these forces so as to avoid interfering with them.

As a logical development of its theories, Taoism turned its back on political activities and advised the individual to find his safety and satisfaction in a meditative return to nature and to abstain from action lest he disturb the Yin-Yang balance. The original Taoist doctrine did not concern itself with social relations, but, in a setting where philosophical thought always eventually turned to problems of government, the Taoists were forced to develop their own theories in this field. The Taoist attitudes toward nature provided the basis for a concept of the natural and therefore happy man. He had big bones, strong muscles and an empty head, qualities to be desired in the subjects of an autocratic state. The duty of the ruler was to see that his subjects were well fed, steadily worked, and maintained in a state of contented apathy. Both for his own good and that of the peasants themselves, the ruler should make no attempt to teach or awaken them. Above all, the governed should be denied any part in or understanding of the processes of government. These tenets naturally aroused strong opposition in the Confucian school.

The school of Mo Tzu dates from the same time as

that of Confucius. Its fundamental principle was that of sympathy, but it ignored the gradations of sympathy based on degrees of nearness which Confucianism insisted on so strongly, and declared that the individual's love should be extended equally to all mankind. In contrast with the other two schools, it was definitely theistic and, indeed, almost monotheistic. The world was not governed by fate but by the conscious will of a supreme being. The existence of other supernatural beings was recognized, but they occupied minor positions. Great stress was laid on the reality of individual survival after death. The love for mankind which the school taught was not regarded as either instinctive or learned but as a religious duty. The attitudes of the school's members were strongly ascetic, and its adherents were expected to sacrifice all comforts and joy to their service to humanity. At the same time they combined a practical attitude with their asceticism and judged the value of various acts on the basis of their utility. For this reason they condemned the teaching of the arts, especially music. The philosophers of this school were noted as fearless and devoted advisors to princes. In accordance with their doctrines, they were willing to sacrifice themselves for the good of the community. Pacifism was an outstanding feature of their doctrine, but they were realistic enough to distinguish between wars of aggression and those waged in self-defense.

Certain parallels can be drawn between the teachings of this school and that of the Quakers. Although the followers of Mo Tzu relied on strict logic and lacked the ecstatic quality which characterized early Quakerism, both were in agreement on the direct relations between man and the deity, and on the obligation of the individual to give his whole energies to the betterment of mankind, while retaining a realistic attitude. In the pacifism of both one can see natural reactions to the sufferings of populations which had been subjected to generations of war.

The three philosophies just described coexisted for centuries and exerted considerable effect, not only on Chinese institutions but also on each other. A number of minor philosophies were born from their interaction. The only one of these which exercised significant influence on the development of Chinese culture was the school of the Legalists. This had as its main aim the development of effective patterns for state administration. Its concepts were worked out most completely in the organization of the state of Ch'in, which, a few centuries later, stepped forward to unite a China enfeebled by the endless wars of a decadent feudalism. The fundamental idea of the Legalists was that of government by law, with human factors eliminated as completely as possible. They devoted their attention to the development of statute law, and to defining its meaning so accurately that individual opinion could not intrude into its administration. They were probably the first group anywhere in the world to insist on the equality of all members of the state before the law. In view of the immunity of the nobles from the Chou imperial code, this was a revolutionary development. The cold impersonality of this school succeeded in welding the state of Ch'in into a formidable weapon and in holding it together during the period of conquest, but understandably, under the new dynasty, it disappeared as a school although its principles remained alive under a veneer of Confucianism. It is interesting to note that during the Chinese republic this philosophy, largely because of its similarity to European concepts of jurisprudence, enjoyed a brief revival.

All the speculations of the philosophers could not arrest the increasing disorder of the closing centuries of Chou feudalism. The sanguinary wars which followed the introduction of cavalry greatly reduced the population, and the systematic killing of prisoners of war resulted in the elimination of a large part of the feudal nobility. The state of Ch'in, lying north of the center course of the Yellow River, was saved from these evils. It was protected from most attacks by a mountain range, and had a series of rulers and councilors who were statesmen of outstanding ability. Although their ultimate aim was the conquest of China, they avoided wars of doubtful outcome and followed a consistent policy aimed at strengthening the state by exploiting its rich natural resources, including its inhabitants. The rulers' advisors were largely Legalists, and under their direction Ch'in was changed from a feudal state of the usual Chinese sort to a totalitarian conquest-oriented nation of surprisingly modern type.

The army occupied a favored position. Every man was liable to lifelong military service, and all officials were also army officers. The leaders of successful campaigns and soldiers of outstanding courage were highly rewarded, while failure or cowardice were usually punished by death. The Legalists saw to it that these regulations were enforced with the greatest severity. The main weakness of the system proved to be that it provided no rewards, only punishments, for the peasantry. Such a system could enforce obedience, but not loyalty, and it could not arouse devotion. When the state of Ch'in, under its greatest ruler, known to history as Shih Huang Ti, finally conquered the whole of China, its control was short-lived.

Shih Huang Ti combined the administrative and organizing ability of an Augustus Caesar with the megalomania of a Hitler. In the long run, the consolidation of China which he accomplished and the models which he set for later imperial rule were a distinct gain, yet his name is still execrated for his excesses, and above all for his attempts to destroy the whole pattern of classical education and scholar administration. Born to the rule of Ch'in, he continued the expansion begun by his predecessors. Whenever a feudal district had been conquered, its hereditary nobility were eliminated, and it was incorporated into one of the provinces of the growing empire. At the end of his conquests there were thirty-six of these provinces, to which four more were added later. Each province, in turn, was divided into districts for administrative purposes.

At the time when Shih Huang Ti came to power, the importance of the Hsiung-nu barbarians was steadily increasing. To defend the newly acquired territory the emperor linked up the existing walls and frontier posts to form the Great Wall. It has been suggested that the Great Wall was quite as much to keep the Chinese peasants in as to keep the barbarians out. The economy of China, in this as in later times, was completely dependent upon a large agrarian population whose economic surpluses could be diverted to the support of the state. The oppression which all the peasants suffered under Shih Huang Ti must have provided a strong incentive to escape from his tax collections and labor pressgangs. Whatever the purpose of the Wall, and no matter how many earlier elements were incorporated into it, it still remains one of the greatest works erected by man and a lasting monument to the superhuman energy and organizing ability of the first authentic emperor of China.

Shih Huang Ti was far too great an egoist to found a dynasty. Men of his type can never tolerate sons who are potentially of their own stature. When he died he left a country seething with discontent, and the feeble son who tried to carry on the dynasty was eliminated in a few months. The imperial peace gave way to struggle between war lords, with mobs of starving peasants wandering from place to place and leaving disaster in their wake. Out of the chaos there finally emerged a strong ruler, whose possession of the Mandate of Heaven was shown by his ability to restore peace and order. This man, Liu Pang, followed the pattern of later war lords, if he did not create it. He was an illiterate peasant who began his career as a brigand, then made himself Duke of P'ei and finally Emperor. His accession marked the beginning of the Han dynasty in which China became, for the first time, a power in world affairs.

LATE DYNASTIC CHINA

FOR two thousand years the Chinese have been the largest politically and culturally unified group in the world. The census made in 100 A.D., during the later Han period, reported a population of 60 million and it should be noted that Chinese censuses are always underestimated, because the peasant quite normally concludes that any official who asks questions is getting statistics for tax purposes and consequently tells as little as possible.

For the next thousand years the population of China was almost static, indicating that it had developed to the limit set by the combined resources and technology at this period. From 1100 A.D. to the census of 1736 the population slowly increased. In 1736 it was 125 million. Between 1736 and 1881 it advanced suddenly to 380 million and has been climbing steadily ever since.

At this particular time in history there was a sudden increase in population throughout the Old World. The reason is not clearly understood. In Europe the increase has been attributed to the beginning of mechanization and opening of colonial markets, but the same phenomenon took place in China and India, which were untouched by the industrial revolution at this time. In any case, China has had for a very long time a tremendous population which was much more united culturally than any other population in the world. Even in times of collapse of the central power, when there was confusion and civil war, the Chinese have maintained their tradition of unity and looked upon such times as mere interludes.

This huge population has been of great advantage to China, for it has made the country really invulnerable. The conqueror who established himself over this huge, cuturally united, civilized population inevitably found himself swamped, acculturated, and ultimately absorbed. However, such a huge population has also set significant social and governmental problems, problems which we in the West have faced for some time but which we are only beginning to solve. Big populations are a fairly new development in world history. Most of the continental nations, up until the eighteenth century, were under 25 million, and Great Britain never exceeded 10 million. The necessity for handling hundreds of millions of people under a unified central government poses new problems for which adequate techniques have not yet been developed.

To understand the background of Chinese political organization, it is necessary to take a look at the general social patterns of the country. With the exception of the northeast part of the country, where families live on large isolated farms, much like the American farm pattern, the single independent homestead is rare in China. The real unit is the village, a collection of families living close together, frequently with a mud wall surrounding the settlement as a protection against wandering bandits. Beyond the villages are a series of cities, which function mainly as administrative centers and as dwelling places for the wealthy part of the population (which in Old China was almost entirely the official class) and for the service occupations, such as the manufacture of luxury objects.

The functioning of the economy differed in certain respects from those of India and the West. There is no suggestion of the Indian caste system, with its hereditary occupational groups. Nor, except within narrow limits, was there the Western pattern of concentrating manufacturing in the cities. There was instead local concentration of particular industries; certain villages in one district would manufacture one item and exchange it for the products of other villages. These exchanges were carried on in market towns, which were intermediate in size between the villages and the cities. The peasants came into the market towns and sold and exchanged their goods for raw materials which they needed, or they came for finished products. This organization of local specialties, by which one small district made all the baskets of a particular type that were used all over China, another concentrating on a special kind of iron too, etc., reflects the pattern of a unified country with strong central control which made safe trade possible. Even in times of confusion, when it did not operate properly, this organization was retained in the minds of the populace as the ideal pattern.

The bulk of the population were free landholders living in villages. There are two great dividing lines in Chinese society: the line between the man who owns land, even if it is only a minute patch, and the man who does not. The landowner is like the captain of a boat: whether it is a battleship or a barge, he is still the captain and distinct from a mere sailor; similarly, the Chinese peasant with his patch of land feels superior to a landless man.

The other dividing line falls between the peasant and arti-
san groups, who work with their hands, and the scholar
and official group.

Since the Chinese peasants do not practice primogeniture but divide their estates evenly among their sons,
there is a constant fragmentation of holdings. This means
that a section of the peasant population is progressively
squeezed off the land and forced to become either city
proletariat or, in recent times, rickshaw boys. China,
whenever the controls of famine or war are not operating,
rapidly builds a larger population than can be maintained
at the level of hand industries and uses this proletariat for
the heaviest and most unskilled labor. It is because of this
constant supply of labor, which will work for anything it
can get in order to live, that slavery has never taken hold
in China. In the large wealthy households there are
women servants who have been bought as children and
might be regarded as slaves, but they are actually brought
up as members of the family, and their master has a definite obligation to find husbands for them when they are of
age. There were slaves in the Imperial Palace, but there
was nothing like the mass slavery of the sort which flourished in the West. That could not develop because it was
cheaper to use the proletariat, just as it was only after the
rise of the machine that our consciences began to trouble
us about slavery. With the machine it was obviously
cheaper to hire a man, treating his labor as a commodity
and throwing him out when he became old or disabled,
than to own him as a slave and be obliged to take care of
him.

One of the most significant things about Chinese society is that there is a high degree of vertical mobility, not
only in theory but in fact, as much as there is in England,
for example, where in spite of strong class distinctions it is
possible for a commoner to make a fortune and buy his
way to knighthood. In China there is a steady turnover in
the population, with families of peasant ancestry gradually
rising into the scholar and official class and then dropping
out again. Until recent times this worked as follows. The
entree to Chinese officialdom was through education and

the ability to pass a series of competitive examinations.

The scholar held a high position in China, the poorest scholar, a village school teacher, for example, taking social precedence over a rich merchant who was illiterate. Therefore, any family who could afford to do so educated its sons in the hope that they might be able to pass the official examinations. These examinations were one of the few things in early China which were kept reasonably free from graft, because they were regarded as the core of the system. It is true that in the later days of the Manchu dynasty and during some other dynasties also, it was possible to buy lower military degrees which were correlated with academic degrees. The Chinese themselves had a term for it: "a degree by the back door." However, an individual with a back-door degree never achieved an official position in the government.

The examinations were first introduced under the Han dynasty, roughly from 200 B.C. to 200 A.D. There was at this time considerable friction between the emperior and the scholar groups, and it is said that the Han emperor who organized the examination declared: "Now I have the scholars fast in my net." However, it proved to be the scholars who had caught the emperor, for the Chinese government was dominated by the scholar class from that time until fairly recently. The examinations assumed their final form under the T'ang dynasty, between 700 and 900 A.D. They usually consisted of two essays and a poem of twelve lines of five characters each, all on a subject assigned at the last minute. This pattern continued with little change in either form or subject matter until 1912, when the so-called Republican Revolution occurred in China.

It was essential that a candidate for any appointive post pass at least the first examination. Usually two degrees were required. There were four examinations in all, but few were able to achieve this highest degree. Those who did so were taken care of, even if they could not be assigned to an immediate post. They were pensioned and held in reserve until a post became vacant. All the administrative officials above the village level were appointed, the appointees being taken from the lists of those who had passed the examinations. The village had a highly democratic type of government run by a village council, comparable to a New England town meeting. It operated with great effectiveness, for the council was a group of men who were family heads and whose opinions carried authority in the village. However, above the level of the village council, government was from above downward.

The successful candidates were usually given jobs in a part of China as remote as possible from their homes. This was done because, as soon as it was known that a member of the Tsu had a government post, everyone who had a kin claim would be around looking for help or minor jobs. The only way to avoid this horde of hungry relatives was to move out of reach. In the old days, when traveling was difficult, an official who was shifted to a distant province left his relatives safely behind. However, with the rise of the motor bus and other handy means of transportation, a flock of poor relations would be sitting on his doorstep by the time a new provincial governor arrived at his post, hoping to make use of the pattern of family loyalty and family obligations for all sorts of graft and patronage.

The examinations covered a broad general field and were designed to demonstrate the scholar's intelligence and ability. The assumption was that a man who was intelligent enough to pass the examinations could soon acquire the special skills needed for a particular job. This is in direct opposition to the American belief that, if a man knows the skills needed in his job, nothing else matters, and to our idea of a politician as an individual who is, not only in his general interest but in his general abilities, as near the common man as possible. The Chinese idea was to devote as much ingenuity as possible to finding a really superior man for legislative and administrative jobs; by superior they meant a man who was honest, disinterested, and devoted to the public good. The rewards were high, unlike the American system where a trained man can make much more money on the outside than he can in a government job, unless he goes in for graft on the side.

The Chinese system was very like that of the British Colonial Service which has been, until recent times, one of the most effective administrative groups in the world. Here too the civil service examinations were directed mainly toward discovering cultured men of high intelligence, and questions varied all the way from one on the book-collecting tastes of Boccaccio to the reading of a weather chart. The Chinese official was a similarly carefully selected man and a man of high I.Q. Any European official who had to deal with the Chinese government in the days when the Manchu dynasty was strong was well aware of the high quality and ability of these men. Occasionally the system might miscarry as, for instance, when a Mandarin of the fourth rank who had never been on the water was appointed to command the Chinese fleet in the first Sino-Japanese war. Naturally the Chinese fleet was rapidly eliminated. The Mandarin followed the best scholarly tradition by writing an excellent literary ode on the subject, transmitting it to the emperor, and then committing suicide. But apart from such emergency situations, the method worked effectively.

Six or seven thousand students would compete in the first examination. From these perhaps less than ten per cent would be chosen. These would then take another competitive examination, and so forth, until not more than one per cent, say sixty out of six thousand, would be given the first degree. Those who passed could go to the prefectural cities and enter universities to prepare for the second examination. A man who had passed the first degree had nothing to worry about. His financial security was assured, for if his family could not help him for further study, the community would pay his expenses on the chance of his passing the second degree and getting a government post. The Chinese have always been gamblers, and they were willing to take the chance of getting a friend in the government who could help the community.

Passing the first degree was a great event. The name of the successful candidate was inscribed on the ancestral tablets of his family. Before the arrival of the telegraph in China there used to be a special group of men who made their living by acting as messengers for such news. They would wait outside the examination rooms until the list of the winning candidates was posted, then ride off to announce the good news to the families in remote villages. The families, filled with good feeling at such times, rewarded the messengers liberally.

The second examination was held in the provincial capital, with examiners appointed by the emperor. The procedure was similar to that of the first examination. The successful candidates were decorated with a collar and a gold flower. The winners then went to the capital, Peking in the old days, for examinations in the third degree. The winners remained to take a fourth examination given, and corrected in red ink, by the emperor himself. The winners of the highest degree were divided into four classes. One group was pensioned and kept in reserve to fill important vacancies. A second group became members of the inner council. A third group was appointed to positions in government bureaus, and a fourth group was sent out as provincial rulers.

Needless to say, the last posts were the ones most sought after, because the ruler was in a position to cut in on the highly organized graft which was an integral part of the Chinese governing system. Since there were not enough posts to go around, getting an appointment, even after passing the final examination, required a combination of skill and influence. The Chinese official who had gone through this process was exceedingly intelligent, and as long as government in China was actually left to this honestly recruited bureaucracy of scholars everything went exceedingly well. The weak spot in the system was that there was no equally rigid arrangement for recruiting emperors. The Chinese did not follow the patterns of primogeniture, although there was a tendency to it in the imperial line. In general, the emperor designated his heir from among his sons. Since the emperor was polygynous and his wives were chosen from various important Chinese families, the scheming and intrigue which this system occasioned can be imagined. When the heir was appointed, his mother worked on him to get appointments for all the members of the family. The sign of impending breakdown of a dynasty was always that the administration began to pass out of the hands of the real scholars recruited by the examinations and into the hands of palace favorites.

The palace eunuchs played a deadly part in the breakdown of Chinese dynasties. The eunuchs in China differed decidedly from those in Islamic countries, where they were usually slaves. In China they were volunteers, in many cases middle-aged men who had already fulfilled their obligations to the clan by marrying and producing sons. They would voluntarily undergo this operation and go into the palace service, where it was possible to rise to a high position. But the eunuchs, in spite of their emasculated condition, had families on the outside, and thus promoted the old Chinese administrative conflict of family claims operating against the national claims. Needless to say, the individuals who abandoned their families to enter palace service on these terms were either men who had been maladjusted or unsuccessful in ordinary life, or those who had such an overweening desire for power that they were willing to make any sacrifice to obtain it. The result was that they were a dangerous group. When the eunuchs became powerful enough in palace administration so that they held administrative posts and brought in their relatives, a dynasty was on the way out.

The weakness of this system was at the top, but as long as the rulers were good, it functioned effectively and made it possible for China to build up and constantly recruit a highly intelligent official class, who were united in education and cultural background. It was, as a matter of fact, the best system for maintaining an aristocracy which has so far been developed. The problem of recruiting really efficient administrators is one of the most exigent problems facing modern nations, and it is also one which we have handled very badly.

The further weaknesses in the Chinese government were the universality of graft and the handling of crime. Chinese graft cannot be judged by Western standards. The Chinese governor was paid a small salary and was expected to take graft. How much he received in this way was rigidly fixed by custom and became a predictable overhead for those who had to deal with him. It was what the old Tammany Hall leaders in New York used to call "honest graft." If the governor of a city squeezed too much, the merchants and craftsmen would send a protest to the central government. A board of examiners then arrived unannounced, sealed the accounts, arrested the officials, and went into the case. If it was shown that the official had been grafting out of reason, action was swift. Instead of letting the case drag on for ten years and then fining him three per cent of his known take, in American fashion, the official was executed. This provided a considerable deterrent to excess.

The Chinese handling of crime, while bad by our standards, was harder on the criminals than on the public, which cannot always be said of our practices. Punishment was meted out swiftly, and there were many ingenious forms of execution. The criminal, however, had little right of appeal. Witnesses who had no active part in the crime were tortured on the principle that a more complete account of the circumstances could be obtained in this way. This, of course, made any witness flee the scene of crime with swiftness, and evidence was very difficult to obtain. If the person charged with an offense was an official, and his crime was not flagrant enough for execution, he would be sent to the capital to await trial. Here he would be kept for months or years, with everyone around him extracting bribes until he was finally milked dry. This, by the way, was a conscious technique for concentrating wealth for the use of the dominating group. The pattern was to let the minor officials graft all they wished and then pick them when they were ripe. It was a method coming into usage in Nazi Germany, and one which is likely to appear wherever there are dictatorships.

China is unique among the great civilizations in that at no time in its long history has it produced a strong priestly group. To be sure, in the early times of Shang, Chou, and Han, the emperor was also a priest who made the sacrifices to heaven on behalf of the entire kingdom, but the religious functions of the rulers have always been secondary to the business of governing, or at least of providing the sanctions for government, the actual procedure being in the hands of experts, the trained bureaucracy. China has never, at any stage, had anything corresponding to the great temple establishments which dominated the intellectual and economic life of such civilizations as Egypt, Mesopotamia, and to a lesser extent, India.

The most significant element in Chinese religion was ancestor worship. Any religion tends to be a projection of those values and interests which the society considers most important. The two things which were most important in Chinese daily life were the patterns of family organization and the continuity of family. Next in importance were the patterns of politeness, the rules for which were provided at great length in the classics. These two dominant interests were reflected very strongly in Chinese religion. The Chinese, no matter to what creed they gave official allegiance, were always fundamentally ancestor worshippers. The Chinese attitudes toward religion are a mixture of superstition and practicality. The folklore abounds in tales of demons and ghosts.

Although there were some mystics during the early periods of developing Chinese philosophy, the general approach of the Chinese is a thoroughly practical one. The Chinese have always been tolerant of various religions and willing to worship anywhere it will do most good. They never persecuted on religious grounds, and there have been few Chinese martyrs. Such persecutions as there were, notably those of the Buddhists, sprang less from religious causes than from the fear of having the Buddhist church continue to siphon off the wealth of the land. The Chinese are quite ready to switch from one deity to another if it seems advantageous to do so. The principal reason that Christianity has never taken hold in China, aside from its being the religion of a foreign power which is felt to be a threat to Chinese integrity, has been that the Christian missionaries objected to ancestor worship.

A wealthy Chinese will frequently have on one side

of his funeral procession a group of Buddhist monks chanting from the Buddhist scripture. On the other side a group of Taoist priests will recite the proper spells to scare away demons and burn paper money to pay off the beggar ghosts. It is believed that these ghosts attend funerals and may cause trouble for the new arrival in the spirit world unless they are placated.

The most significant contribution which China has made to world culture is its importance as a center for the development and diffusion of civilization. It maintained great city populations when the rest of the world was living in small villages. It met most of the problems of government which confront a huge modern state and found working solutions for them, even to the proposition of how to deal with a small ruling minority. China not only affected all the civilizations of the East, providing a center from which the neighboring cultures were constantly reinforced, but it also influenced Europe. The situation of China with regard to neighboring cultures was much as though the Roman Empire, with its imperial institutions, had endured for three thousand years instead of five hundred, influencing all the barbarians within radius.

China at various times in her history has been one of the richest and most powerful countries in the world. During the seventeenth and eighteenth centuries, the period of European flowering, China was incomparably richer, and by most standards, more civilized than Europe. Europeans traded extensively with China, bringing back fine silks and porcelains which gave the name "china" to all English tableware. In the early 1700's things Chinese introduced a new style and enjoyed a great vogue in Europe. Wallpapers, cabinets, furniture, and paintings done in this manner were called Chinoiserie. French nobles built Chinese summer houses in their gardens. Many French Jesuits were sent to China with the hope of converting the Emperor Ch'ien Lung to the faith. They were well received at court, but the emperor was more interested in the scientific, mathematical, and military contributions which the Jesuitical scholars were able to furnish than in their religious offerings. The French Jesuits, however, studied Chinese philosophy and classics. There is good reason to believe that many of the ideas of the period of enlightenment that formed the background of the French revolution actually percolated into French thinking from Chinese sources. The belief that, while the ruled owed allegiance to the ruler, the ruler in turn had an obligation to protect the welfare of his subjects, and that the subjects had the right to revolt if he failed in this obligation, is straight Confucianism. It is difficult to prove at which point this idea came into the European thought stream, but we do know that it makes its first appearance at a time when there was a burst of interest in Chinese art and Chinese philosophy. From what we know of the mechanics of diffusion, we can at least speculate that China was its source.

It is also interesting to note that in the writings of Rousseau, who was brought up by Jesuits at a time when the order was permeated with Chinese thought, the concept of the natural man is highly reminiscent of the ideal of Taoist philosophy. However, the natural man of the Taoists, based on realistic observation of the oriental peasantry, differs from that of Rousseau, who endowed his mythical man with infallible instincts and a superior understanding of moral values.

China at the present time is in a state of confusion and domination. It will probably take them about a hundred years to throw off the Russian yoke and refocus their energies, but they have always in the past been able to absorb or drive out their conquerors. It is improbable that the Chinese will ever become thoroughly converted to Marxism. They have been civilized for too long to be able to embrace any political ideology with the religious fervor with which the Russians took to Communism. The Chinese psychology is that of the wise old gentleman who has seen too many happenings and too many changes to get truly excited about anything.

One advantage which they have over the West is that they have been civilized so much longer. We of the West are only a race of villagers recently introduced to city living. We are still making adjustments, physically and sociologically, to living in large aggregates. The Chinese, on the other hand, have been exposed for over three thousand years to the most terrific processes of natural selection, through famine, disease, and competition of all kinds. The cold fact is that they can underlive us. This is something to be reckoned with in the future, particularly when the question arises as to what is to be done about a series of large continents occupied by a sparse white population while one large continent is occupied by a huge Mongoloid population increasing at a rapid rate. We can be reasonably sure that within another two hundred years a strong dynasty will again emerge in China, and that the Chinese will, as in the past, become an important world power.

10 JAPAN

THE origins of the Japanese population are still in dispute. We do not know when the first humans came to the islands. No prehuman remains have been found in Japan, nor even any very early human fossils, in spite of the fact that during the Pleistocene Japan was intermittently linked with the Asian mainland. Remains of Indian elephants and other tropical forms have been found. If these animals could have got across, humans certainly would have been able to do so.

The curtain does not lift archaeologically until the Neolithic. Around 1000 B.C. the northern two-thirds of Japan were occupied by a curious people called the Ainu. These were regarded for a long time as being marginal remnants of a Caucasic race. More recent studies have linked them with the Australian aborigines. They are probably an old, undifferentiated human type from eastern Asia, which, living in a cloudly northern environment, became more bleached out than their southern ancestors. They are light-skinned, with long heads, broad faces, and stubby noses. Their eyes are round rather than almond-shaped. They have liberal whiskers and much body hair. The later Japanese, being a relatively smooth-skinned and beardless people, have always referred to them as the hairy Ainu. The culture of these earliest inhabitants can be reconstructed partly from archaeology and partly from the life of the Ainu who still survive in northern Japan.

The Ainu culture was a part of the Circumpolar co-tradition. They were fishermen and food-gatherers. They lived in pit-houses and used Neolithic tools: ground stone celts, ground bone projectile points, etc., and made grit-tempered, cord-marked pottery, almost indistinguishable from that made by the American Indians of the eastern woodlands, in other words, the typical Circumpolar pattern of early cooking ware.

The social organization of the Ainu was one of small villages with an exogamous totemic group; that is, each group had a sacred animal for which they were named and toward which they held special attitudes. Their religion was a worship of nature spirits, not merely the elements such as the sun and rain, but also waterfalls, rocks, trees, and other elements of nature. Their most important cult centered around the bear, which was the one dangerous animal in this environment and also the largest meat animal. Bears were regarded as people of a different tribe who, when no outsiders were present, took off their fur overcoats and behaved like other human beings. Special rites were performed, whenever a bear was killed, to placate its spirit so that it would pass the word along to other bears that if they let themselves be killed by the Ainu they would be well treated. In fact, even today the Ainu follow the practice of capturing a bear cub which is brought up as a village pet and treated with honor and deference until it is finally sacrificed.

In contrast to the Ainu, the early inhabitants of the southern part of Japan seem to have been agriculturalists from very early times. They brought in taro and probably rice, but they also relied heavily on fishing and built their settlements in coastal areas. The archaeological evidence of their culture is scarce, for they used bamboo and wood for building and implements, made no pottery, and used little stone. Apparently this southern group were physically much like what we call proto-Malay, a stockily built, brown-skinned people with little body hair. They had broad faces, small noses, thin lips, and straight eyes.

Between these people and the Ainu, who were at approximately the same cultural level, the frontier fluctuated for some time. Both were good fighters, but the southern people, having agriculture and therefore being able to support larger populations, gradually moved northward, pushing the Ainu back. Still later, somewhere in the third of fourth centuries B.C., there was another invasion of people coming from Korea. These people brought with them bronze weapons, pottery, and well-developed agricultural techniques. In spite of their smaller numbers, they managed with their superior culture to spread out as conquerors over the southern territory occupied by the Neolithic Indonesian group, whom they organized and absorbed. The ancestors of the Ainu were pushed farther north, where they remained, making little cultural contribution aside from forcing their neighbors to the south to maintain military vigilance. Japanese culture has had a military caste from the beginning. Throughout their history the soldier class has been in control, whereas in China the soldier was of minor importance, considered an unfortunate necessity for the defense of scholars, farmers, and merchants.

The early history of Japan is difficult to reconstruct, for there has been little good archaeological work done there, and the Japanese learned to write and keep records very late. Legends and traditions were handed down by word of mouth. Written history does not begin until after 552 A.D., when there were a number of Korean scribes and Buddhist missionaries coming into Japan. Moreover, Japanese history has been exposed from its very beginning to propagandistic activities, reinforced by religious and patriotic enthusiasm, and this background is not conducive to the keeping of accurate records. In the sixth century, when the Japanese came into contact with the historically minded Chinese, they felt that they should have a history of their own, and tried to manufacture it from the various legends which had been handed down. Japan was at this time split into a great number of localized clans. Each scribe set out with the pious intention of writing a history of Japan which would show his own clan as having been the ruler of all Japan throughout its history. When the clan which was the founder of the present imperial line became dominant, it was obviously to its advantage to falsify the records and claim that it had always been on top. In the same way the ancestor goddess

of this clan, Amaterasu, the sun goddess, from whom the
present emperor claims descent, was exalted and put high
in the pantheon of gods, although there can be little doubt
that she was originally a minor deity.

The Japanese Empire came into existence when one
clan finally established dominance over the others and its
chief arrogated to himself the title of emperor. The society which emerged was a feudal system, with numerous
clan survivals. The Japanese nobles were originally clan
chiefs but, as the empire was centralized, the clan organization broke down. It was replaced by an extended family
organization, patrilineal kin groups which included a number of persons but which were smaller than the original
clans and which did not cut across class lines. Society was
organized into four classes. At the bottom were the *Eta,*
or outcastes. The origins of this group are unknown. Its
nucleus was probably the war captive slaves of the pre-
Imperial period, but it was gradually extended to include
outcastes of all sorts: criminals, and even occasional
members of the noble class who had not had the courage
to commit hara-kiri when good manners required it.

Above the Eta were the commoners, who were divided into cultivators, artisans, and merchants. The cultivators, although they were economically unfortunate in
that they tended to be taxed by everybody, nevertheless
had social prestige. Farming *per se* was an honorable
occupation. Even a *Samurai* could become a farmer without losing caste. Artisans ranked below farmers.

The merchants originally held a debased position in
Japan, but during the "sealed" period in the seventeenth
and eighteenth centuries they came into more and more
importance. During this period a strong central government developed and, in order to control the nobles, the
ruling clan insisted that every noble either should be in
the capital himself or send some responsible member of
his family there. The old feudal economy, which was a
production economy, was thus transformed into a luxury
and money economy because the nobles and their families
who were settled in the capital had to have cash in order
to buy elaborate costumes demanded for court rituals

and to keep up the establishments that their prestige required.

Throughout Japanese history there were trade guilds and unions, which operated mainly in the larger centers where the luxury manufactures were located. The Japanese city-workers who made up these guilds had never been a docile lower class, and the organized guilds often fought back if they felt the nobles had mistreated them. As there came to be more concentration of population in the cities, the merchants began to acquire wealth, while the nobles kept the prestige. Gradually the merchants began to acquire prestige also. In the last hundred years before the opening of Japan, an impoverished nobleman could recoup his fortunes by marrying the daughter of a wealthy merchant and becoming the adoptive husband in the merchant's family. When there was no son in a Japanese family, it was customary to marry a daughter to a promising young man who would be adopted as a son and given the family name. Some of the greatest of the Japanese merchant houses have been built up in this way in the last hundred years.

The nobles constituted a hereditary military class, the *Samurai*. Since a noble's sons by peasant concubines were rated as noble, this class was constantly increasing. The highest noble was the *Shogun*. This title, meaning "victorious general," was originally conferred by the emperor on the noble in charge of the northern frontier region, where the Japanese were carrying on their endless war with the Ainu. Later it became the title of the secular ruler who pre-empted the powers of the emperor. Beneath the Shogun were the great military lords, *Daimyo*, and attached to these in turn were minor chiefs and knights. The feudal system differed from the European one in that there was much more concentration of power at the top. In Europe, the knight lived by the direct exploitation of the serfs on his manor. In Japan, taxes were collected by the overlord and then disbursed down to the lower ranks of nobles. This made the nobles highly dependent upon their overlords. The eldest son succeeded his father in receiving this allowance, and, if there was no son, the family lost its right to the allowance. Expropriated Samurai formed a distinct group called *Ronin,* which meant "wave men," and served as mercenary soldiers under various lords. They were readily recruited for attacks on the mainland, and many of them served outside Japan. Thus, for centuries the royal bodyguard of the kings of Siam consisted of Japanese Ronin.

The Samurai evolved their own code of ethics, called *Bushido,* and had their special dress and social ritual. Their armor, made from plates intricately lashed together with silk cords, was effective against the Japanese sword, which was used exclusively for slashing. The swords themselves were among the finest examples of metal-working to be found anywhere in the world. They were made from alternate layers of high and low carbon steel, which were repeatedly pounded out, folded, and welded, until some of the finest blades might have as many as two thousand laminations.

The patterns of obedience and personal discipline imposed by the feudal system proved a distinct advantage when the Japanese came in contact with the West. They provided the nation with a group of patriotic leaders whom the masses had been trained to follow. The long years of feudalism made it possible for the Japanese to mobilize national energies for the assimilation of those elements of Western culture which appeared valuable to them. Needless to say, the Western military tactics were among the things most eagerly accepted.

At the top of the social scale was the imperial family, who were a social class in themselves. Originally the imperial family had been the chiefs of one of the powerful noble clans, but, as they came to be regarded as of divine origin and became sanctified, they were set apart from the other nobles. Although marriages in the imperial group were permitted only within the imperial clan, an imperial prince could take concubines from among the daughters of the nobles. The children of such unions, according to Japanese rules of patrilineal descent, were regarded as of divine origin and had full imperial powers. The imperial line thus became quite extensive. If the Shogun had trouble with the emperor, there was always a collection of imperial princes, one of whom could be substituted for the refractory ruler. The usual technique was to request the emperor to resign in favor of a young and docile prince.

The first relatively certain date in Japanese history is approximately 200 A.D., when the Japanese invaded Korea under the Empress Jingo. We have this, not from the Japanese records, for there were no scribes in Japan at this time, but from Korean and Chinese historians. She seems to have been a powerful ruler in central Japan, who succeeded in uniting enough clans to make large-scale continental expeditions possible. It was Jingo who first brought a more or less centralized Japan into contact with the Asian mainland, and prepared the way for the flow of Korean and Chinese culture into Japan.

In 284 A.D. the Emperor Ojin called in a Korean sage as his advisor. This man brought writing to Japan for the first time. However, writing did not become established in Japan until two or three centuries later. Japan took on culture and learning from the mainland and became civilized only in the seventh century A.D. The first Buddhist temples in Japan were built just before 600 A.D. under the direction of Shotoku Taishi, the Crown Prince Regent, who is known as the founder of Buddhism in Japan. In 645 the Emperor Kotoku, the great reformer, began his campaign to educate and improve his people. This reforming emperor may appear under other names, as the Japanese custom was to give a child one name at birth, another when he matured and took office, and a third, or divine name, after his death. However, under any name, this emperor recognized the inferiority of his own people as compared with the civilizations of the mainland, and set out deliberately and purposefully to do something about it. This bears the stamp of the sort of Japanese psychology which has persisted up to the present time. The Japanese have always been willing to borrow and benefit by other people's ideas and inventions, though remaining essentially Japanese in their attitudes and loyalties.

Kotoku not only tried to civilize and educate the

people but also worked to reorganize the loose tribal government by strengthening the central power, that of his own clan, of course. He also tried to give more recognition and freedom to the common people. The chief contact for this borrowing and organization was Korea. In the next century, when the Japanese were going farther afield from their own islands, they discovered that the real center of civilization was not Korea but China, and that the Korean culture which they had been imitating was a second-hand version of the Chinese. The emperor then sent commissions to China to study and report on Chinese institutions. This was a unique event in human history, the only case on record, except for a Japanese parallel many centuries later, in which a nation deliberately set out to remake its formal structure on a pattern taken from another country. The Japanese commission in China stayed for about twenty years, during which time they selected the most promising craftsmen of all kinds and encouraged them to carry their skills in lacquer work, porcelain, enamel, and so forth, over the sea to Japan. They also sent over many Korean and Chinese scholars, and even persuaded scholars and craftsmen from India and Indo-China to go to Japan.

During the seventh and eighth centuries in Japan, therefore, there was a making-over of Japanese life comparable to that which took place in the late nineteenth and early twentieth centuries. This reorganization was characterized by the same psychological needs: the feeling of intense inferiority and a desire not merely to catch up with the rest of the world but to exceed it.

The attempts to remake Japanese culture along Chinese lines failed at certain points. In China at this time the system of competitive examinations and the establishment of a professional bureaucracy was assuming the form which it was to hold for the next thousand years. Although the Japanese made some attempt to introduce this system into their own country, they were unsuccessful because the bulk of the Japanese aristocracy was still illiterate. There were few Japanese scholars, and no Japanese literature or philosophy upon which an arrangement of the Chinese sort could be established. In China the feudal aristocracy had practically destroyed themselves during the wars preceding the emergence of the Han dynasty. In Japan the feudal aristocracy was never destroyed, and the central government succeeded in bringing them under control only for short periods. The result of this situation was that the Japanese officials were appointed through favor without preliminary selection. Given the Japanese pattern of strong family and clan loyalties, there was a tendency for government offices to be hereditary, with no consideration given to honesty or ability.

The attempt to center rule in the emperor also broke down, following this period of reform. After a series of able emperors, the line began to die out. The Japanese met this in very characteristic fashion. They retained the emperor as a sort of figurehead, making him more and more sacred, while turning over the central control to first one and then another of the great Japanese clans. From the ninth through the nineteenth centuries the emperor was immobilized by his own sanctity and the taboos which surrounded him. For example, when the emperor sat in state he had to hold himself rigid, for if he turned his head he would cause an earthquake in the direction toward which he looked. His person was so sacred that his hair and nails could be cut only when he was asleep, and his personal belongings or anything he had touched were taboo. The emperor had to be fed out of new dishes at each meal, and the dishes were destroyed after he had finished with them. This was an excuse to use poor and cheap equipment in the imperial palace.

At first the secular rulers showed great respect for the emperor, but later this declined and they regarded him more and more as merely a symbol. The institution of the sacred emperor and the secular rulers was crystallized under Yorimoto, who ruled from 1185 to 1199. At this time there was a terrific war between two of the great clans, with most of the minor clans being drawn in on one side or the other. Yorimoto, whose group emerged victorious, proceeded to reorganize the empire so that he would be able to control it. Up to this time Japan had not been particularly warlike. There were the usual clan feuds, but after this reorganization, which involved also changes in the patterns of inheritances of offices and income, a definite military caste emerged, which remained dominant until the reformation of Japanese politics which took place after Commodore Perry's visit in the middle 1800's.

In 1192 Yorimoto was given the title Shogun. This was not a new title, but, after Yorimoto, it took on a new significance and came to mean military dictator. He preserved the emperor and the court at Kyoto. However, without destroying the older civil officialdom, he established a military administration under his control. He made peace with the powerful Buddhist monks and appointed military constables and tax collectors in all the provinces. Yorimoto was a political genius, and his dual form of government lasted until the middle of the nineteenth century, a period of 650 years.

In the eighteenth century the Shoguns themselves became puppets. Another ruling house seized power, and another ruling office was established. In the last two hundred years before Europeanization and reform, the governmental setup consisted of the sacred emperor in the extreme background and completely immobilized, next to him the sacred Shogun largely immobilized, and then the real rulers, who were successors of Hideyoshi, who had overthrown the Shogunate and had established what was to all intents and purposes a totalitarian state. This government gave the Japanese good training for what was to come later.

The first Europeans to reach Japan were the Portuguese. They arrived in 1542, shortly followed by the Spaniards, Dutch, and British. Some commerce was established between Japan and Europe, and the Europeans brought with them two things which profoundly influenced the culture of Japan: firearms and Christianity. Firearms gave new strength to the feudal lords, who could now become more independent of the central power. Their old simple wooden houses were replaced by stone castles in more or less European style, for they now needed strong-holds which could withstand gunfire.

The Jesuit, Francis Xavier, was the first missionary to Japan. He arrived in 1549, accompanied by some other members of the Society of Jesus. The missionaries found an immediate response among the Japanese. The doctrine and ceremonial of the Roman Catholic Church was similar to that of the Buddhist religion. The once powerful Buddhist priests were at this time losing their hold on the people, who were ready to turn to new spiritual leadership. The new faith was favored by the central government, for it facilitated trade with the West. Within a generation after Xavier's arrival there were reported to be 200 Christian churches and 150,000 Christians in Japan. The feudal lords sent embassies to Rome, and for a time it seemed that Japan might become a Christian country.

During this period three great leaders arose in Japan: Nobunaga, Hideyoshi, and Iyeyasu. Nobunaga was a feudal war lord who successfully overpowered his neighbors and made himself master of the capitol. He was followed by Hideyoshi, a man of humble rank, not even of the Samurai class, the only instance in Japan's history in which a commoner rose to the highest position open to one not of divine descent. Hideyoshi, having unified Japan under his military dictatorship, undertook foreign conquest also. He overran most of Korea, which he regarded as a gateway to China. It was Hideyoshi who announced that he was going to roll up China as one rolls up a mat. However, the Japanese were no more successful than they were recently in their attempts to conquer China. China does not roll up easily. The Japanese soldiers arrived at a time when the Ming Dynasty was in confusion and there was no strong central power. In spite of this the Chinese rallied under attack.

The Koreans also, although they had never been a particularly warlike or brilliant people, showed unexpected strength and ingenuity in combating the Japanese onslaught. They invented the first "ironclads," and a fleet of these new "turtle boats" sank the Japanese fleet and cut their supply lines. The Koreans also invented at this time the first mortar to throw an explosive shell, an improvement which had not yet come into use in Europe, although it appeared shortly thereafter. Hideyoshi's attack ground to a halt, and after his death the Koreans managed to throw off Japanese control.

This expansion to Korea was actually a diversion which took the military out of Japan and enabled the new government to seat itself more firmly. A war which arouses the patriotism of the population has long been observed to be the best way to unite a nation. This conquest, although unsuccessful in the long run, brought Japanese to the mainland. Also, considerable numbers of Ronin went south and spread through Indonesia and southeastern Asia, where they served as mercenary soldiers. These migrants were, for the most part, men of the noble class who, through poverty, disgrace, or over-adventurousness, and forfeited their connection with the noble house and were on their own. The recent Japanese expansion into Indonesia actually followed an old pattern, in which the Japanese surplus military population spilled over into the mainland territories.

Hideyoshi was followed by Iyeyasu, who had originally been his opponent, but became his chief lieutenant. Iyeyasu turned his attention to internal affairs rather than foreign conquest, and under his leadership the country was finally consolidated. He had himself appointed Shogun in 1603 and was thus in charge of the feudalized military system which had been inaugurated by Yorimoto four hundred years earlier. He set up a military capitol at Edo, the present Tokyo, away from the imperial court. Iyeyasu was succeeded by his son and grandson, and under the rule of his family Japan had peace for over two centuries.

During this time the Japanese not only abstained from foreign conquest, but shut themselves away from the outside world entirely. The Japanese rulers did not want their people to know what was going on outside the country, and, in particular, they did not want them to leave. A Japanese who left the island and returned again was put to death. The central powers instituted a complete police state, with innumerable road blocks. Passports were required of people moving from one province to another, and there were local customs charges, as in France. It was a bureaucratic arrangement very reminiscent of the Russian iron curtain.

Before this time the Japanese had always been a sea people. Within a generation after their first contact with Europeans they were building vessels which could cross the Pacific, and were trading on the west coast of America. When Japan was closed, a law was passed making it punishable by death to build ships above a certain burden. There were also regulations limiting construction so that vessels seaworthy for transoceanic shipping could not be built. All foreigners were excluded, except for a few Dutch merchants who were allowed to occupy a small island in one of the harbors. The only outside skill for which the Japanese admitted a need was that of medicine. They permitted medical students to study Dutch so that they could read Dutch medical books.

However, during the time when Japan had been open there had been a surprising amount of borrowing of European technology and ideas. The Japanese, behind their self-imposed barriers, went on perfecting many of the European forms. They developed firearms based on European models but modified in accordance with Japanese manual habits. They made elaborate armor, a modification of European plate armor, made up of lacquered metal and rawhide put together with silk lashings. Metal work was raised to a high art. Their swords would take a razor edge but would also stand heavy service. The Samurai lord would have a variety of sword fittings for his blade, some simple and refined for religious occasions, and some inlaid with gold for court ceremonials.

The Japanese have always been a beauty-loving people, with a desire for aesthetic perfection. Their art has been basically dependent on importations from abroad, mainly from China, which were then gradually transformed to satisfy the native sensitivity for harmonious proportions, decorative pattern, and humor. Thus, from the seventh through the eighth century, and again in the fourteenth and fifteenth centuries, when a new wave of Chinese influence brought with it calligraphic painting, art in Japan was almost purely Chinese in character. Around 1600, in Hideyoshi's time, this style of painting was once more synthesized, this time into the brilliant decorative screens that adorned the imperial castles and temples. With the rise of a bourgeois merchant class a new art was developed through the inexpensive medium of the color woodblock, which was employed mainly to depict trivia of everyday life. The woodblock was the first Japanese art form to capture the attention of the West. More recently we have been influenced by the sophisticated simplicity of the paraphernalia used in the tea ceremony, which originally derived from Zen Buddhist ritual. Another profound influence on modern art has been Japanese domestic architecture.

The Japanese, like the Chinese, have shown tolerance for all sorts of beliefs. Buddhism was the first world religion to be superimposed on the aboriginal nature worship. It did not become powerful until the seventh century, when it began to develop various local sects. Christianity had considerable influence in the sixteenth and early seventeenth centuries, but was banned by the Shogunate and practically wiped out. Side by side with Buddhism and Christianity was the truly native Japanese religion, Shinto, which developed from the aboriginal nature worship. During most of Japanese history Buddhism has been the religion of the intellectuals and aristocrats. Zen Buddhism, with its emphasis on the development of the individual personality, had wide influence, especially among the Samurai. Attitudes created by this sect permeated the aesthetics and ethics of all Japan. Shinto was carried on as an unorganized back-country cult. After the opening and modernization of Japan, Shinto was made the state religion.

During the Shogunate the population of Japan was pretty well stabilized. This was accomplished partly by considerable ingenuity in sexual matters and techniques of contraception, and partly by a process, which the Japanese dislike to acknowledge, called "thinning the family." The Japanese did not practice the usual sort of infanticide, in which a superfluous child is done away with shortly after birth. The Japanese family head who had more children than he could properly provide for would wait until the child was two or three years old and his potentials of health and intelligence were becoming obvious. The least promising ones would be eliminated. This "thinning" was done in the same way that one would thin a growing crop, removing the poorer plants so that the surviving ones would have a better chance. However, when the Japanese became mechanized and the developing commercial interest needed cheap labor and the emperor needed soldiers, the people were encouraged to breed rapidly. Being a well-disciplined and patriotic people, they proceeded to do so, and the population took a rapid upswing.

The country was closed in 1636 and remained closed until 1853 when it was opened, so to speak, with a can opener. What happened was that the Americans sent to Japan a fleet of war vessels vastly superior to anything the Japanese had and politely suggested that they would like treaties permitting trade—or else. It was much like the suggestion of an offensive and defensive alliance between Russia and Finland, and the Japanese liked it about as much. They would have preferred to stay comfortably isolated from the world.

A few years after Perry's arrival some of the Japanese shore batteries opened fire on some European armed steamers, which returned the fire with a speed and precision astonishing to the Japanese. It brought home to them very definitely that they were helpless against the modern equipment of European forces, and made them realize that if they were to be drawn into the world once more they would have to modernize themselves as rapidly as possible. The Japanese already had the pattern of deliberately imitating other countries, and China, their previous model, was at this time in a state of confusion and was itself being rapidly brought under European control. The Japanese turned to the West. They sent delegates to various parts of Europe to bring back the skills which had made the Europeans successful. They recognized that different countries excelled in different things. Therefore they organized their army along German lines, the navy along British lines, and finance and manufacturing on French and English models. The United States they ignored at this time as not being far enough advanced to warrant study and imitation.

Perry's visit was in 1853, and by 1867 the internal revolution had been accomplished. Feudal dues had been formally abolished, and the emperor was reinstated as an actual political ruler, not merely a divine symbol. Fortunately, the emperor of this Meiji era was an able man. The Japanese set up a new government which looked democratic and constitutional enough to win the respect of Europeans, although actually it was handled on a sound Japanese basis of family control. It is interesting that in the reorganization, for instance, one of the great clans took over the army, another the navy, while still others went into various businesses.

For a time all the old aspects of Japanese life were devaluated. The population was so dazzled by European pre-eminence that they attached little importance to their own culture. Many of the finest pieces of Japanese art were sold for a song to knowing Europeans, and the Japanese strove to acquire an appreciation of pre-Raphaelite Victorian painting.

A long period of discipline had prepared the Japanese for acting with a united will upon orders. They laid out a careful plan for modernization, for the conquest of world markets, and then, as part of the long-range program, for the conquest of the world so that all races should be brought under the benevolent shadow of the emperor. These plans were carried well forward during World War I, but foundered on Japanese miscalculations in World War II.

CONCLUSION

THIS book is not concerned with history of civilization in the usual sense. In culture development, the victories of Alexander the Great are of less consequence than the invention of the loom or the discovery of how to smelt metals. Throughout the marvelous age of the Renaissance, just as throughout the Dark Ages, kings came and went, scholarship rose and degenerated, but the peasant went on patiently tilling his land. In the cities that arose, wherever the stable economy necessary for city living developed, the pattern of Sumer was repeated, the pattern of the organized guild craftsmen who were both manufacturers and salesmen. Even technology remained strikingly similar except for some minor developments. For instance, early technology was dependent on bronze as its principal metal; later, this gave place to iron, which was cheaper and more abundant and which, in a way, proletarianized metal-using. The early complex hieroglyphic types of writing, in which only professionals were skilled, were revolutionized by the invention of the alphabet, which made possible a wide spread of literacy. China, of course, provides one of the few exceptions to this development.

In the course of human culture there have been three basic mutations. The first was the use of tools, fire, and language. The second was the discovery of how to raise food and domesticate animals, which brought about a whole series of social and technological advances. Within a thousand years of these discoveries the basic patterns of our civilization were established and culture reached an effective adjustment in technology, patterns of economic distribution, and social forms, the sort of adjustment which can be achieved only by centuries of experimentation. The third mutation came about less than two hundred years ago through the discovery of how to obtain power from heat and how to use scientific method; we are still struggling, not very successfully, to adapt our institutions and economic life to the new elements introduced.

Until this third mutation, the Old World civilizations were fundamentally very much alike. Everywhere the chief pattern of life was agricultural; the economy depended on men's muscles, with a little help from the animals, the ox pulling the plow, the donkey carrying burdens. The craftsmanship of the world depended on the skill of human hands in carving wood, forging metals, and weaving cloth. However, as we have seen, each great civilization made its own unique contribution to world culture. All cultures develop disharmonically; that is, they elaborate those elements which seem important to them and lag behind or completely reject others. So Mesopotamia gave us the first patterns for city living and legal control. The Code of Hammurabi is still echoed in much of our modern legal procedure. The mysticism of the Egyptians is reflected in many elements of world religions. China was first to evolve a system for governmental control of a huge population of both city and rural peoples. Our own culture has made great contributions in technology, but we have been so preoccupied with them that we have done little to adapt our social and economic systems to the new situations created by the Machine Age. This book has attempted to show how these specializations came about and how they have been integrated and diffused to make the richness and variety of modern world culture.

The third mutation got under way with the invention of the steam engine and the internal combustion engine and with all the technological advances that followed in their train. Along with this evolved the use of scientific method. The Greeks are credited with this development, but they developed it only to a limited degree. When the Greek scientist came to an impasse, he fell back upon philosophy and pure reason, not recognizing that when one is dealing with multiple phenomena operating in configurations, the logical results are not always the correct results. When the Greeks tried a thing once and received a satisfactory result, they stopped. The essence of the scientific method is that experiments are rigidly controlled, results and techniques being recorded so that they can be checked by other scientists. This method has made it possible for results to be used and improved by other workers. All these basic discoveries were made in Europe, and because this was a region in which the necessary deposits of coal and iron were available, European culture got a head start over the rest of the world in the third mutation; the real basis for the theory of white supremacy.

The recent discoveries of how to make use of atomic energy and the penetration of space may well bring about a fourth mutation before we have become fully adjusted to the third one. At present, however, the power of these new basic inventions is largely political: the tremendous destructive possibilities must force nations to revise their attitudes toward war. The atom's potentialities for changing the basic structure of our culture are not yet explored, for this terrific source of power has not yet been harnessed in a way that makes it a dynamic factor in everyday economy. But unless we are so mad as to use this new force to destroy ourselves, we may be sure that the world will go on changing and developing and life will become richer and longer for the individual.

INDEX

At the time of his death in 1953, RALPH LINTON, Sterling Professor of Anthropology at Yale University, had an established reputation as one of the two or three greatest anthropologists in the world. Born in Philadelphia in 1893 of Quaker parentage, he attended Swarthmore College and pursued graduate studies at the University of Pennsylvania, Columbia University, and Harvard (Ph.D., 1925). He devoted sixteen years, beginning in his undergraduate days, to work as a museum and field anthropologist, which took him to, among other places, New Mexico, Colorado, Guatemala, the Marquesas Islands, and Madagascar. He entered academic life in 1928, teaching first at the University of Wisconsin, then at Columbia (1937–46), and finally at Yale.

Linton was President of the American Anthropological Association in 1946, Vice President of the American Association for the Advancement of Science in 1937, and a member of the National Academy of Science. He received the Viking Fund medal and award in general anthropology in 1951, and in 1953 was honored by the American Medical Association as giver of the Thomas William Salmon Lectures for that year. In 1954 he was awarded posthumously the Huxley Medal of the Royal Anthropological Institute of Great Britain and Ireland. He was editor of the *American Anthropologist* (1939–44) and of the *Viking Fund Publications in Anthropology* (1947–51). His writings include *The Cultural Background of Personality, The Study of Man,* and *The Tanala.*

The text of this book was set on the Linotype in a face called Times Roman, designed by Stanley Morison for *The Times* (London), and first introduced by that newspaper in 1932. Composed, printed, and bound by THE COLONIAL PRESS INC., Clinton, Massachusetts. Paper manufactured by S. D. WARREN COMPANY, Boston. Cover design by JOSEPH LOW.

VINTAGE RUSSIAN LIBRARY

V-708	Aksakov, Sergey	YEARS OF CHILDHOOD
V-715	Andreyev, Leonid	THE SEVEN THAT WERE HANGED *and Other Stories*
V-705	Bauer, Inkeles, and Kluckhohn	HOW THE SOVIET SYSTEM WORKS
V-725	Carr, E. H.	MICHAEL BAKUNIN
V-723	Chernyshevsky, N. G.	WHAT IS TO BE DONE
V-704	Deutscher, Isaac	STALIN: *A Political Biography*
V-722	Dostoyevsky, Fyodor	THE BROTHERS KARAMAZOV
V-721	Dostoyevsky, Fyodor	CRIME AND PUNISHMENT
V-709	Fedin, Konstantin	EARLY JOYS
V-707	Fischer, Louis	THE SOVIETS IN WORLD AFFAIRS
V-717	Guerney, B. G. (ed.)	AN ANTHOLOGY OF RUSSIAN LITERATURE
V-727	Ilf and Petrov	THE TWELVE CHAIRS
V-716	Kamen, Isai (ed.)	GREAT RUSSIAN SHORT STORIES
V-710	Kohn, Hans	PAN-SLAVISM: *Its History and Ideology*
V-706	Leonov, Leonid	THE THIEF
V-726	Marcuse, Herbert	SOVIET MARXISM
V-720	Mirsky, D. S.	A HISTORY OF RUSSIAN LITERATURE
V-703	Mosely, Philip E.	THE KREMLIN AND WORLD POLITICS: *Studies in Soviet Policy and Action*
V-718	Nabokov, Vladimir (trans.)	THE SONG OF IGOR'S CAMPAIGN
V-714	Pushkin, Alexander	THE CAPTAIN'S DAUGHTER *and Other Great Stories*
V-719	Reed, John	TEN DAYS THAT SHOOK THE WORLD
V-701	Simmons, Ernest J.	LEO TOLSTOY, Volume I
V-702	Simmons, Ernest J.	LEO TOLSTOY, Volume II
V-713	Tolstoy, Leo	THE KREUTZER SONATA
V-711	Turgenev, Ivan	THE VINTAGE TURGENEV Volume I: SMOKE, FATHERS AND SONS, FIRST LOVE
V-712	Turgenev, Ivan	Volume II: ON THE EVE, RUDIN, A QUIET SPOT, DIARY OF A SUPERFLUOUS MAN
V-724	Wallace, Sir Donald Mackenzie	RUSSIA: ON THE EVE OF WAR AND REVOLUTION

A free catalogue of VINTAGE BOOKS will be sent to you at your request. Write to Vintage Books, Inc., 457 Madison Ave., New York 22.

VINTAGE POLITICAL SCIENCE
AND SOCIAL CRITICISM

A free catalogue of VINTAGE BOOKS will be sent to you at your request. Write to Vintage Books, Inc., 501 Madison Avenue, New York 22, New York.

VINTAGE HISTORY
AMERICAN

VINTAGE HISTORY
EUROPEAN

A free catalogue of VINTAGE BOOKS will be sent to you at your request. Write to Vintage Books, Inc., 501 Madison Avenue, New York 22, New York.